Studies in the Psychosocial

Series Editors
Stephen Frosh
Department of Psychosocial Studies
Birkbeck, University of London
London, UK

Peter Redman
Faculty of Arts and Social Sciences
The Open University
Milton Keynes, UK

Wendy Hollway
Faculty of Arts and Social Sciences
The Open University
Milton Keynes, UK

Studies in the Psychosocial seeks to investigate the ways in which psychic and social processes demand to be understood as always implicated in each other, as mutually constitutive, co-produced, or abstracted levels of a single dialectical process. As such it can be understood as an interdisciplinary field in search of transdisciplinary objects of knowledge. Studies in the Psychosocial is also distinguished by its emphasis on affect, the irrational and unconscious processes, often, but not necessarily, understood psychoanalytically. Studies in the Psychosocial aims to foster the development of this field by publishing high quality and innovative monographs and edited collections. The series welcomes submissions from a range of theoretical perspectives and disciplinary orientations, including sociology, social and critical psychology, political science, postcolonial studies, feminist studies, queer studies, management and organization studies, cultural and media studies and psychoanalysis. However, in keeping with the inter- or transdisciplinary character of psychosocial analysis, books in the series will generally pass beyond their points of origin to generate concepts, understandings and forms of investigation that are distinctively psychosocial in character.

More information about this series at
http://www.palgrave.com/gp/series/14464

Julian Manley

Social Dreaming, Associative Thinking and Intensities of Affect

Foreword by Lita Crociani-Windland

Julian Manley
University of Central Lancashire
Preston, UK

Studies in the Psychosocial
ISBN 978-3-319-92554-7 ISBN 978-3-319-92555-4 (eBook)
https://doi.org/10.1007/978-3-319-92555-4

Library of Congress Control Number: 2018947634

Cover illustration: 'Rhizome' (digital photograph) by Nicole AL Manley

This Palgrave Macmillan imprint is published by the registered company Springer Nature Switzerland AG
The registered company address is: Gewerbestrasse 11, 6330 Cham, Switzerland

To Nicole
For Gabriela

Foreword

My relationship to social dreaming, like this book's author's, goes back to the 1990s when I was introduced to it as a Master's student at the University of the West of England. Like him I found the experience of the social dreaming matrix refreshing and intriguing and have taken part in many such events since as both participant and host. As an early doctoral student of the then newly formed Centre for Psycho-Social Studies I share an intellectual lineage with Julian, that has seen both of us linking what have been seen by some as incompatible frameworks, namely psychoanalysis and continental philosophy, particularly the work of Deleuze.

Reading the first part of this book on the history of social dreaming reminded me of the initial scepticism of colleagues in relation to bringing a Deleuzian perspective to the field of group relations and psychoanalysis. We were both fortunate enough to be in an environment that was open to cross-fertilisation of different approaches in the development of psycho-social studies, which included neuroscience and philosophy. At UWE Bristol 'psycho-social' has always been spelt with a hyphen. This spelling was much debated in a special issue of Psychoanalysis, Culture and Society journal (2008), as Manley reminds us (refer Chap. 1) and while it may seem a pedantic distraction to mention it at this juncture, it is a useful sideways move to tackle one of the issues in the development of social dreaming offered by this book.

The reason for the hyphen is to acknowledge the space between the 'psychological' and the 'social' as being the key focus of this new field of studies. There is something about this that links to concepts such as Bion's 'O' (1965, 1970) and Winnicott's transitional space (1971). As indicated in this book, the dreams in the social matrix can be seen to reside in a transitional space that is neither about the individual nor purely about the social environment. As in transitional spaces of any kind it is about both, yet the focus in the social dreaming matrix is on the latter aspect, which goes beyond the individual level. In that sense, as Gordon Lawrence claimed, it is also about more than the social and by reaching to an unconscious level reaches to the many forces and tensions that in a Deleuzian or Bergsonian sense reside in the 'virtual'. The Tavistock tradition has Bion to thank for his concept of 'O' as reaching towards that realm, yet Bion's concept of 'O' while reaching for the 'infinite', something Lawrence also struggled to establish (see Chap. 2), remains at a poetic level of negatives: 'without memory and desire', 'the unknown' and 'negative capability'.

In order to offer a more positive appreciation of such slippery and seemingly un-encompassable aspects it seemed necessary to some of us, myself and Manley in this case, to go beyond the traditional psychoanalytic and group relations frameworks, something that Lawrence may have found hard to do in his lifetime of belonging to that community and its established paradigm. In some way he was expanding and reforming that paradigm, yet may have been unable to go beyond it to another set of ideas outside that tradition. It has fallen to another generation to do so. This is this book's contribution and the reason the work had to go Deleuzian.

Lawrence disliked interpretation, his intuitions that the unconscious is more than just an individual aspect or just related to repressed psychic material seems to go directly to the Deleuzian/Bergsonian formulation of the 'virtual'. Lawrence was frustrated with Oedipal concerns. This is something Deleuze and Lawrence shared and is indicated by the now classic text by Deleuze and Guattari (1972) titled Anti-Oedipus, that Manley uses extensively as a resource for his own unpacking of the workings of the social dreaming matrix. The Anti-Oedipus title should alert us to its aspect of critique, yet critique is not the same as wholesale rejection of the psychoanalytic project (see also Chap. 2). Guattari, a psychiatric practitioner, underwent analysis with Lacan and can be seen to have found inspiration in the work of Winnicott (Genosko in Guattari 2000: 110–114). Deleuze and Guattari's aim was not to deny the unconscious, but to un-domesticate it, to bring it out of the familial Oedipal drama and allow for its wildness (Deleuze and Guattari 1980: Chap. 2, see page 38 in particular). Their aim is to broaden its reach to the non-human and therefore include all the forces and tensions that affect our existence, with or without our awareness of them, drawing and developing Spinoza and Bergson's philosophical concept of duration and the virtual (see Chap. 5, also Chap. 10 for other influences). This is reminiscent of what Lawrence may have been reaching for when referring to the 'ecology' of social dreaming (see Chap. 1). The idea of the 'virtual' encompasses individual unconscious milieus as well as aspects of our environment, i.e. nature, as well as social and political conditions that are real, while not all coming to direct expression as actual events. To make this more comprehensible let me use a simple example: the potential for electrical events is part of nature, lightning however requires certain conditions of tension in the atmosphere. It does not require our consciousness of these conditions to occur, though it does if we are to harness its power and reproduce those conditions to light our houses and so on. We can live without understanding why flicking a switch turns something on, but that does not mean the forces in tension that result in lighting a bulb are not real. The light is the sign, the outer expression of that tension. Our bodies and minds likewise are complex and governed by aspects we don't need to understand in order to live, yet influence us. As the Socratic saying goes 'the unexamined life is not worth living' and the most interesting aspects are the hardest to explore.

The work of Deleuze has often been regarded as difficult. Its difficulty lies in two main factors. Firstly, its focus is on what I have termed as fluidity (Crociani-Windland 2011) to encompass movement and process, unconscious aspects of reality, transformations at a molecular level, hard to perceive and register consciously, though not impossible as Bergson (1913), Deleuze and Guattari's work attests. The nature of what they are exploring means that clear cut definitions, the bread and butter of academic work, do not serve the purpose as they would not be able to encompass that which is trying to find expression and be brought to a level of consciousness. Secondly, all this goes against our Western mind set, based on linear logic and is what makes their work (and the work of psychoanalysis) both difficult and controversial. In spite of the success these continental philosophers' work has received over time, it remains a niche, even elite, academic pursuit. This is also the case of processes such as social dreaming and its offspring the visual matrix (Manley et al. 2015; Manley and Roy 2017; Roy and Manley 2017; Manley 2018; Froggett et al. 2015).

Working with these processes, as will be evident in this book, requires an appreciation of the positive creative potential of allowing affective processes to run in free associative ways, suggesting, rather than defining, possible understandings in an emergent way. In addition to possible understandings arising within the matrix event as a whole, the experience and images often linger in participants and hosts and work beyond the matrix, combining with other external impressions to offer further insights. The process is one of resonance, analogical modulation; it is about topological transformations (Massumi 2002: Chap. 8), where, in what Massumi (ibid) terms non-Euclidean geometry as a shorthand, the form of a doughnut and a cup are about the same because one can be made into the other, without cuts or additions. They are transformations of the same. Social dreaming works, in my experience, in a similar way, while adding to the complexity by not just working with one cup or doughnut form, but many topologically related images. What I have termed insight is I believe just a glimpse of the underlying pattern that has given rise to the many images and associations offered as partial stops in the potentially limitless transformations of it. That is what I have made of my own experiences of the social dreaming matrix and another way of thinking about the 'unthought known'. My own hypothesis in this respect is that the time boundary of the matrix and its location in a particular social and historical moment is what limits the limitless, in addition to the unusual spatial snowflake chair arrangement, in other words the relative stopping of time itself has a part to play. The partly actualised expression of the dream, in that it is a visual artefact of the mind while not following rational linear rules, is what allows us to utilise it as a window into the underlying tendencies of an actual moment that is not just about an individual expression of both conscious and unconscious elements of experience, but links to the shared experience of what is shaping, both known and 'unthought known' (see Chap. 3), the social and historical conditions of that time.

One of the insights offered in this book that I found particularly poignant is the idea that the web of associations and linking of dreams is able to create a Body without Organs (Deleuze 1969, see Chap. 7). My association was to the wondrous patterns of flight of starlings. The murmuration (isn't that a wonderfully appropriate term in this context, where we are not after loud proclaiming of results?) of starlings shape-shift as if one body in a coordinated pattern of group mind. In the spirit of social dreaming I would like not to elaborate further, but allow the beautiful image to stand for itself in linking what I have tried to express thus far. Attractive though this image and thought may be, it would only be part of the picture.

We use the word dream to relate to our wishes and aspirations, but dreams can also be nightmares. Fluidity is something we relish and are terrified of. Many of the images offered in social dreaming matrices speak of delight and terror, vitality and death, sometimes almost in the same breath, so to speak. In order to reconnect to the idea of topology and the problem of how to work with social dream matrix content I will use some of the case study material offered in Chap. 9, which exemplifies the ambivalence of affect very well and where there are recurrent images or themes, before offering my own take on this aspect of the matrix. In the first transcript extract a person speaks of the pleasure of supporting someone to float and glide through the water, like a parent does to teach a child to swim; not long after others speak to the terror of water, the sensation and possibility of drowning, disorientation and annihilation taking one over. It may not be surprising that many more extracts of such negative associations to fluidity are given: the theme of that event was related to climate change. What could be more primal than the fear of flooding, now a real possibility given the melting of polar ice and consequent sea level rise? The real, actual and virtual environmental conditions combine with/in the associated dream images and life experiences in what Manley terms the social dreaming collage or rhizome (see Chap. 6). The etymology of the word nightmare itself seems to link to some of the themes that recur as associations to the art exhibition that had been linked to the social dreaming event, the problematic of breathing is part of that etymology: a mare is old English for an evil spirit lying on top of one, constricting breathing, the Latin incubus has the same meaning and in Italian incubo is the word for nightmare. The constriction or impossibility of breathing, running out of air, recurs in that particular matrix event, whether linked to being immersed in water or polluted air, being squashed or drowned. As we are reminded in Chaps. 10 and 11, I should be wary of generalisations and the problem that language poses in attempting to express affective experiences. As Manley puts it, interpretation can be a trap, an imposition of standardised categories on what may be very different, or on difference in itself to put it in Deleuzian terms (1968). Deleuze and Guattari, however, did not shy away from using what I would like to term 'topoi', used here not in terms of a traditional topic, but in relation to the topological aspect mentioned earlier: 'becoming' in Deleuze is associated with woman/child/animal for example. Are these themes? Not quite, they are signs. Becoming woman signals a state of existence characterised by connectivity, sensitivity, even falling in love, that is not about sex or gender, but is about bodily affects at a subtle molecular level. Becoming child has nothing to do with age, but everything to do with finding the youthfulness of any age. Becoming animal has a less positive association as Manley's reference to Moby Dick, taken from A Thousand Plateaus (Deleuze and Guattari 1980), attests along with werewolves and other obsession/possession examples offered there. Tracing the topological in other words does not preclude the identification of difference in the repetition, rather it is about tracking transformations that may be signs of underlying processes and since the main mean of communication (though not the only one) is language then this requires us to name them.

But is this all fanciful stuff with little relation to serious scientific work? As Manley points out in his final chapters not all scientific work has to be reductionist and we now have work in complexity theory that attests to non-linear processes, that shows how order can emerge spontaneously from chaos or a pattern emerge from a thousand starlings flying. I leave you with that image and hope you enjoy the book.

Bristol, UK Lita Crociani-Windland

References

Bergson, H. (1913) *Time and Free Will-An Essay on the Immediate Data of Consciousness*, [Reprinted 2001]. Minneola, N.Y.: Dover Publications.

Bion, W. (1965) *Transformations*. London: Heinemann.

Bion, W. (1970) *Attention and Interpretation*. London: Tavistock Publications.

Crociani-Windland, L. (2011) *Festivals, Affect and Identity*. London: Anthem Press.

Deleuze, G. (1968) *Différence et répétition* (Paris: PUF); tr. as *Difference and Repetition*, by Paul Patton, New York: Columbia University Press, 1994.

Deleuze, G. (1969) *Logique du sens* (Paris: Minuit); tr. as *The Logic of Sense*, by Mark Lester with Charles Stivale, New York: Columbia University Press, 1990.

Deleuze, G. and Guattari, F. (1972) *L'Anti-Oedipe* (Paris: Minuit); tr. as *Anti-Oedipus*, by Robert Hurley, Mark Seem and Helen R. Lane, New York: Viking, 1977; reprint University of Minnesota Press, 1983.

Deleuze, G. and Guattari, F. (1980) *Mille plateaux* (Paris: Minuit); tr. as *A Thousand Plateaus*, by Brian Massumi, Minneapolis: University of Minnesota Press, 1987.

Froggett, L., Manley, J. and Roy, A. (2015) 'The Visual Matrix Method: Imagery and Affect in a Group-based Research Setting', *Forum: Qualitative Social Research./ Forum Qualitative Sozialforschung / Forum: Qualitative Social Research*, 16 (3).

Genosko, G. (2000) 'The Life and Work of Felix Guattari' in Guattari, F. *The Three Ecologies*, tr. Ian Pindar and Paul Sutton, London: Athlone Press.

Manley, J., Roy, A. and Froggett, L. (2015) *Researching Recovery from Substance Misuse Using Visual Methods*, in (Eds.), L. Hardwick, R. Smith and A. Worsley, Innovations in Social Work Research, London: Jessica Kingsley.

Manley, J. and Roy, A. (2017) 'The visual matrix: A psycho-social method for discovering unspoken complexities in social care practice', *Psychoanalysis, Culture and Society* 22(2), pp. 132–153.

Manley, J. (2018) 'Every human being is an artist': From social representation to creative experiences of self. In Cummins, A.M. and Williams, N. (Eds.), *Researching Beneath the Surface*, Vol. 2. London: Routledge.

Massumi, B. (2002). *Parables for the Virtual*. Durham, USA: Duke University Press.

Psychoanalysis, Culture and Society, Volume 13, Issue 4, December 2008, Special Issue: British Psycho(-)Social Studies.

Roy, A. and Manley, J. (2017) 'Recovery and Movement: Allegory and 'journey' as a means of exploring recovery from substance misuse'. *Journal of Social Work Practice.* Vol. 31, Issue 2, pp 191–204.

Winnicott D. W. (1971) *Playing and Reality*. London: Routledge.

Preface and Acknowledgements

Social dreaming was invented or 'discovered' by Gordon Lawrence, working with Patricia Daniels, in 1982. Lawrence is widely acknowledged as being responsible for promoting, disseminating and developing social dreaming until his death in 2013. This book intends to provide a much needed development of its ontological and epistemological underpinnings which have hitherto remained obscure and undeveloped. This is a volume in three parts. Part I introduces the basics of social dreaming, the problematic of dreams and the shared nature of dreams in social dreaming; Part II considers social dreaming from a freshly conceived ontological and epistemological perspective, viewed chiefly through a Deleuzian lens, which will simultaneously focus forwards to a future understanding of social dreaming emerging from Deleuzian and associated thinking, and backwards to retain and encompass its origins in psychoanalytical thinking. Part III further develops the Deleuzian paradigm and introduces new ways of conceiving social dreaming.

The book is fruit of many years of social dreaming work, leading up to a PhD thesis in 2010, the development of a related method, the 'visual matrix', and continuing work since then. Just before Lawrence's death in 2013 a foundation was set up – the Gordon Lawrence Foundation for the Promotion of Social Dreaming (GLF) – to continue supporting the practice and development of social dreaming. I am grateful to have known Gordon Lawrence personally, and I am indebted to his knowledge and the richness of his creative imagination that made social dreaming possible in the first place. I have shared many dreams with my colleagues at the GLF, and I thank them all for their continued enthusiasm, insights and support. A few years ago now, I was grateful for the support and guidance of my PhD supervisors, Simon Clarke and Jem Thomas of the University of the West of England. That thesis gave birth to many of the ideas in this book: I'm still grateful today. I also acknowledge the general contribution of the rich and creative atmosphere that imbued the Centre for Psycho-Social Studies, as was, at the University of the West of England. This was truly one of those rare 'potential spaces' that one comes across in life from time to time, and then they are gone. My teachers then have become my valued colleagues: Anne-Marie Cummins, Paul Hoggett, Nigel Williams, Herbert Hahn, Sean Watson, and the late Robert French. In addition to the staff, many thanks to my fellow students at the time, who were a joy to be with. Like me, in those days, in transition from student to staff member, many thanks to my colleague, Lita Crociani-Windland, who wrote the Foreword to this book, and gave me some exquisitely presented advice in the book's latter stages. Special thanks to Wendy Hollway for reading through the text before publication and especially for advice given in redrafting sections of Part I. To those people I have shared the hosting of social dreaming events with, it has been a rich learning journey and I thank them all. To name but a few, some of the ideas in this book would have struggled to find their final form without the conversations I have been privileged to share with David Armstrong, Hayley Berman, and Jacqueline Sirota, among others, too numerous to list. Many are colleagues in the Gordon Lawrence Foundation for the Promotion of Social Dreaming, of which I am privileged to be a Trustee. My recent work with Susan Long in the first of a post-Lawrence series of books on social dreaming due for publication in 2018, has been invaluable to me in refreshing and revitalising ideas on social dreaming, old and new. And of course, I have fond memories of discussing social dreaming with Gordon Lawrence himself. My debt to his thinking and above all his enthusiastic embracing of the social dreaming project should also be acknowledged. Last but first, thanks to Nicole, who always has the best dreams.

Preston, UK Julian Manley

Contents

List of Figures

Part I

Social Dreaming: Background and Origins

1

How It All Began

Introduction: The Very Idea!

Many years ago, when I walked into the room where, as a Master's student at the University of the West of England (UWE), I was to experience my first social dreaming matrix, hosted by Herbert Hahn, my heart sank. I was at that time immersed in the theory and practice of group relations of the Tavistock kind, and the thought of sitting in this room with my fellow students filled me with dread and frustration. For what could be more futile and boring than sitting in a room listening to other people's dreams? There was plenty of potential for embarrassing moments too. Surely I wasn't the only one with 'funny' dreams! Knowing something about group dynamics, I couldn't imagine that the sharing of dreams would do anything more than further exacerbate the psychodynamic tensions in the group and create scapegoats at both ends of the spectrum: those who were open and frank with offering their personal dreams and those who were mute and retired.

How wrong I was! To my astonishment, the group settled into a strange sense of harmonious, almost meditative communion of gentle thoughts and feelings punctuated by dreams of others that –inexplicably – seemed to feel very close to my own life and experiences. The session was calm and a feeling

J. Manley, *Social Dreaming, Associative Thinking and Intensities of Affect*,
Studies in the Psychosocial, https://doi.org/10.1007/978-3-319-92555-4_1

of human warmth pervaded the group. I was flummoxed! This perplexity engaged my curiosity and turned it into a quest to find out what exactly was going on. I have since dropped the 'exactly' from that quest, but I still endeavour to unveil the reasons for the effects of the social dreaming matrix on myself and others. After many years of study and practice, this book represents my attempt at answering the general question "what is going on?"

Although the question might be simple, the answers are not. Although dreams might have become a legitimate source of discussion after Freud's *Interpretation of Dreams*, they have rarely been used beyond the couch, and even in the psychoanalytical encounter, they have most frequently been described as a source of uncovering the repressed and more often than not, sexual thoughts and desires of a patient undergoing treatment for mental health issues. The issues of the couch in Freudian analysis are frequently interpreted as having their origins in childhood distress or trauma. Crucially, in the context of social dreaming and the critical ambition of this book, dreams have only been conceived as sources of knowledge within this dyadic psychoanalytical context, never in a shared group or social environment. There are, therefore, considerable impediments to the use of social dreams in academic research. Even in the field of psychosocial studies, where debates sometimes emerge over the difficulties or even the desirability of fusing the 'psycho' and the 'social', (see the sometimes acrimonious debate highlighting this polemic in a special issue of *Psychoanalysis, Culture and Society* journal (2008), Chancer and Andrews (2014) and recently Cummins and Williams (2018)), social dreaming has remained on the fringes of intellectual respectability. When a widely respected academic in the field, precisely one that tends towards the 'psycho' of psychosocial studies, Wendy Hollway, asks whether social dreaming may be a method which is 'too far outside social science research method', (Hollway 2015, pp. 97–98), you know you have a lot of exploring, thinking and reflecting to do!

A Brief Summary of the Principal Features of Social Dreaming

For the reader who is new to social dreaming, I provide the following précis of the main features of social dreaming that make it essentially different from other methods that might be used in psychosocial and qualitative research. This is a brief description that has the aim of providing a foundation for the book as a whole. For a complete summary of social dreaming as perceived by its originator, Gordon Lawrence, see Lawrence (2005) and Manley (2014).

The Basics

In social dreaming, a group of people sit together in a quiet room to share their real, night-time dreams; these are shared in no particular order, when it 'feels right' to one of the participants. Participants may also free associate to each other's dreams or to other images and emotions that arise in the course of the matrix. The dreams and associations are offered anonymously, with no names mentioned or recorded. The number of participants varies from about 6 to about 35, with an optimal average being 12–18 (although there have been social dreaming events at conferences that have included even more participants). The number of hosts (the name given to the person who explains the task, keeps the time and provides low key facilitation) can also vary, with more being added according to size of matrix. Often, there is only one host. The host does not interpret the material in the course of the matrix; s/he guides and facilitates the enunciations in a neutral fashion. Each session can last between 40 and 75 minutes, depending on circumstance and size of matrix.

Gathering in a 'Snowflake Pattern' Seating Arrangement and Facilitation

The participants sit in a snowflake pattern distribution of chairs, the purpose of which is to break up the lines of vision of the participants while still retaining a sense of belonging to a shared space. In Fig. 1.1 below, the arrows indicate that no matter how much a participant might want to look at another directly in the face, this is made difficult through the distribution of the seating arrangement.

This arrangement encourages the idea that in social dreaming we are interested primarily in the dream material rather than the individual person who is telling the dream. The deliberate patterning of the seating in

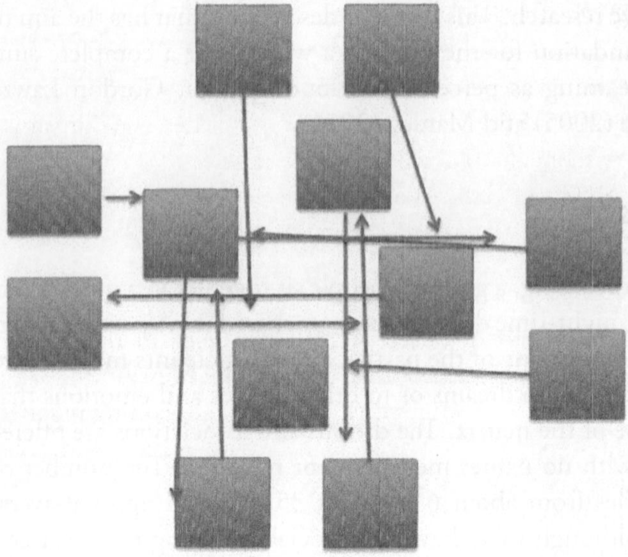

Fig. 1.1 The chairs for the social dreaming matrix are arranged in a snowflake pattern to provide containment but also to disturb the sense of addressing others directly. The arrows indicate the possible averted gaze of participants

this way for the social dreaming matrix also implies a change of role for the host compared to a facilitator or consultant to a group. In the case of social dreaming, the host is not managing the anxieties and psychodynamics of a group process (Bion 1961; Bion Talamo et al. 1998; French and Vince 2002), but rather attempting precisely to avoid these dynamics. The host needs to hold a space that allows for the telling of dreams and associated images through free association. This is achieved through refraining from interpretation and judgment and by linking and making connections between disparate dream images for the purposes of illuminating emergent meaning. When the host invites participants to speak their spontaneous and emerging associations to the dreams and images, the matrix often becomes a space that resembles a 'stream of consciousness'. The host's two main tasks are (1) to select relevant connections between what might otherwise appear to the participants as being an irretrievably unconnected welter of images; and (2) to offer working hypotheses intended to clarify and aid understanding without ever resorting to overt interpretation.

Post-Matrix Session

The post-matrix session that I conduct for research purposes differs slightly from traditional practice. Following the social dreaming matrix, after a short break, the chairs are rearranged into a more conventional distribution (e.g. a circle or a horseshoe configuration), for a post-matrix reflection session, the purpose of which is to allow the participants to debrief and find meaning in the images and associations that have emerged from the previous social dreaming matrix session. The host takes notes on a flipchart or board of the most relevant themes, images and ideas that have emerged from the matrix. This session may last between 30 and 60 minutes. In some versions of social dreaming practice, this session might often be a dialogue or reflection session without the note-taking aspect.

It has always been recognised that there is a need for something to happen after the social dreaming matrix, even though it is the matrix itself that has captured our attention. The need arises from the fact that participants in the matrix may be left with a bewildering sense of a mass of dream images and associations that are felt to be in various degrees of comprehension and confusion. The post-matrix events, therefore, are designed to help participants in their transition back to a more everyday manner of thinking and to attempt to make some sense of the dreams and images of the matrix.

There are various other possibilities for the post-matrix sessions. Typically, matrices are followed up by some form of 'dream reflection group' (Lawrence 2007b). The shifting away from the 'reverie' space of the matrix to this 'dialogue' space is emphasised by rearranging the chairs in a rectangle so that they are neither the 'snowflake' of the matrix, nor the circle of the small group recognisable as typical of a group relations conference. The sense of 'dialogue' in the reflection group has been closely associated to David Bohm's use of the word as defined in his book *On Dialogue* (1996), where he talks about 'participatory thought' and the 'infinite'. Recently, however, the tendency has been to try to go back to the dreams themselves, for example, by some sort of 'synthesis' of the dream images in a 'dream reflection group', (or 'systems synthesis'). These are opportunities for the participants, with the help of the host, to reflect upon the dream images, which are linked together to form a 'collage' of images, from which working hypotheses are postulated. Another example of a post-matrix event is the Creative Role Synthesis (Lawrence 2007c), where an individual presents to a small group from the bigger social dreaming matrix, a problem or puzzle from the workplace and any associated dreams that the presenter feels may be relevant. Then the group is invited to free associate to the puzzle and its dreams in a way that can allow meaning to suggest itself.

The Data

If data collected from social dreaming is to be used for research, both the matrix and the post-matrix session have to be audio recorded and transcribed for later data analysis. The data analysis begins with the post-matrix session, but most of the work is in the analysis of the matrix transcript between researchers, who have normally been either hosting or participating in the matrix.

The questions that arise in terms of research include:

- How to make sense of dream material and associations to that material
- How to apply the data to a research question
- How to justify any conclusions that are drawn from complex material that is open to interpretation
- How can we be sure that the conclusions drawn from analysis are representative of all the participants, and if not all, then which ones?

What Does the Data Look Like?

I quote an extract below from the beginning of a typical social dreaming matrix for the purposes of illustrating the nature of the material, especially for the reader who is unfamiliar with social dreaming. In the extract below, 'D' at the beginning of a contribution signifies 'dream', while 'A' signifies 'association' (or any other contribution that is specifically not a dream). I have highlighted the moments when either through dream or association the images start to resonate and interconnect with each other in ways that are normal features of social dreaming. As the matrix develops (beyond this extract), these links and connections become greater and more complex and start to suggest meanings to each participant.

1. D: it involved water; a famous person had drowned in a river and leeches were found on her face; then I am travelling back in time and visiting this person – and then the accident happens again, but this time there were no leeches; I was looking for leeches to complete the dream.
2. D: travelling with a young woman in her car; I have a contemptuous attitude towards her, ignoring her; I was standing in the passenger place, the door was open; this seemed normal in the dream; something strange (with the antenna?) is happening… in the road; brake, brake: there is a dead body in the road; she couldn't brake; I wondered: shall I drive? but didn't have insurance.
3. D: a confusing dream, repeated once; there are two levels of knowledge: (1) something like news/ TV images; and (2) knowing of something that had led to these images or that these images led to; **the image is of a horse's head** (Damian Hirst?), and **I don't know what the extra knowledge was.**
4. A: its the **400th anniversary of Guy Fawkes' death… what is behind the news is difficult to apprehend**.
5. D: **a man was attacked and lost his arms and feet**; I couldn't remember who he was; I led him away off the scene; he found some children's shoes, they were his daughter's, he had been looking for them.
6. A: **Falfalla (a fairy-tale about a faithful horse, which could speak)**
7. D: going up elevators; I went in to go to the top floor, but it went to the bottom and the doors didn't open; it moved, but didn't open; then the doors worked for others, but not for me; I couldn't get out.
8. A: **a race horse died this week, 'Best Mate'.**
9. D: **I had a dream of 3 horses, small ones; I killed them by skinning them, which was supposed to kill them, but one horse wasn't dead; I was ashamed that I had not done it properly; I then cut its throat to put it out of its misery.**
10. A: **dismembering …Guy Fawkes.**

(Beginning of a social dreaming matrix, Bristol, UK, 05.11.05)

Already in this short extract, ideas, or what Lawrence would have called new thoughts, are emerging within the images of the horse, Guy Fawkes and 'extra knowledge'. The dreams and associations work together. For example, the association to Guy Fawkes in 4 emerges from the dream in 5. A connection is made between not knowing the nature of 'extra knowledge' and 'what is behind the news is difficult to apprehend'. The dream in 5 seems to allude to the Guy Fawkes association previously. The horse's head in the dream at 3 and the unknown knowledge and news seem to connect with the association at 6, with both the horse and something spoken (the knowledge?) combined in 'Falfalla'.[1] The intimate and loving relationship between human and horse is transmitted in the association in 8, all of which leads to a significant dream in 9 and the following association in 10 about horses and death and Guy Fawkes.

I have summarized this very briefly to give the reader a flavour of the nature of the data both in itself and also in the way it works in linking and connectivity. Actual interpretation of the material would require the post-matrix reflection session and an analysis of the entire matrix transcript. I give examples of the potential results of such a process in the Case Studies in Part III.

Purpose of Social Dreaming

The purpose of social dreaming in whatever context is to gain an understanding of participants' shared feelings and thoughts that remain submerged, unseen, unspoken and temporarily unknown until they are expressed in dreams and associations. The theory depends on the idea that the participants share a social environment that they are able to reflect upon both consciously, in daily life and discourse, and unconsciously, through dreams. It is in the dreams of each individual that this unconscious is expressed and in social dreaming that this expression is given a forum for sharing. In this book, I am primarily concerned with its

[1] I am not sure about the fact of this story of the horse. However, it is a good example of how in social dreaming we are not concerned with veracity in an objective sense. What matters is how this was spoken and presented in the context of the matrix.

usefulness in providing research data of the kind that would otherwise be difficult to access; that is to say, wherever the research is directed at difficult topics where explicit debate or verbal communication may not necessarily unearth people's innermost feelings and thoughts about the topic in question. This might be due to the intrinsic difficulty of the subject matter, negative and unwelcome emotions associated to it or the desire of research subjects – 'defended subjects' (Hollway and Jefferson 2013) – to provide answers that they believe the researchers want to hear. An example of such a research topic is people's relationship to climate change (see Chap. 9), where the emotions elicited by confronting the effects of climate change on an individual's sense of personal responsibility are so negative – including, for example, anger, shame, despair, humiliation, fear, guilt, hopelessness, melancholy, mourning and regret – that they can only authentically be faced up to through providing a containing forum for the expression of unconscious thinking. Other examples might include the complexities of racial and national identity (Karolia and Manley 2018); coping with extreme violence and trauma (Berman and Manley 2018); dealing with unexpected feelings arising from the experience of challenging museum exhibitions (Manley 2010a; Manley and Trustram 2018). There will be many more similarly complex research areas that require a forum that can allow for investigation of complexity within a contained space. The social dreaming matrix is such a forum.

Sources of Social Dreaming

First among Lawrence's sources for social dreaming is Charlotte Beradt's *Third Reich of Dreams* (1968). Her work was frequently mentioned by Lawrence as being the first indication of the possibility of understanding dreams socially instead of individually. Second, Freud's *Interpretation of Dreams* (1991 [1900]) is key to our understanding of free association. Lawrence showed how it was possible to use free association applied to social dreaming matrices. Third, Bion's works were also a fundamental source for Lawrence's understanding of social dreaming's roots in group relations. Bion's *Experiences in Groups* (1961) is the source of Lawrence's conception of social dreaming being a manifestation of what Bion denominated 'Sphinx', that is, shared intellectual knowledge. Lawrence was clear in linking Bion's naming of the unconscious as Sphinx to the unconscious of social dreaming as opposed to the Freudian Oedipus. The Sphinx represents the idea of intellectual problems and knowledge appropriate to group work, while Oedipus is concerned with pairing in group work or the dyadic relationship in analyst–analysand work (Bion 1961, p. 8). Taking this as a basic starting point, Lawrence went on to identify four areas belonging to this unconscious 'Sphinx-like' space: 'being', 'becoming', 'unthought known', and 'dreaming', which could be represented as four faces of a single three dimensional pyramid (Fig. 1.2) where: 'being' is what we are; 'becoming' is the future; the 'unthought known' is what is in the unconscious but has yet to be thought; and 'dreaming' is the bringing of this unthought known to the consciously thinking mind.

The unthought known as part of these four modes of thinking, was taken from Christopher Bollas' *The Shadow of the Object* (1987), representing knowledge that was known to people but unavailable for thought. Once this unthought known has emerged in the matrix, it is made concrete through dialogue. The idea of dialogue in social dreaming was influenced by David Bohm's book *On Dialogue* (1996). Another book by Bohm, *Wholeness and the Implicate Order* (1980) is essential reading to understand Lawrence's more 'scientific' leanings when he talks about social dreaming in terms of the 'infinite' and quantum physics. The link

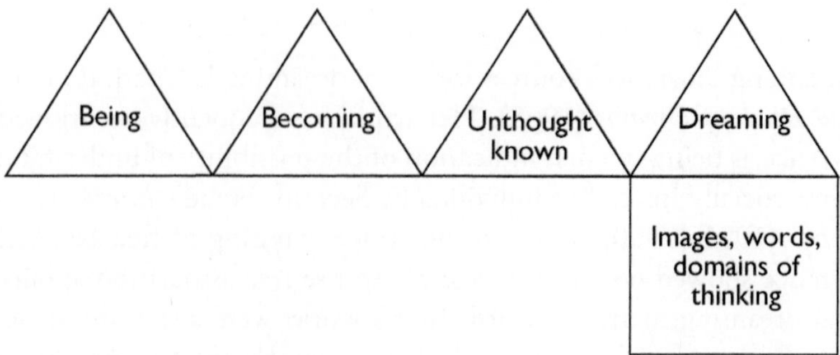

Fig. 1.2 The four modes of thinking. (Lawrence 2005, p. 22)

between Bohm's implicate order and how dreams convert this into 'explicate' was inspired by Montague Ullman's work. In particular, Lawrence cites Ullman's dream process diagram, 'making the implicit explicit', first published in 'The transformation process in dreams' (Ullman 1975). For further scientific ideas, systems thinking, theories of chaos and complexity, which represented an expansion of the 'social' into the 'universal', Lawrence relied on Fritjof Capra's work, notably *The Web of Life* (1997). Lawrence often acknowledged his debt to the work of Matte-Blanco, in particular *The Unconscious as Infinite Sets* (1975) and *Thinking, Feeling, and Being* (1988).

Theory of Social Dreaming

'Matrix' Versus 'Group'

The word 'matrix' came about for both positive and negative reasons. In a negative sense 'matrix' was simply a reaction and defence against the possibility that, in the early 1980s, dream participants and Lawrence's colleagues would understand any group gathering of people at the Tavistock Institute's Group Relations Programme, of which Lawrence was then joint Director, as a 'group' in the 'group relational' sense of the word and all the group dynamics that would entail. A more positive reason for the word 'matrix' was the suggestion that it could define a containing space of potential birth, the birth of new thought and ideas. This was expressed by Lawrence in an almost transcendental way:

> Matrix describes the space from which everything that exists in our Universe, indeed the cosmos, has its origins. Matrix exists before mankind developed groups. And it may well be that group is a defence against the experience of the formlessness of matrix. The social dreaming matrix, purposely convened in the here-and-now, is a reflection of the primordial matrix of humanity. (Lawrence 2003a, p. 3)

In one of Lawrence's early edited books, Claudio Neri pointed out that Foulkes had used the idea of matrix in his development of groups that were representative of the social and not just the individuals within the group (Neri 2003, p. 21). Lawrence himself also suggested that the idea of matrix came from Foulkes (Lawrence 2003b, p. 617). Foulkes' original description of the matrix reads as follows:

> The matrix is the hypothetical web of communication and relationship in a given group. It is the common shared ground, which ultimately determines the meaning and significance of all events and upon which all communications and interpretations, verbal and non-verbal rest. (Foulkes 1964, p. 292)

The 'Infinite' and the 'Unthought Known'

For Lawrence, the concept of the infinite in social dreaming is connected to the unconscious and the unthought known. Lawrence has recourse to Christopher Bollas' discussion of the 'unthought known' (Bollas 1987; Lawrence 2005), and applies this idea to the way the participant in the social dreaming matrix 'knows' and shares the 'known' with others in the matrix, and suggests that this 'known' is 'unthought' (because it resides in the unconscious) until it is brought into the conscious realm through the sharing of dreams in the matrix. In *Introduction to Social Dreaming. Transforming Thinking* (2005), Lawrence attempts to link thinking-as-dreaming to thinking-as-an-unthought-known. And this unthought known is both the knowledge located in the unconscious and the acknowledgement of some transcendental understanding located where the unconscious becomes 'infinity':

> As the dreams are recounted and the participants free-associate, the infinite becomes immanent; it begins to be in the participants' grasp, and not as something imagined to be transcendent. The infinite is the unknown, and the dream introduces us to this: it questions what we have assumed, and accepted, to be social knowledge. (Lawrence 2005, p. 11)

I understand by this that the 'infinite' is what is unknown to the conscious mind because it has not been thought. In this sense, the matrix becomes the container of the infinite. What is unknown to conscious thought might yet be known unconsciously. Once we are introduced to the infinite in this sense through the dreams in the matrix, this unknown becomes potentially known and translated into conscious thought. This thought is then a challenge to accepted social knowledge. Here, then, Lawrence questions the quality of knowledge in the 'social' and equates it with conscious thought that is then challenged by the unthought known as it is revealed through the dream work in the matrix. There is a knowledge in this context that is conscious knowledge ('thought known'), and that can be challenged or enriched by another kind of knowledge, that is not merely 'social' but somehow more transcendental and unconscious ('unthought known'). Here too, it is worth noting that there is an implied difference between what is known or can be known and what is commonly termed 'knowledge', the latter being that which is agreed by society, recorded and handed down from generation to generation in the form of accepted norms. This difference is also part of many people's experiential understanding of the social dreaming matrix. For many participants, there is a sense of a shared knowing in some other, transcendental realm that feels closer to the sensation of the matrix. This sensation suggests that participants in a matrix share a form of knowledge, thoughts, and feelings about complex matters of humanity that are difficult to extrapolate in the course of 'normal' conscious thought.

Lawrence's psychoanalytical ideas of the infinite have their roots in Bion's view of the unconscious and can be linked to Bion's O and theory of thinking. As Crociani-Windland has pointed out, Bion's O – not-knowing – has some resonance with Bergsonian and Deleuzian philosophy (Crociani-Windland 2009), especially as a way of dealing with the unknown and ultimately unknowable, as a result of an ontology of complexity without boundaries. In this way, Lawrence was seeking an understanding of social dreaming through an infinite that could be justified through reference to Bion, who himself sought to understand at least part of his ideas on infinity through recourse to the mystical and transcendental. Lawrence, however, was not to develop the idea of the infinite beyond this tradition, and the concept remained ambiguous.

The 'Social' in 'Social Dreaming'

The word 'social' was used as a way of distinguishing the 'social' dreams as they are presented in the matrix from the 'individual' dreams that are normally associated with dream interpretation in the context of psychoanalysis.

'Social' in this way is the opposite of personal. The emphasis in the social dreaming matrix is on the dreams, not the dreamer, that is to say, the 'social' and not the individual. However, Lawrence himself struggled to define a meaning for social that could embrace other aspects of what is beyond the individual. In 2003, Lawrence was able to write about an ecology in social dreaming that would have us move beyond the social:

> The ecology of forgotten dreams is the infinite. What comes to be known when it is thought depends on the opportunities and the impediments presented by the eco-niche that each of us inhabits. By "eco" I am referring to the whole natural world in which we are located. Loosely, I am using it in the sense of ecological. By "niche" I mean the slice of the environment that we occupy. I have the idea that even a single-cell organism dreams, or participates in proto-dreaming. Thus, evolution comes about in the context of the eco-niche the organism inhabits. (Lawrence 2003a, p. 11)

It seems probable here that the idea of 'proto-dreaming' is akin to Bion's 'proto-mental phenomena' (Bion 1961, p. 101). It would be interesting to understand what Lawrence meant by a 'single-cell organism' dreaming and the idea of 'evolution' in this context. Through using an ecology of dreams, Lawrence touches upon the idea of the shared dream space as being comparable to our natural environment; in other words, the 'whole natural world', that takes us away from the social and towards nature in a way that suggests an intimate link between the unconscious and the environment.

Social Dreaming and Derivatives Today

Gordon Lawrence held centre stage with regards social dreaming in all its aspects before his passing away in 2013. This was important in some ways for the development of social dreaming as a practice that he himself had instigated and was driven to explore and claim as his own. In other ways, however, Lawrence may have occasionally been an overzealous protector of the 'brand' (as he sometimes called it), ensuring that all social dreaming roads led back to his person and therefore his ideas. It made the expression of other explorations of social dreaming very difficult for others and it is no coincidence that nearly all the books published on social dreaming since 1998 have been either edited or written by Lawrence himself (1998, 2003a, 2005, 2007a, 2010). The one exception is Clare and Zarbafi's 2009 *Social Dreaming in the 21st Century*, and even this is indebted to Lawrence, including a lengthy foreword by him. One of the consequences of this has been that it has taken until 2018 for a further edition on social dreaming, in the style of Lawrence's original series, to be published (Long and Manley, in press). And it is in this edition that we are beginning to see a further epistemological development of Lawrence's social dreaming matrix. This edition explicitly introduces a philosophical approach that Lawrence was not disposed to develop himself, and opens out the possibility of social dreaming as a method in research. This is important because the nature of the differences between social dreaming and other, more conventional, psychosocial research methods has made it difficult to apply social dreaming as a method for academic research. This is what initially motivated me to suggest an alternative method of image and group-based investigation, later in collaboration with colleagues, called the 'visual matrix', based on principles of social dreaming but focused more on unconscious visual images and affect:

> Psycho-social research needs to take the assessment of visual imagery in our shared human expression into greater account and consider adapting or rethinking methodology. We need a greater understanding of how these unconscious images are intimately linked to our strongest emotions or 'affects'. (Manley 2010b, p. 195)

The visual matrix and other derivatives of social dreaming – in particular Sievers' social photo matrix – are described in Chap. 13 below. It is precisely this new push towards situating social dreaming within frameworks recognizable and usable by researchers that the present volume seeks to address, moving away from the unwitting self-exile that Lawrence imposed on social dreaming created in his own image.

References

Beradt, C. (1968). *The Third Reich of Dreams. The Nightmares of a Nation 1933–1939.* Chicago, IL: Quadrangle B.

Berman, H. and Manley, J. (2018). Social Dreaming and creativity in South Africa: Imagi(ni)ng the unthought known. In Adlam, J., Gilligan, J., Kluttig, T., and Lee, B.X. (Eds.), *Creative States: Overcoming Violence.* Vol 1, Part 4, Ch. 2, pp. 221–237. London: Jessica Kingsley.

Bion, W.R. (1961). *Experiences in Groups and Other Papers.* London: Routledge.

Bion Talamo, P., Borgogno, F., and Merciai, S.A. (Eds.). (1998). *Bion's Legacy to Groups.* London: Karnac.

Bohm, D. (1980). *Wholeness and the Implicate Order.* London: Routledge.

Bohm, D. (1996). *On Dialogue.* London: Routledge.

Bollas, C. (1987). *The Shadow of the Object.* London: Free Association.

Capra, F. (1997). *The Web of Life. A New Synthesis of Mind and Matter.* London: Flamingo.

Chancer, L. and Andrews, J. (Eds.). (2014). *The Unhappy Divorce of Sociology and Psychoanalysis.* Basingstoke: Palgrave Macmillan.

Clare, J. and Zarbafi, A. (2009). *Social Dreaming in the 21st Century.* London: Karnac.

Crociani-Windland, L. (2009). How to live and learn: Learning, duration, and the virtual. In Clarke, S. and Hoggett, P. (Eds.), *Researching Beneath the Surface*, pp. 51–79. London: Karnac.

Cummins, A.M. and Williams, N. (Eds). (2018). Further *Researching Beneath the Surface.* London: Routledge.

Foulkes, S.H. (1964). *Therapeutic Group Analysis.* London: George Allen & Unwin.

French, R. and Vince, R. (Eds.). (2002). *Group Relations, Management, and Organization.* Oxford: Oxford University Press.

Freud, S. (Strachey, J. (Trans.). (1991 [1900]). *The Interpretation of Dreams.* London: Penguin.

Hollway, W. and Jefferson, T. (2013). *Doing Qualitiative Research Differently: A Psychosocial Approach.* New Delhi: Sage.

Hollway, W. (2015). *Knowing Mothers.* Basingstoke: Palgrave Macmillan.

Karolia, I. and Manley, J. (2018). 1 in 5 Brit Muslims' Sympathy for Jihadis': An insight into the Lived Experience of UK Muslims following the Terror Attacks in Paris. In Adlam, J., Gilligan, J., Kluttig, T., and Lee, B.X. (Eds.), *Creative States: Overcoming Violence*, Vol. 1, Part III, pp. 161–177. London: Jessica Kingsley.

Lawrence, W.G. (Ed.). (1998). *Social Dreaming @ Work*. London: Karnac.

Lawrence, W.G. (Ed.). (2003a). *Experiences in Social Dreaming*. London: Karnac.

Lawrence, W.G. (2003b). Social dreaming as sustained thinking. *Human Relations*, 56(5), pp. 609–624.

Lawrence, W.G. (2005). *Introduction to Social Dreaming. Transforming Thinking*. London: Karnac.

Lawrence, W.G. (Ed.). (2007a). *Infinite Possibilities of Social Dreaming*. London: Karnac.

Lawrence, W.G. (2007b). Dream Reflection Group. In Lawrence, W.G. (Ed.), (2007). *Infinite Possibilities of Social Dreaming*. London: Karnac.

Lawrence, W.G. (2007c). Creative Role Synthesis. In Lawrence, W.G. (Ed.), (2007). *Infinite Possibilities of Social Dreaming*. London: Karnac.

Lawrence, W.G. (Ed.). (2010). *The Creativity of Social Dreaming*. London: Karnac.

Long, S. and Manley, J. (Eds.), (in press). *Social Dreaming: Philosophy, research and practice*. London: Routledge.

Manley, J. (2010a). The slavery in the mind: Inhibition and exhibition. Chapter 6 in Lawrence, W. Gordon (Ed.), *The Creativity of Social Dreaming*. London: Karnac.

Manley, J. (2010b). *Untold Communications: A holistic study of social dreaming*. Unpublished PhD thesis. Bristol: UWE.

Manley, J. (2014). Gordon Lawrence's Social Dreaming Matrix: Background, origins, history and developments. *Organisational and Social Dynamics*, 14(2), pp. 322–342.

Manley, J. and Trustram, M. (2018). 'Such endings that are not over': The slave trade, social dreaming and affect in a museum. *Psychoanalysis, Culture and Society*, 23(1), pp. 77–96.

Matte-Blanco, I. (1975). *The Unconscious as Infinite Sets*. London: Duckworth.

Matte-Blanco, I. (1988). *Thinking, Feeling, and Being*. London: Routledge.

Neri, C. (2003). Social dreaming: Report on the workshops held in Mauiburg, Raissa, and Clarice Town. In Lawrence, W.G. (Ed.), *Experiences in Social Dreaming*, pp 15–36. London: Karnac.

Ullman, M. (1975). The transformation process in dreams. *American Academy of Psychoanalysis*, 19(2), pp. 8–10.

2

Problems in Conceptualising Social Dreaming

While the previous chapter has provided a foundation for the further development of an epistemology for social dreaming that this book intends to pursue, there are still some conceptual issues that need to be addressed before continuing. These difficulties give rise to a need to question some of the assumptions made in considering the nature of social dreaming. These include: the occasional claims that are made for social dreaming as being significantly rooted in Jungian concepts of the collective unconscious and/or the wisdom of dream sharing among indigenous populations; the extent to which social dreaming can be understood as a therapeutic practice; and the difficulty of introducing an alternative Deleuzian paradigm (the subject of Parts II and III of this book) when Deleuze and Guattari are so frequently interpreted as being opposed to psychoanalytic thinking.

Differences Between Jungian Dream Interpretation and Social Dreaming

The case is sometimes made for the social-not-individual aspect of social dreaming as being a version of a Jungian collective unconscious. Certainly, Jung demonstrated that dreams were not entirely features of the individual

J. Manley, *Social Dreaming, Associative Thinking and Intensities of Affect*, Studies in the Psychosocial, https://doi.org/10.1007/978-3-319-92555-4_2

dreamer. The first step in Jung's release of the dream from the individual to the collective was to point out that not all dreams were rooted in the patient's own past, but that they could be indications of other aspects of thinking. For example, Jung suggested that dreams could be the opposite of delving into a personal past experience, they could be anticipatory (Jung 2002 [1931], p. 92). In establishing this, Jung was also able to debunk, as he saw it, his old mentor's theory of dreams that saw them as being about personal repression:

> The view that dreams are merely imaginary fulfilments of repressed wishes is hopelessly out of date. There are, it is true, dreams which manifestly represent wishes or fears, but what about all the other things? Dreams may contain ineluctable truths, philosophical pronouncements, illusions, wild fantasies, memories, plans, anticipations, irrational experiences, even telepathic visions… The dream is specifically the utterance of the unconscious. (ibid., p. 95)

He therefore concluded that the unconscious was not a repository of negative repressed traumas, which he claimed Freud had established, but a natural aspect of the human psyche, neither good nor bad, but valuable to individuals in order to understand the completeness of the human psyche. Thus far, Jung resonates with social dreaming. However, Jung then goes on to formulate his theory of collective dream archetypes, and this is not so clearly part of the social dreaming domain. For example, for Jung, the Freudian phallic symbol should or could be interpreted as a commonly shared archetype:

> That which underlies all the analogies, and sexuality itself, is an archetypal image whose character is hard to define, but whose nearest psychological equivalent is perhaps the primitive mana-symbol.' (ibid., p. 104)

It is this affirmation that permits Jung to discuss a collective unconscious: such 'mana-symbols' or archetypes, when discovered in an individual's dreams may well have a significance that is collectively shared and/or understood. However, such an understanding of the collective meaning of the archetype is only used to explain, ultimately through dream interpretation, the unconscious aspects of an individual's mind, which, for Jung, is still the patient on the couch. Instead of dreams harbouring repressed desires and wishes, Jung suggested that they contained knowledge buried in archetypal symbols. Furthermore, Jung insisted on focusing directly and only at the dream and its inherent symbols rather than using the dream as a starting point for free-association, in a Freudian manner (Jung 1978, pp. 8–14). These details of Jung's thinking demonstrate the distance between his view on the use of dreams and that of social dreaming. In social dreaming, the ideas that emerge from the shared dreams are rarely understood as archetypal or symbolic in a Jungian sense. That is to say, they are not experienced as expressions of some primordial archetype that each of us inherits from our ancestors, thus providing us with a collective understanding of their meanings. Instead, as this book will discuss, social dreaming is a sharing of a social or associative unconscious, of what the participants in a social dreaming matrix are thinking unconsciously. This may include images that appear to be symbols or even archetypes, but not exclusively so. And most importantly, these dream images in social dreaming are felt to belong not to the individual that has expressed them, but the shared space of the matrix as a whole. Furthermore, it needs to be emphasised that social dreaming is as much about the sharing of free association as it is about dreams. It is the use of shared free association that binds the participants in a social dreaming matrix together, thus providing the sensation of shared experience. If images emerge that become symbolic in social dreaming, they are often, not always but to a certain extent, created by the participants in the matrix. For Jung, however, the symbol was eternal and could be interpreted in a historical and cultural context. The primordial, which could not be explained as belonging to the individual was the result of 'aboriginal, innate, and inherited shapes of the human mind' (Jung 1978, p. 57). The following example illustrates both this and the sense that Jung's interpretation could end up sounding unfortunately definitive and unarguable:

> "Horse" is an archetype that is widely current in mythology and folklore. As an animal it represents the non-human psyche, the subhuman, animal side, the unconscious… Also, it has to do with sorcery and magical spells – especially the black night-horses which herald death./ It is evident, then,

that "horse" is an equivalent of "mother" with a slight shift of meaning. (Jung 2002 [1931], pp. 106–107)

It is both fascinating and instructive to compare Jung's description of the horse as an archetype to the occurrence of the horse in the sample extract from the previous chapter. In that extract, it is clear that even if the image of the horse has some of Jung's interpretation in it, the image, in its intertwining with the previous dreams and associations, becomes more nuanced and complex than the rather simpler mythical representation suggested by Jung.

An essential skill in dream interpretation for Jung, therefore, was an in-depth knowledge of mythology, folklore and religion, which is not needed in social dreaming. Jung of course did not limit his interpretations to archetypal symbols, but the cases of dream interpretation that didn't include those archetypes were located back to the individual. The shared aspects of dreams, for Jung, were based on a collective unconscious that was populated with symbolic archetypes. Individual dreams were acknowledged to contain 'emotionally charged pictorial language' (Jung 1978, p. 30), but this aspect of the dream belonged to the individual unless it could be seen as an archetype. In social dreaming, the emotions (that later we shall define as 'affects') that are held in an image belong to the shared space of the matrix rather than being the sole property of the individual. Although Jung adopted Lévy-Brühl's idea of 'mystical participation' (ibid., p. 7) to describe tribal people's sense of collaboration with their environment, this almost invariably emanates outwards from the individual rather than vice versa. In contrast to this, social dreaming removes the personal aspect of the dream and free associative images from the individual and reboots the experience as starting from the shared social space. Hence the insistence in social dreaming that participants in a matrix are interested in the dream and not the dreamer. This is why Jung's 'collective unconscious' is not a version of social dreaming. Jung's collective archetypes, according to Jung himself were inborn, primordial, and common to all (Jung 1991). They are connected to myths and fairy tales and identifiable through generally recognised symbols (the Mother, the Trickster, the Cross, and so on). Unlike these archetypes, the shared images of the social dreaming matrix are only occasionally reminiscent of the Jungian universe. Most of the images and how they inter-relate with each other in the process of the social dreaming matrix appear to emerge from a shared experience of life (the 'social') that we all experience, which is not the primordial archetype that we share through inheritance.

This different shared source has been variously described as the 'social unconscious' (Fromm 1962; Hopper 2003), the 'political unconscious' (Bermudez and Silverstein 2013), the 'cultural unconscious' (Henderson 1988), the 'potential space' (Winnicott 1991) and the 'associative unconscious' (Long 2013), and for some commentators interested in a Jungian perspective, these third spaces have been placed in between the personal and the Jungian collective unconscious. It was the social unconscious that most appealed to Lawrence, but as was often the case, he refrained from explaining the nature and quality of this social unconscious in any depth:

> Social Dreaming makes possible the examination of the social unconscious, which comes into existence when three or more people relate through their individual unconscious. Through their unconsciousness they discover an added quality to their unconscious mind which would be beyond the capabilities of their individual unconscious. This is the social unconscious. (Lawrence 2007, p. 6)

So although he did not develop or situate in context the idea of the social unconscious, Lawrence clearly did not conceive of the social aspect of social dreaming as being similar to Jung's collective unconscious. Despite the interest of some Jungians in social dreaming, (Noack 2010; Morgan 2007; Tatham 2003, 2007; Tatham and Morgan 1998), the idea of social dreaming being an example of Jungian dream work is unsubstantiated. For some, it has been a source of conflict: 'One participant…was a distinguished professor with a Jungian background. She pointed out that there was nothing new in this programme because the Jungians had been doing it for years. I let her remark pass' (Lawrence 1998, p. 20).

Other aspects of Jungian thinking that have been claimed as being part of social dreaming are the Jungian method of amplification of dream interpretation and the concept of synchronicity (Noack 2010). While it is true that a form of amplification seems to occur in the social dreaming matrix (and Lawrence also accepted this to some extent, (Lawrence 1998, p. 1, 2005, p. 13)), this is not exactly what Jung originally proposed. The amplification that tends to occur in the social dreaming matrix refers to a kind of further thought or development of an image from a dream or association. It implies something more than a simple association, and yet it is not quite a Jungian amplification that relied on making parallels with and developing the meanings of dreams according to mythical symbols, or historical and cultural archetypes that would be evidence of the collective unconscious.

Indigenous Dream Sharing and the Western Tradition

Implicit and explicit in Jung's primordial or archetypal work is the idea that the western world has somehow lost an ancient wisdom that indigenous populations have traditionally held and may still possess today. This wisdom is, according to Jung, partly located in the archetypes of our dreams. The reason this is of interest to the study of social dreaming is that it would give a precedent and a historico-cultural basis for social dreaming data. As Lawrence points out, 'anthropological studies of dreaming focus on the relationship between dreaming and culture, not on aspects of the individual dreamer' (Lawrence 2005, p. 2). Gosling and Case, in their study of the use of social dreams to presage an ecological crisis to come, refer to this indigenous dream wisdom, and cite a range of anthropological literature that makes the case (Gosling and Case 2013, p. 7). I have discussed elsewhere the origins of dream sharing in relation to the 'discovery' of social dreaming, and concluded that social dreaming more likely arose from an increased sensibility to the possibility of dreams and the sharing of dreams and the creative potential of free association as expressed through the art and poetry of the early twentieth century, in particular through the influence of André Breton's 'automatic writing' (1997), which used a version of free association; Salvador Dalí's paranoic-critical method, that encouraged the linking of unrelated objects; the

Surrealist Manifesto (Breton 1992); and the Surrealist movement in general (Manley 2014). At approximately the same time, 1933–1939, Charlotte Beradt was collecting the dreams of German people as the Nazi regime was being developed. Her book, *The Third Reich of Dreams* (1968), demonstrated the potential for personal dreams to be applied to the social and is acknowledged by Lawrence as being the prime catalyst for the idea of social dreaming.

The indigenous dream-sharing theory of the origin of social dreaming is maybe the source of the claim made by Lawrence and others that social dreaming is none other than a continuation of a lost mode of communication among people. This thinking forms the basis for Lawrence's claim to be the 'discoverer' rather than the creator or inventor of social dreaming. That dreams have always been shared among some indigenous communities is worth mentioning here in order to point out that the sharing of dreams which does not focus on the individual may have echoes of practice elsewhere and in other cultures and times, but this is not the same as making special claims for these cultures as being primary sources of the origins of social dreaming.

Social Dreaming Is Not Therapy

Since Freud's *Interpretation of Dreams* (1991 [1900]), dreams in a psychoanalytic context have been associated with the clinical relationship between psychoanalyst and patient, and, therefore, with therapy. Social dreaming, however, is not concerned with therapy, even though participants in social dreaming sessions sometimes report sensations of wellbeing as a result of attending a social dreaming matrix (see Manley 2014 for a discussion of the differences between the use of dreams in therapy and the 'social' dream, and Thomas (2018) for a discussion of the differences between psychoanalysis and the psychosocial and, by implication, between therapy and research). Lawrence himself was clear about these differences and drew up this helpful table illustrating what he thought were the differences between therapeutic dreaming and social dreaming (Table 2.1).

The key to the difference lies in the removal of the source of the dream from its apparently individualised root to the shared social space of the

Table 2.1 The difference between therapeutic dreams and social dreams

The Therapeutic Dream (TG)	The Social Dream (SDM)
The dreamer is in the centre	The dream is in the centre
The individual aspect	The social aspect
Profound exploration of the past	Looking to the future
Dramatising the personal biography	Facing life as a tragedy
Oedipus	Sphinx
Egocentric	Sociocentric
Finite	Infinite

Lawrence (2002, p. 224)

social dreaming matrix. A social understanding of dream sharing is difficult to align with therapy, as, for example, the widely assumed relevance of the dream to the individual and therefore to the individual's life story that connects to a Freudian-influenced use of the dream as being 'Oedipal' in nature, in other words as harbouring repression that is linked to mental illness. According to Lawrence, therapeutic dreaming was 'finite', meaning that it was boundaried within the individual. The 'infinite' in social dreaming refers to the social unconscious and the never-ending possibilities of associative thinking that can be maintained by the social dreaming matrix. Lawrence was given to an understanding of the unconscious as a neutral or benign aspect of human thought. As such, the unconscious is open to sharing in a way that is comparable to conscious thought.

A Deleuzian Philosophy That Can Also Be Psychoanalytically Informed

If social dreams are neither the stuff of the dyadic encounter between psychoanalyst and analysand, nor just historical and cultural dream records of an indigenous kind; and if they are not essentially Jungian and not focussed on therapeutic practice, it is not immediately clear where they belong. The premise of this book is to provide an epistemological framework to relocate social dreaming in a new place. As we shall see in Parts II and III, this new location is within a broadly Deleuzian paradigm. For some psychoanalytically informed readers, this may already be interpreted as anti-psychology, given the radical and provocative anti-Freudian views very often attributed to Deleuze and Guattari, not without reason, since their work *Anti-Oedipus* (2004) specifically rejects the Freudian 'tripartite formula – the Oedipal, neurotic one: daddy-mommy-me' (p. 25). This question is discussed in Chap. 4. Suffice to say at this juncture, that a psychoanalytically informed approach to social dreaming can also be a Deleuzian approach, though not a traditional one, and this book intends to demonstrate this.

As Deleuze later explained, the Deleuzian-Guattarian project in *Anti-Oedipus* was not anti-psychology but very precisely anti-Oedipus. It was opposed to the psychoanalytical emphasis on the individual and the total rejection by the psychoanalyst – a kind of censorship even – of the wider cultural and environmental ambit of each individual. The exact truth of this position is not my concern here, but I note, rather, the explicit call for bringing the social into psychoanalytical awareness in a way that easily resonates with social dreaming. This is how Deleuze puts it in an interview:

> Psychiatrists and psychoanalysts hear nothing of this [delirious anxiety and confusion about the political, cultural and social state of the world they inhabit], on the defensive as much as they are indefensible. They crush the contents of the unconscious under prefab statements: "You speak to me of the Chinese, but what about your father? No, he isn't Chinese? Then do you have a Chinese lover?" It's at the same level of repressive work as the judge in the Angela Davis [political activist] case who affirmed: "Her behaviour can only be explained by her being in love." And what if, on the contrary, Angela Davis's libido was a social, revolutionary libido? What if she were in love because she was a revolutionary? (Deleuze, quoted in Guattari 2009, p. 51)

This dramatic relocation of the individual psyche into the social context came together with the 1960s' and 1970s' demand for thought (and therefore the psyche) to be revolutionary. In other words, there was a suspicion that an individual (psyche) might be turned into itself and tuned inwards to a sense of the individual which could too readily be associated with capitalism. If this happened, a collective revolution would never be possible, and revolution was an essential part of the intellectual thought of the time. This is how the political sphere, for Deleuze and Guattari, is also a psychological space. In order to create this new space, as I will describe below, the sanctuary of the unified object of the individual Self would have to be rejected in favour of a disunified distribution of part objects that are not only belonging to the individual but to all individuals together, forming an ever-changing mass that can be more readily identified as a shared cultural, political, social and psychological space.

As an illustration of how widespread this view of psychoanalysis might have been at the time, it is worth comparing this Deleuzian psychological space with the opinion of Deleuze's philosophical and intellectual ally, Michel Foucault, who was able to affirm that it was no longer possible to consider the historical, political and social without psychology. In fact, he went as far as to say that 'all there is now, basically, is psychology' (Foucault 2000, p. 252, also quoted below). The spirit of the present book's exploration is to challenge one's intellectual 'negative capability' through this kind of revolution, to ask the reader to accept a temporary discomfort while walking unchartered territory and to watch out for new landscapes and vistas. This resonates with Lacan's definition of psychoanalysis as 'something that psychoanalysis keeps to itself, something that gives it this dignity, gives it some weight', a 'position that I have sometimes called by the name it deserves: 'extraterritorial'' (Lacan 2008, p. 14). Psychoanalysis, in this book, will be open to extraterritorial spaces, allowing for the possibility of fresh insights into the possibility of the use of social dreams to create new ways of using the knowledge of the shared or associative unconscious discussed below.

However, before moving to the extraterritorial spaces that occupy Parts II and III, the next chapter summarises the better known spaces inhabited by Bion, Winnicott, and Bollas as spaces of knowledge that would have been recognisable and close to Gordon Lawrence as the discoverer of social dreaming. Chapter 3 brings together many of Lawrence's ideas on a theory of social dreaming that are distributed throughout his work.

References

Beradt, C. (1968). *The Third Reich of Dreams. The Nightmares of a Nation 1933–1939.* Chicago, IL: Quadrangle B.

Bermudez, G. and Silverstein, M. (2013). Social Dreaming Applications in Academic and Community Settings. *Other/wise*, 1(Spring), pp. 33–54. (https://ifpe.wordpress.com/2013-issues/volume-1-spring-2013/) Accessed 07.05.18.

Breton, A. (1992). First manifesto of surrealism 1924. In Harrison, C. and Wood, P. (Eds.), *Art in Theory 1900–2000*. Padstow: Blackwell.

Breton, A., Eluard, P., and Soupault, P. (1997). *The Automatic Message*. London: BCM Atlas Press.

Deleuze, G. and Guattari, F. (2004). *Anti-Oedipus. Capitalism and Schizophrenia*. London: Continuum.

Foucault, M. (2000). Philosophy and psychology. In Faubion, J.D. (Ed.), *Essential Works of Foucault 1954–1984, Volume* 2. London: Penguin.

Freud, S. (Strachey, J. (Trans.). (1991 [1900]). *The Interpretation of Dreams*. London: Penguin.

Fromm, E. (1962). *Beyond the Chains of Illusion: My encounter with Marx and Freud*. NY: Simon & Schuster.

Gosling, J. and Case, P. (2013). Social dreaming and ecocentric ethics: Sources of non-rational insight in the face of climate change catastrophe. *Organization*, pp. 1–17.

Guattari, F. (2009). *Chaosophy. Texts and interviews 1972–1977*. South Pasadena, CA: Semiotext(e).

Henderson, J.L. (1988). The cultural unconscious. *Quadrant: Journal of the C. G. Jung Foundation for Analytical Psychology*, 21(2), pp. 7–16.

Hopper, E. (2003). *The Social Unconscious*. International Library of Group Analysis 22. London: Jessica Kingsley Publishers.

Jung, C.G. (2002 [1931]). The practical use of dream-analysis. In *Dreams*, pp. 85–109. London: Routledge.

Jung, C.G. (1991). *The Archetypes and the Collective Unconscious (Collected Works of C. G. Jung)*. London: Routledge.

Jung, C.G. (1978). *Man and his Symbols*. London: Picador.

Lacan, J. (2008). *My Teaching*. London: Verso.

Lawrence, W.G. (Ed.). (1998). *Social Dreaming @ Work*. London: Karnac.

Lawrence, W.G. (2002). The complementarity of social dreaming and therapeutic dreaming. In Neri, C., Pines, M., and Friedman, R. (Eds.), *Dreams in Group Psychotherapy*, pp. 220–233. London: JKP.

Lawrence, W.G. (2005). *Introduction to Social Dreaming. Transforming Thinking*. London: Karnac.

Lawrence, W.G. (Ed.). (2007). *Infinite Possibilities of Social Dreaming*. London: Karnac.

Long, S. (2013). *Socioanalytic Methods*. London: Karnac.

Manley, J. (2014). Gordon Lawrence's Social Dreaming Matrix: Background, origins, history and developments. *Organisational and Social Dynamics*, 14(2), pp. 322–342.

Morgan, H. (2007). Shedding light on organizational shadows. In Lawrence, W.G. (Ed.), *Infinite Possibilities of Social Dreaming*, pp. 106–112. London: Karnac.

Noack, A. (2010). Social dreaming: Competition or complementation to individual dreaming? *The Journal of Analytical Psychology*, 55(5), pp. 672–690.

Tatham, P. (2003). Social dreaming and the senior managers' programme. In Lawrence, W.G. (Ed.), *Experiences in Social Dreaming*. London: Karnac, pp. 179–189.

Tatham, P. (2007). Social Dreaming at the Jung Congress. In Lawrence, W.G. (Ed.), *Infinite Possibilities of Social Dreaming*, pp. 113–120. London: Karnac.

Tatham, P. and Morgan, H. (1998). The social dreaming matrix. In Lawrence, W.G. (Ed.), *Social Dreaming @ Work*. London: Karnac.

Thomas, J. (2018). "As easy as to know...": On the tensions between psychoanalysis and psychosocial research. In Cummins, A.M. and Williams, N., *Further Researching Beneath the Surface*. London: Routledge, pp. 3–26.

Winnicott, D.W. (1991). *Playing and Reality*. London: Routledge.

3

From Group Relations to the Social Dreaming Matrix

Although the circumstances of Lawrence's life and his own intellectual background impeded him (and others, in part due to Lawrence's own fierce possession of his idea) from developing a complete theory of social dreaming, he nevertheless seeded many interesting thoughts and clues about his own way of seeing the process, and many of these are still useful and relevant. This chapter considers these ideas as a starting point towards a theory for social dreaming.

Group Dynamics and Bion's Unconscious

Lawrence emerged with his social dreaming from the world of group relations and organisational consultancy. He sometimes seemed to hold an aversion to group relations, especially the interpretive and therapeutic aspects of group relations work. People who attend group relations conferences are often warned of the emotional struggles that await them and advised to not attend a conference if they are going through a difficult period in their lives. None of this is relevant for social dreaming, because according to Lawrence, and to a certain extent corroborated in practice

J. Manley, *Social Dreaming, Associative Thinking and Intensities of Affect*,
Studies in the Psychosocial, https://doi.org/10.1007/978-3-319-92555-4_3

and through experience, social dreaming moves away from the ego and the historical/biographical past and moves towards the social and the future.

It was imperative, as Lawrence saw it, to move away from a therapeutic use of the dream – which, according to him in 1982 was only possible in the consulting room – to the use of dreams outside the dyadic psychoanalytic relationship and within a group setting where the dream moves away from the individual and becomes part of the shared space of the group. This move from psychodynamic group to social dreaming matrix, also obliged Lawrence to consider what else was going on in a group that was detrimental to social dreaming matrix work. This is why interpretation in a group context was disliked by Lawrence, where this interpretation would be 'omnipotent' on the part of the consultant, and would be directed at a group member's personal, individual way of being with others, with the roots of that interpretation finding its way to that individual's personal biography. In the case of working with dreams in a matrix, an interpretation would also foreclose the potential for the dream to become a shared dream of relevance to the others in the matrix. The interpretation would belong to that individual, and the dream would similarly be assigned to that person. This was the basis for Lawrence's insistence on the 'working hypothesis' replacing interpretation. This working hypothesis, would also be about what the dreams were saying concerning the participants' combined thinking in the context of the current shared social situation. It includes a potential for shared future imaginings, rather than being related to either an individual or the psychodynamics of the group. It was in these circumstances that he partially borrowed from Wilfred Bion, ignoring Bion's psychodynamic interpretations of group work, which were about the whole group behaving in ways that could be interpreted psychoanalytically, and working only with Bion's theory of thinking. This theory of thinking, which was applied to the matrix, and implicitly sanctioned somehow by Bion's work with groups, led to Lawrence being able to justify the idea of the sharing of unconscious material as if that material were a single piece as opposed to a collection of individual fragments, which would be as relevant to the social space as conscious thought. Lawrence removed the group dynamics and introduced the idea of dreams as being products of unconscious thinking that are processed not only within the individual but also through a shared environment, in exactly the same way as people are able to share thoughts which arise in a similar environment but in the conscious domain. The unconscious, in this context, is not the individual repository of biographical struggle with childhood adjustments to the world, but an intimately shared social space where thinking continues to develop, albeit in another way. In this sense, dreaming is thinking. The social dreaming matrix creates a new space where these unconscious thoughts in the form of dreams, can be shared and combined with conscious thinking. The whole experience is almost like removing a sense of an individual body and replacing this sensation with another, quite uncanny, of a profoundly shared and interconnected 'body' with others forming part of this new 'body'. This sensation and what it means for a theory of social dreaming will be discussed in Parts II and III.

Bion's Theory of Thinking, Dreaming and Social Dreaming

Returning to Bion, it becomes clear that by accepting Bion's conceptualisation of the unconscious, and therefore drawing together his theory of the psyche with Lawrence's own view of the social, Lawrence was able to turn social dreaming into a psycho-social phenomenon. As mentioned above, Lawrence interpreted the unconscious in social dreaming according to Bion's concept of the 'Sphinx' as opposed to the Oedipal unconscious, with the latter, for Lawrence, being irredeemably linked to Freud and the consultant's couch. The Sphinx, in Bion's mention of it in his introduction to *Experiences in Groups* (2000), is the aspect of the psychoanalytic approach that relates to the group and 'problems of knowledge and scientific method' (p. 8), while the Oedipal is related to the individual. Bion understood that both approaches could be used in group work, with different but appropriate results, in what he called a 'binocular vision' (p. 8). Lawrence believed that in social dreaming, the psychoanalytic approach being adopted was only that of the Sphinx. For this to be so, the dream has to be extracted from its individual focus and made social. For Lawrence it follows, therefore, that the dream is the centre of a shared social unconscious. The main point here is not so much whether this unconscious is 'social' but rather that it is not individual. If we take Bion's Sphinx and literally apply it to the social dreaming matrix, we can say that the sharing of dreams brings with it the shared working out of life's puzzles, just as the puzzle of the Sphinx, which spans the lifetime of a human being had to be worked out to avoid destruction. The solving of life's puzzles through the knowledge engendered through thinking can lead to a future that does not depend on a past. This is the crux of the matter. This is what Lawrence meant when he suggested that the thinking of the matrix 'looks to the future'; it was not dependent on a biographical and individualised past. This also explains the strangely prophetic nature of some of the dream work in the matrix. Clare, in writing about apparently prophetic dreams of the 9/11 attacks points out that it is 'not that dreams were magical predictions of future events of which people had no prior knowledge… they were dreaming about the future but it was a future that lay dormant in the present' (Clare and Zarbafi 2009, p. 39).

The conceptualising of the unconscious as a thinking zone in this way, enabled Bion to create his own theory of thinking that became directly useful for Lawrence's way of understanding social dreaming. As is well known, Bion (1967, 1970) assumed that the unconscious contained what he denominated Beta elements, which were raw, unprocessed information and sensations in the mind. He then suggested that partly through a process of reverie these Beta elements could undergo a process of change and be transformed into so-called Alpha elements which were the Beta information transformed into a form that could be experienced, reflected upon, potentially made sense of, and remembered. In this way the unprocessed Beta elements are given a form such as visual images in dreams or other sensory symbols. Dream work, therefore, provides the conditions of meaning-making and activates the aesthetic dimension of mind (Pistiner de Cortiñas 2009). The shared dreams in social dreaming activate an aesthetic capacity in the matrix, and transform raw sensory material into communicable thoughts. Bion postulated the existence of a 'contact barrier' that separates the conscious and unconscious world, where Alpha elements as 'visual pictograms' can be consciously thought while still retaining qualities of the unconscious (Ferrero 2002, p. 598). This description seems to come close to the sensation of taking part in a social dreaming matrix, occupying the space between the conscious and unconscious worlds that human beings inhabit.

Bollas' Unthought Known

It will be remembered that Lawrence's idea of thinking included two aspects of the unconscious, dreaming and the unthought known (see Fig. 1.2). This latter concept is not necessarily easy to understand and is used slightly differently in social dreaming to Bollas' use of it in a clinical setting (Bollas 1987). Bollas' definition of the unthought known is firstly related to early personal memories that have been forgotten in adulthood, but nevertheless survive as memories that are 'known', in the sense that they are memories with potential, but they are not yet 'thought' into consciousness, the process of which is evidenced through the relating of such thoughts into language ('the reliving through language of that which is known but not yet thought' (ibid., p. xv)). Unlike Bion's Beta Elements, these are not necessarily raw sensations, but more akin to forgotten memories. Lawrence, however, despite his separation in Fig. 1.2 above of unknown thought and dream thinking, actually finds it difficult to separate the unthought known from the process of sharing a dream in the social dreaming matrix. Therefore, although he discusses the difference in *Introduction to Social Dreaming* (2005, p. 21), his example dream evokes the unthought known as being something that people knew but somehow had not consciously registered, which is certainly true in his example, (p. 10), but is not a forgotten memory in Bollas' use of the term. In the way that Lawrence gives his example, the unthought known is actually part of dream thinking, thereby fusing the two modes of thinking that he himself is at pains to separate.

As in much of Lawrence's work, his intuition was sound, even if its redaction was flawed. What I believe Lawrence meant but did not articulate was that the unthought known represents part of the associative work in social dreaming. Lawrence was so preoccupied with the dreams themselves that he often relegated the work of associative thinking in the social dreaming matrix, possibly because he was so determined to move away from linking social dreaming to group work, as discussed above. The role and importance of associative thinking and the associative unconscious has recently assumed a greater importance in studies on social dreaming, especially in the work of Long (2013, in press) and Manley (in press).

It seems to me that the lost memories that constitute Bollas' unthought known are triggered by dreams and expressed as associations to those dreams in the course of the social dreaming matrix. This would account for the feeling of the transformative nature of the matrix, how people frequently leave a session feeling, if not necessarily transformed, often re-energised and significantly different to when they started the matrix. This feeling emerges not only from the dreams, but in how the dreams are linked and intertwined with each other through a process of association that combines dreams and the unthought knowns that they trigger. It is a process that resonates with Bollas' description of the aesthetic experience as constituting an experience in adult life that can ignite the expression of early transformative memories of the relationship between infant and mother:

> … the infant's experience of his first object. This is, of course, the mother, who is nevertheless known less as a discreet object with particular qualities than as a process linked to the infant's being and the alteration of his being. For this reason, I have termed the early mother a 'transformational object'. And the adult's search for transformation constitutes in some respects a memory of this early relationship. There are other memories of this period of our life, such as aesthetic experience when a person feels uncannily embraced by an object. (Bollas 1987, p. xv)

The feeling of being embraced by another person's dream in the social dreaming matrix is similarly uncanny, and it is this sensation that is conveyed in the flow of associations in the matrix.

Helpfully, Bollas describes the object here as being more like a process. Again, this resonates with the sensations evoked through social dreaming, where one is just as connected to abstract affects – that emerge and become interlinked with each other, almost creating a formless object, a relational process object – as the definable objects that form part of the dreams in the matrix. Helpfully, again, Bollas also describes the importance of dreams in supporting our thinking about ourselves, with these dreams being a place where subject and object can be joined, thus enabling the subject to contemplate itself as an object and therefore think differently about the self.

> The relation to the self as an object is clearly an important feature of our lived life, but it is no more explicit than in the dream, when the dreaming subject (the experiential subject inside the dream) is the object of the dream script. I consider the fact that in the dream we are subject and object… (ibid., p. xv)

This is why and how, if we follow Bollas' theory, the dreams as expressed in social dreaming can resonate with others and lead to associations that bring into active memory and expression the unthought knowns into the thinking process, becoming '*thought* knowns'. When a dream is expressed and shared with others, therefore, they are not just the dreams of their subjects, but the subject objectified, so to speak, and therefore the dreams become more readily available to others. I will pursue this idea in greater detail in Part II below.

Winnicott's Potential Space and Transitional Object

Bion and Bollas, especially the former, have been pivotal for a psychoanalytically informed understanding of social dreaming in Lawrence's world. However, it would seem to me remiss not to mention Winnicott. Clare, in his book with Zarbafi (2009) dedicates some space to Winnicott, and summarises what he describes as key elements of the social dreaming experience as understood through a Winnicottian lens:

- the *potential space* of the matrix
- *transitional objects* (dreams) which can be used
- the capacity for *play* emanating from the dream telling
- glimpses of the *true self* in the spontaneous gesture of free association
- articulation of the *relationship between self and culture* as the dreams are both internal and external, personal and social. (Clare and Zarbafi 2009, p. 14, author's italics)

It seems to me that we have in these fundamental ideas from Winnicott, some interesting ways of understanding social dreaming. It is curious, for example, to see Clare suggesting that a dream can be a transitional object, which, in Winnicott is always a specific physical object into which the baby's good thoughts and wishes are projected. This, it seems to me, resonates with Bollas' idea that the object can be a process. Similarly, the dream can be an object, which, as it combines and recombines itself interconnectively with other dreams and associations in a state of continuous flux, can be felt as if it were an object, like a collage. Furthermore, this object can be used in a transitional way, in the sense that it can provide the focus for our transition from our pre-matrix state of being to a new state of thought and knowledge. Both pre- and post-matrix states are 'reality', while the social dreaming matrix state itself is more akin to Winnicott's potential space, where these dreams can be used in the shared imagination to make hitherto unforeseen connections between ourselves and reality. It is worth pointing out in this context that Winnicott regarded the mature human being's cultural life as the equivalent to the child's potential space of play. In this way, the social dreaming matrix can be considered a potential space for development through creativity and the aesthetic culture of the matrix. Additionally, it should be noted that the sharing aspect of social dreaming is also supported by Winnicottian theory:

> There is a direct development from transitional phenomena to playing and from playing to shared playing, and from this to cultural experiences. (Winnicott 1971, p. 51)

In the same context of his discussion of the use of play in the potential space, Winnicott summarises his chapter in a way that resonates very closely with the process of social dreaming, even referring to the space of play as being enacted as a dream sample in order to distinguish it from either the child's inner or any other external reality:

- This area of playing is not inner psychic reality. It is outside the individual, but it is not the external world.
- Into this play area the child gathers objects or phenomena from external reality and uses these in the service of some sample derived

from inner or personal reality. Without hallucinating the child puts out a sample of dream potential and lives with this sample in a chosen setting of fragments from external reality.
- In playing, the child manipulates external phenomena in the service of the dream and invests chosen external phenomena with dream meaning and feeling. (ibid., p. 51)

If this were to be somehow 'translated' into the process of social dreaming, it is clear to see how the social dreaming matrix occupies this potential space, neither inside nor outside; how without hallucinating, the participants in a matrix feel that they are becoming deeply involved in each other's dream images and how through association, the participants are able to make connections between chosen fragments of external reality and between the dreams and associations; and finally, in the social dreaming matrix, the participants see external phenomena through the lenses of the collage of dreams and associations that are being created within the potential space of the matrix.

References

Bion, W.R. (1967). *Second thoughts*. London: Maresfield.
Bion, W.R. (1970). *Attention and interpretation*. London: Karnac.
Bion, W.R. (2000). *Experiences in Groups and other papers*. London: Routledge.
Bollas, C. (1987). *The Shadow of the Object*. London: Free Association.
Clare, J. and Zarbafi, A. (2009). *Social Dreaming in the 21st Century*. London: Karnac.
Ferrero, A. (2002). Some implications of Bion's thought. The waking dream and narrative derivatives. *The International Journal of Psychoanalysis*, 83(3), pp. 597–607.
Lawrence, W. G. (2005). *Introduction to Social Dreaming. Transforming Thinking*. London: Karnac.
Long, S. (2013). *Socioanalytic Methods*. London: Karnac.
Long, S. (in press). Dreams and Dreaming: A Socioanalytic and Semiotic Perspective. In Long, S. and Manley, J. (Eds.), *Social Dreaming: Philosophy research and practice*. London: Routledge.

Manley, J. (2018). 'Every human being is an artist': From social representation to creative experiences of self. In Cummins, A.M. and Williams, N. (Eds.), *Researching Beneath the Surface*, Vol. 2. London: Routledge.

Manley, J. (in press). Associative thinking: A Deleuzian perspective on social dreaming. In Long, S. and Manley, J. (Eds.), *Social Dreaming: Philosophy, research and practice*. London: Routledge.

Pistiner de Cortinas, L. (2009). *The aesthetic dimension of the mind*. London: Karnac.

Winnicott, D.W. (1971). *Playing and Reality*. London: Routledge.

Winnicott, D.W. (1991). *Playing and Reality*. London: Routledge.

Part II

Deleuzian Approaches

4

Social Dreaming in a New Key

Symbols and Facts

When Susanne Langer wrote her seminal work *Philosophy in a New Key* (1948), she justified what she claimed was a new turn in philosophy by emphasising and differentiating the rational from the empirical fact, especially the fact of scientific positivism. In doing so, she questioned the nature of scientific observation that, according to her, was tending to observe secondary material (e.g., instruments of observation) as opposed to the primary source of observation.

> The promiscuous collection and tabulation of data have given way to a process of assigning possible meanings, merely supposed real entities, to mathematical terms, working out the logical results, and then staging certain crucial experiments to check the hypothesis against the actual empirical results. But the facts which are accepted by virtue of these tests are not actually *observed* at all. (Langer 1948, p. 15 (author's italics))

She pointed out that mathematics was a respected mode of thinking in the sciences but that it was based on logic and symbols rather than observable fact. In this way, she opened out a new line of philosophical

J. Manley, *Social Dreaming, Associative Thinking and Intensities of Affect*,
Studies in the Psychosocial, https://doi.org/10.1007/978-3-319-92555-4_4

approach based on symbols and their interpretation that should be as acceptable to knowledge as the facts of positivism. The importance of this resides in Langer's insistence that one does not necessarily require either facts or empirically defined objects to write rationally acceptable material. In terms of psychosocial attitudes, it is not necessary to definitively separate subject and object, or inner and outer worlds, with the 'inner' representing the psyche and the 'outer' being interpreted as the social. The human subject does not necessarily observe an object in a way that is clear-cut. The boundaries are blurred. In object relations terms, the internal object relations are in constant contact and intercommunication with external objects in ways that make a definite distinction between the inner psyche and the outer social worlds difficult to hold. This harks back to previous debates on the nature of the psychosocial, which is only relevant here inasmuch as the work of social dreaming seems precisely to entail the moving away from the inner individual psyche – the dream of the individual – to the shared unconscious and the external world that justifies this shift – the social dream. And yet, the dream is always a psychic phenomenon. In social dreaming, the dream is indissolubly both inside and outside the individual who dreamt it. This necessarily obscures the differentiation of subject and object which, as we have already noted, Christopher Bollas defined as a peculiarity of the dream: to have the self as subject become the object of the one's dream. As Frosh has said as part of this debate, by combining the inner and outer worlds implied in psychosocial, we are opening out the possibility of introducing a Deleuzian perspective as part of the psychosocial, a possibility that will be explored in this book. Frosh advocates an understanding of the psychosocial

> that sees "inner" and "outer" as run through by a series of forces or perhaps by a field of force that constitutes them as domains that can be experienced as well as studied. The paradigm for such an understanding is not necessarily discursive or Lacanian; it could just as easily be Deleuzian or be theorized through the turn to affect. (Frosh 2008, pp. 420–421)

The principle that needs highlighting here is that in discussing social dreaming it is reasonable and necessary to discard any notion of fact, reality or even empiricism. For Langer, what we 'see' is not necessarily a thing in itself but a form that is created to help a person perceive sense-data:

> I believe that our ingrained habit of hypostatizing impressions, of seeing *things* and not sense-data, rests on the fact that we promptly and unconsciously abstract a form from each sensory experience, and use this form to conceive the experience as a whole, as a "thing". (Langer 1948, p. 72 (author's italics))

This relationship between the senses and the formulation of 'things' is important to the discussion of a dream image and its connection to affect, discussed below. Langer goes on to discuss the symbol at length, but symbols per se are not uniquely important in a discussion of social dreaming. Indeed, a thinker like Jung (1978) equated symbol with archetype, and I have already suggested that social dreaming is not primarily concerned with archetypes. Langer herself is amenable to a general 'notion of symbolization' that could be 'mystical, practical or mathematical, it makes no difference' (Langer 1948, p. 19), and this more generalized notion of the symbol is more relevant to this reflection on social dreaming. Most of all, for these purposes, a symbol is not a fact or even necessarily representative of fact.

Image-affects

It is useful, therefore, to view the dreams and associations in social dreaming as consisting of forms that encapsulate and give shape to sensation or 'affect', the latter suggesting a complex multiplicity of holistic emotional intensities in the Deleuzian or Spinozian sense of that word, which will be discussed at greater length below (see also Manley 2009). This giving of form to affect I have previously denominated the 'image-affect' (ibid., 2009), which is a reminder that the visual images we are discussing are not representations of things that we can see as observable facts but rather affects in visual attire.

The idea of forms of intensity or image-affects being part of the process and production of social dreaming can be illustrated by returning to

Bion's idea, as adapted by Gordon Lawrence, of the unconscious processes of social dreaming being understood as a Sphinx-like rather than as an Oedipal process. The image-affects and the unconscious panorama from where they emerge in their Sphinx-like configurations are knowledge puzzles in constant processes of bringing forth or giving shape to consciousness as they move through strata of thinking, with these thoughts flowing in incessant and ever-emerging forms of ephemeral creation. The image-affects are ephemeral because they are never conclusively defined. Instead, they flow in augmentations or diminutions of intensities according to the circumstance of their relative configurations. In social dreaming, because the images in the dreams are shared, their sense is similarly shared. There can only be a sense in the happenings between each of the image affects, for which there need to be at least two in mutual relationship. If these were words only, as opposed to descriptions of image-affects, they could be understood as rendering meaning through the spaces between the words rather than in their explicit connections that attempt to bridge those gaps, in Derridean fashion. By adding a third image-affect from a dream to the previous two, the complexity of affect is multiplied and senses may fluctuate in intensity between image-affects in ways that are never stable, yet always authentic, and with no preconceived pattern of linearity between them.

As a social dreaming process continues, the sense in the image-affects becomes progressively multiplied and the fluctuations in intensities become ever more sophisticated. It is the containing aspect of the matrix that enables this complexity to be held in the minds of the participants, who otherwise would be faced with a potentially overwhelming accumulation of image-affects. Through the shared containing process of the matrix, participants are able to support each other's image-affects and allow these to exist in their complexities without undue simplification or reduction that might otherwise be necessary in order to feel comfortable about holding such uncertainty. This feeling of holding meaning in the container of the social dreaming matrix is akin to Bion's oft cited idea of 'negative capability' (Simpson and French 2006), the acceptance of living with the uncertainty that arises from the image-affects of the dreams, with no foreclosing explanations or interpretations, and therefore allowing the exponential growth of complexity to emerge and to create its own interlinking possibilities within the minds of each participant and without a need to come to an overt agreement with one's neighbour as to the exact meanings of these dreams, images and associations. The lived uncertainty of the image-affects resides in the agreement – stated at the beginning of each social dreaming matrix and re-iterated in the actual practice of the social dreaming process – that in the course of the social dreaming session, there will be no cognitive interpretation of the dreams offered to the space. This does not mean that participants are awash in a meaningless activity, however. If that were the case, the social dreaming matrix would soon disintegrate. The meanings that hold the matrix together are, rather, internally and affectively processed by each participant, and in this way, the affective nature of the dream images is respected and maintained during the course of the social dreaming matrix. Allusions to meaning are sometimes offered to others, and are therefore externalised, through association rather than interpretation. Such associations may trigger intensities of affect in the collage-like puzzle of image-affects that are at any given moment floating in the matrix, or they may not; furthermore, they may do so in some of the participants and not in others. But if they do not trigger such intensities in some of the participants, that does not make them any less valid, because the matrix is not being conducted in a cognitive or factual mode. Instead, the matrix is formed through the knowledge of affect, where feelings of importance are noted and become 'true' or meaningful through the intensity – and therefore the authenticity – of an affect to one or more of the participants in the matrix. There is no demand for meaning except that which is felt, and when a participant is 'capable of being in uncertainties, mysteries, doubts, without any irritable reach after fact & reason……' (Keats [1817] 1970, p. 43).

It is precisely the maintaining of this mysterious and uncertain collage of image-affects of social dreaming that is one of its defining factors. It also helps to define that sense of playfulness and creativity that people feel they have engaged with in social dreaming. It is almost describable as a sense of meaning in suspension, a state wherein the mind is in continual flux from one affective combination to the next, in a series of possibilities of meaning that never settle. In this scenario, we are close to Deleuze and Guattari's idiosyncratic critique of Kleinian and object relations theory in *Anti-Oedipus* (2004); and although they never mention this in terms of

Bion's Sphinx as opposed to Oedipus, the potential parallels between the Deleuizan position and that of the Sphinx become intriguing if we bear them both simultaneously in mind.

Anti-Oedipus

In discussing Deleuze and Guattari's understanding of the anti-Oedipus in the context of social dreaming, I will take up Foucault's warning that their writing is full of 'games and snares scattered throughout the book' which might provoke the reader to 'take one's leave of the text and slam the door shut' (Foucault, in Deleuze and Guattari 2004, p. xvi). But a little patience will take us far.

Like Lawrence, Deleuze and Guattari were suspicious of the Oedipal. For Lawrence, it was the idea of the unconscious as a repository of repressions that was not suitable for understanding the role of the unconscious in social dreaming. Lawrence was disposed to see the positive in the shared unconscious experience of social dreaming. Similarly, Deleuze and Guattari were opposed to the negativity they thought was implied in the Freudian Oedipal position. Unlike Lawrence, however, they went to great lengths to attempt to debunk, in their view, the Oedipal myth.

Desiring-machines

Deleuze and Guattari begin and continue their work by lauding desire as opposed to the feelings of repression that are associated with it from a Freudian perspective:

> Oedipus presupposes a fantastic repression of desiring-machines. And why are they repressed? To what end? Is it really necessary or desirable to submit to such repression? (Ibid., p. 3)

By describing 'desire' in terms of a 'machine', they refer to the interconnected links between all things and the difficulty of separation between elements. As mentioned above in discussing the image-affect, any meaning inherent in the dreams and associations of social dreaming are emergent in the links and interconnections between the dreams, images and affects rather than each of these in isolation. This, which is a knowledge of affect is quite distinct from any cognitive knowledge, as Deleuze and Guattari immediately point out at the beginning of their book:

> Can we possibly guess, for instance, what a knife rest is used for if all we are given is a geometrical description of it? (Ibid., p. 3)

Non-linearity

Although Deleuze and Guattari locate their initial discussion within a Marxist framework, their descriptions of the desiring-machines and the creative ('production') process that provides for their functions are immediately relevant to a knowledge process that is liberated from cognitive (and in Deleuzian terms, 'striated') thought. As part of this different way to knowledge, Deleuze and Guattari reject linearity and bind together opposites in a way that closely resembles the way the image-affects interconnect to make collages of potential meaning:

> ...man and nature are not like two opposite terms confronting each other – not even in the sense of bipolar opposites within a relationship of causation, ideation, or expression (cause and effect, subject and object, etc.); rather they are one and the same essential reality, the producer-product. (Ibid., p. 5)

Partial Objects

According to Deleuze and Guattari, whole objects cannot exist if that implies, therefore, that they are essentially separated. The way to connect fragmented objects from a Deleuzian perspective, is to connect them through the creative process which they call 'desire':

> Desire constantly couples continuous flows and partial objects that are by nature fragmentary and fragmented. (Ibid., p. 6)

It is not difficult to see how this desiring process could be applied to social dreaming, where the dreams, images and affect are fragmented in the sense that they are offered to the matrix as single or personal image-affects that acquire richness and sense through the interconnectivity of the dreams within the container of the matrix, what I have been calling the collage of image-affects.

It is in refusing to unify wholes except as different unities of partial objects that Deleuze and Guattari make their important critique of Melanie Klein. Deleuze and Guattari reject a belief in the parts as being necessarily destined for a pre-determined whole, and in doing so praise Klein's discovery of the importance of part objects and yet at the same time deny her theory that part objects are a negative cause of the paranoid schizoid position that should be remedied in maturity through a reunification of the parts into the whole and thereby lead the mature adult into the depressive position. Instead, they declare, 'we live today in the age of partial objects' (Ibid., p. 45). For Deleuze and Guattari, partial objects legitimately exist as such and are not dependent on any sense of reunification with any whole. Similarly, they refuse to limit desire to the Oedipal paradigm and the implications for the unconscious. In this they are deliberately provocative in the way that Foucault warned in his preface:

> Partial objects unquestionably have a sufficient charge in and of themselves to blow up all of Oedipus and totally demolish its ridiculous claim to represent the unconscious, to triangulate the unconscious, to encompass the entire production of desire. (Ibid., p. 48)

Desire and the creativity that for Deleuze and Guattari is implicit in that word, is the energy that connects partial objects in non-definitive ways 'by connecting themselves to other partial objects' (Ibid., p. 49). They continue by emphasising the non-representational nature of part objects, denying that the Kleinian 'good breast' is part of the mother in the infant's perception, but that rather it is part of a 'desiring-machine connected to the baby's mouth, and is experienced as an object providing a nonpersonal flow of milk' (Ibid., p. 50), the point being, in this case, that the partial object is a thing in itself and not a representation of something. The most interesting aspect of this iconoclastic critique of Klein, and especially of Freud, for the study of social dreaming is that the Deleuzian framework provides a range of interesting ways of understanding the social dreaming process that have never been perceived in this way before and which can help to illuminate both the Deleuzian voice and the developing theories of social dreaming.

This is the 'new key' borrowed from Langer and referred to in the title of this chapter, which will be developed in the course of this book. Some of these aspects of Deleuzian philosophy will be further developed and others will be added, placing social dreaming in a specifically Deleuzian context which retains its connections to its psychoanalytic Lawrencian roots but at the same time develops theories and ways of understanding social dreaming that Lawrence and others have struggled to develop within the confines of the approaches that are largely reliant on Kleinian perspectives.

References

Deleuze, G. and Guattari, F. (2004). *Anti-Oedipus. Capitalism and Schizophrenia*. London: Continuum.

Frosh, S. (2008). On negative critique: A reply. *Psychoanalysis, Culture & Society*, 13, pp. 416–422.

Jung, C.G. (1978). *Man and his Symbols*. London: Picador.

Keats, J. (Gittings, G. Ed.). (1970). *Letters of John Keats*. Oxford: OUP.

Langer, S. (1948). *A Philosophy in a New Key*. NY: Mentor New American Library.

Manley, J. (2009). When words are not enough. In Clarke, S. and Hoggett, P. (Eds.), *Researching Beneath the Surface*, pp. 79–99. London: Karnac.

Simpson, P. and French, R. (2006). Negative Capability and the Capacity to Think in the Present Moment. *Leadership*, 2(2), pp. 245–255.

5

From Thinking Linearity to Feeling Non-linearity

Non-linearity, Again

The concept of non-linearity is fundamental to social dreaming and yet it goes against an understanding of thinking that is underpinned by natural inclinations of linear time and linear expressions of thoughts through words and sentences that begin and end in a line, and which would seem to indicate a natural place for rationality, logic and a confidence in the validity of the sequentiality of thoughts. Inevitably, such linearity is also connected to ideas of cause and effect, plans and outcomes and to pre-conceived ideas about the sequential structure of existence. Most research methods in the social sciences depend on this assumption, even creative visual research methods such as photovoice which, although their starting point is a photo, is used in documentary fashion to build narratives and encourage dialogue.

Social dreaming, however, defies this assumed logic of thoughts and sequences that 'lead somewhere'. In social dreaming, thoughts, ideas, images and feelings meander in loosely defined fashions and in ways that may at first appear to be erratic and devoid of direct meaning, at least the meaning that we expect as a product of discourse. It is only in the course of a social dreaming event and within the container of the matrix that

J. Manley, *Social Dreaming, Associative Thinking and Intensities of Affect*,
Studies in the Psychosocial, https://doi.org/10.1007/978-3-319-92555-4_5

indicative forms of affect emerge, only to disappear and re-emerge in different guises and in unexpected and often erratic ways. In other words, any narrative sense is disturbed and substituted by an extended and interconnected pattern or collage of affects submerged in images, whether through dream or association. In this chapter I explore how the non-linear patterns of thought in social dreaming may be understood in ways that situate social dreaming in a philosophical context that supports the experience of participating in a social dreaming matrix.

I begin by discussing Spinoza and the explicit links between his philosophy and that of Deleuze. I discuss how a Deleuzian perspective applied to social dreaming provides a different epistemological approach to that implied through Cartesian linearity and its consequent cause-and-effect duality. While I make no claim to discuss this non-linear approach in sufficient depth due to limitations of space, I also touch upon Deleuzian intellectual allies, such as Foucault (and his concept of history), Bergson (on time and memory) and another less allied thinker such as Lacan (on language), all of whom together express the complexity of the non-linear in some of their writings and in ways that are illustrative of the social dreaming process.

Finally, to be clear, I am of course aware and the reader will be aware that none of these thinkers knew anything about social dreaming, but my argument regards social dreaming primarily as being a way of thinking, non-linear thinking, and therefore, the discussion that ensues should be regarded in that light.

Spinoza and Process

Spinoza was persecuted and ignored in the seventeenth century and for years afterwards due to a misunderstanding of his ideas of process – that there is no beginning leading to a definitive final product that can be observed and recorded and possibly consumed, but rather that process is at once the combination of internal and external objects, or more appropriately affects, that are in states of undirected flows – and it is only recently that his philosophy has been reassessed, largely thanks to the appreciation and acknowledgement of Gilles Deleuze and, intriguingly due to the more recent attention given to him by the renowned neuroscientist, Antonio

Damasio (2003). Through Damasio's attention to Spinoza, it is possible to begin to perceive the relevance of Spinoza's non-linear philosophy to the modern, scientific world. Although I will not be pursuing the neuroscientific line in this book, it is nevertheless fascinating and worth pointing out that according to Damasio, Spinoza's philosophy largely constitutes a prediction of scientific discoveries today related to perception and affect. For example, Damasio is able to talk about feelings as 'interactive perceptions', where affect is compared to visual perception in a way that is close to the idea of the image-affect that I am proposing in this study of social dreaming (Damasio 2003, pp. 91–93). It is, I propose, through a Spinozian/Deleuzian approach that the relevance of the non-linearity of social dreaming in psychosocial research can be understood and highlighted.

The dangers of interweaving different intellectual disciplines leads me to reiterate that although this chapter looks to illumination in a Spinozian/Deleuzian perspective, it does not seek to repudiate the roots of social dreaming in the work of Wilfred Bion as identified by Gordon Lawrence (see Lawrence 1998 for first thoughts on Bion and social dreaming). Bion's demand that the psychoanalyst should approach the world of a patient without memory or desire in order to allow for negative capability and the flow of holistic 'affect' that moves non-linearly 'as links in a circular series' (Bion 2000, p. 101) is completely pertinent to the understanding of social dreaming.

Cartesian Postulates

I cannot delve into a profound investigation of Descartes in this chapter, so I will simply state that by 'Cartesian postulates' I mean the general idea that thought and understanding is necessarily understood in terms of cause and effect. In sum, by Cartesian, I mean the following:

- A conception of the world as governed by a logic of dualities and a linear sense of causes and effects;
- An understanding of nature and man as being intelligible as mechanical constructs; and
- The consideration given to the existence of God as a separate entity to Man.

For Descartes, the very thinking process and the definition of life was reduced to the action of the brain. The thought of the brain is the cause of our awareness of existence. Existence is the 'effect' caused by the thinking process. Consequentially, existence without thinking would not be possible. This led to the sweeping aside of the importance and value of a wider, more embracing attitude to existence, which might have included, for example, emotion and feeling as part of an 'embodied mind' and as legitimate ways of 'thinking', learning and understanding. The alternative idea, that we might learn and therefore understand through processes which were not founded in the thinking brain, has not been generally acceptable as science and only admitted in the expression of the creative arts, that is to say in the 'unscientific' world. Cartesian concepts of duality and processes of linearity became accepted as necessary truths in our understanding of the world, for development, evolution and progress. In this way we made the machines of the industrial revolution as logical constructs that depended on each part being causally connected to the next, its 'effect'. Machinery as a concept was applied equally to science and people. In science, 'the world as a perfect machine governed by exact mathematical laws', was epitomised by Newtonian mechanics (Capra 1997 p. 20); and in human organisation, 'Taylorism' converted people management into a 'science' and human collectives into 'systems' (Taylor 1911). The mechanical flowering of human life in all its aspects gave people hope of being able to control the human environment, and created the appearance of understanding. We were given the opportunity of creating causes for all observable effects in never ending linearity.

Foucault and the Move Away from Descartes

Foucault's work in general moves away from the linear, with a concept of history that rejects the idea of a timeline of progress. The very basis of Foucault's work – the facts of history – is in itself a questioning of Cartesian 'truths'. Does Foucault really present us with the history of society's approach to the problem of madness? On the face of it, yes he does. A book such as *Madness and Civilisation* (2001), for example, appears to be researched as a history and is full of data of the kind you would expect to find in a history text. However, the 'history' soon becomes unsatisfactory as a 'history'. The reader soon becomes aware of a kind of subtext, as this history becomes more and more open to interpretation, as Foucault opens out the facts and, almost indirectly, as if we were thinking a history but feeling something else, we become aware of a profound understanding of the nature of 'civilization' and 'madness' and its relationship with the error of Cartesian thought. By studying 'madness', Foucault disturbs the foundation of its opposite, sanity, in ways that seem to resonate with the 'madness' of the dream, precisely the aspect of shared social dream thinking that can be difficult to accept at first encounter.

In *Madness and Civilisation*, Foucault demonstrates how Cartesian thought could not bear the presence of folly, and called it 'madness'. In doing so, the madness became dangerous so that mad people were treated firstly as a diseased kind that had to be expelled from society, secondly as criminals that had to be locked away and finally as an illness that needed treatment, but this last solution was a kind of self delusion imposed by the thinking brain as an excuse to rid our thinking society of such anomalies which were unacceptable to rational thought, threatening, even. Foucault suggests that instead of sanity being the opposite of madness, actually 'civilization' was attracted to the fantasy and imagination of the 'mad', and hence the morbid interest in Sade, to take Foucault's example.

Foucault's style is as important to his message as his facts. His use of history to create a semblance of 'fact' is brilliantly used to contrast 'facts' with the affective reactions about the 'mad' victims of those 'facts'. As we read the 'facts', they are presented to the reader in such a way that we suddenly realise that we are participating in a sensual voyeurism that intellectually we would reject. In this way we get to feel what we could not have thought, which resonates with the unthought known of social dreaming. This is why Foucault's 'history' is full of dates and names on the one hand (the 'facts') and on the other hand a plethora of quotations that describes the spectacle of madness. We ourselves, intellectual representatives of Cartesian society as we read Foucault, are drawn into that very mode of thought that is being criticised because, as Foucault says,

> ... madness is not linked to the world and its subterranean forms, but rather to man, to his weaknesses, dreams, and illusions...it insinuates itself

within man, or rather it is a subtle rapport that man maintains with himself. (Foucault 2001, p. 23)

Consider, for example, the horrid attraction of being able to see something prohibited, a thing securely confined, away from the safety of reason, in fact with 'reason' giving the spectator a good excuse for surreptitious enjoyment, in the following example:

> … in 1789, the dream of the Abbé Desmonceaux, in a little work dedicated to National Benevolence; he planned to create a pedagogical instrument – a spectacle conclusively proving the drawbacks of immorality: "these guarded asylums…are retreats as useful as they are necessary…The sight of these shadowy places and the guilty creatures they contain is well calculated to preserve from the same acts of just reprobation the deviations of a too licentious youth; it is thus prudent of mothers and fathers to familiarize their children at an early age with these horrible and detestable places, where shame and turpitude fetter crime, where man, corrupted in his essence, often loses forever the rights he had acquired in society". (Foucault 2001, p. 197)

What could be more inviting to the spectators' morbid yet 'civilised' imaginations? Elsewhere, Foucault makes it clear to the reader what it is we are experiencing. By being 'rational' the sane close themselves into their minds to think their thoughts and to stave off the insane imagination. The quoted 'historical' example given above is a metaphor of a similar process: the reasoning of rational thought turns the viewing of the irrational into a learning process: the exterior vision of the madmen is kept in a separate compartment from the inner vision, a splitting, as it were, of the individual mind: the sane, rational Cartesian mind is able to view the danger of the insane mind and its passionate imagination at a safe distance:

> The savage danger of madness is related to the danger of the passions and to their fatal concatenation. (Foucault 2001, p. 80)

The Cartesian link in relation to this idea is also made clear by Foucault:

> Descartes closes his eyes and plugs up his ears the better to see the true brightness of essential daylight; thus he is secured against the dazzlement of

> the madman…In the uniform lucidity of his closed senses, Descartes has broken with all possible fascination, and if he sees, he is certain of seeing that which he sees. (Foucault 2001, p. 102)

In order to understand Foucault's message we have to become voyeurs ourselves, as readers, we have to feel the sensations that are being denounced. We find ourselves moving away from the idea of a 'pure thought' in a Cartesian sense and towards a more embracing and holistic way of thinking, a feeling thought, so to speak. It is not simply a question of the objectified 'content' that is presented in these texts, but the process of expression too.

By questioning the subjective sanity of the exterior perception of objects, through the quasi historical example of the way the mad were perceived in his examples, Foucault points to the complex intrinsic value of understanding the role of the inner imagination in the construction of knowledge. The truth of Foucault's example resides in the understanding of inner perceptions rather than exterior observations, all of which militate against any stated civilised sanity defined as separate and distinct from madness. Such a conclusion prepares the ground for an understanding of the value of the felt, inner visions of social dreaming that combine the perceived objects of the exterior world with the inner images of the felt world as expressed in shared social dreams and the irrationality or 'madness' of the dream.

It is this idea that drives Deleuze and Guattari to interpret the schizophrenic as an alternative vision of the imagination, in other words to give validity to what might otherwise be foreclosed as 'mad'. While it is sometimes difficult to distinguish between the Deleuzian provocation and the actual serious discussion of what constitutes an alternative ontological position in Deleuze and Guattari's *Anti-Oedipus*, the following quotation, which describes the 'schizophrenic's walk', with its dream-like qualities, indicates an openness to the validity of thoughts that are creative and imaginative as opposed to purely rational:

> He thought that it must be a feeling of endless bliss to be in contact with the profound life of every form, to have a soul for rocks, metals, water, and plants, to take into himself, as in a dream, every element of nature, like flowers that breathe with the waxing and waning of the moon. (Georg Büchner, quoted in Deleuze and Guattari 2004, p. 2)

The reference to the dream in this quotation indicates the potential for the dream or the social dream, to provide a window into 'insanity' without having to be or becoming insane.

Affect: The 'Feeling Thought'

The idea of a 'feeling thought', which is important in social dreaming through its connection with the unthought known, that is to say the feeling that resides in us before it becomes a thought, is another way of defining 'affect'. It is a term that has acquired a sense of complexity largely due to a conceptual difficulty in translation. Deleuze uses the term 'affect' from the Spinozian use of the Latin word 'affectus'. Spinoza, who wrote *The Ethics* in Latin (1992), uses a word that has no direct translation into English, although it is usually translated as 'emotion'. In the words of Samuel Shirley, the translator of one of the more recent editions of *The Ethics*,

> … 'emotion' is the usual translation of 'affectus', and the translator had best retain it in default of a more accurate term. It certainly seems odd to speak of 'the emotion of desire', and this is sufficient indication that 'affectus' is not quite the equivalent of our 'emotion'. (Spinoza 1992, p. 28)

The best definition of 'affectus' is, naturally, Spinoza's own:

> By emotion (affectus) I understand the affections of the body by which the body's power of activity is increased or diminished, assisted or checked, together with the ideas of these affections. Thus, if we can be the adequate cause of one of these affections, then by emotion I understand activity, otherwise passivity. (III, def. 3) (Spinoza 1992, p. 103)

The essential nature of 'affectus' then is that it combines body and mind, and it is always in activity, in other words, the 'process' described above. This is the way Deleuze understands Spinoza and therefore adopts the term 'affect'. In Deleuze, the idea of 'affect' always being active, never passive, is connected to the concept of 'becoming'. Affect is always in a state of becoming, always in transition between other states that may be passive. Similarly, for Spinoza, the principal emotions ('affects') are pleasure, pain and desire, and are only existing in activity. In this way, they too are 'becoming', although Spinoza never used this term. So, pleasure is the movement away from less pleasure, pain, a movement away from less pain, and desire only existing in a hunger for what the subject has not. These, Spinoza calls 'primary' affects and all other secondary 'affects' arise from them, (see (III, Definition of the Emotions, 1, 2 and 3) (Spinoza 1992, p. 141)).

The holistic understanding of 'affect' as part of a Deleuzian process that is heavily influenced by Spinoza, combines mind and body in a single activity. As part of this combination, any dream or associated image in the mind is also an emotion and as relevant to the reality of the body as the mind. There is, in this affective process, no difference between the image of the inner mind and external reality. The affect is somewhere in between inner and outer, and constantly moving between the two, never passive. Affect implies a harmony of behaviour based on a union of the actions of the body and the elicitation of images in the mind that are in active communion with the exterior world. These images in the mind are also the dream images and associations of the social dreaming matrix. In this state, affect does not 'belong' to either the subject or the exterior world, it is a thing in itself. In Deleuze's words:

> Affects are no longer feelings or affections; they go beyond the strength of those who undergo them. Sensations, percepts, and affects are *beings* whose validity lies in themselves and exceeds any lived. (Deleuze and Guattari 1994, p. 164, Deleuze and Guattari's italics)

Later, Deleuze defines affects as '*nonhuman becomings of man*' (Deleuze and Guattari 1994, p. 169, authors' italics) and gives an example from *Moby Dick*:

> Ahab really does have perceptions of the sea, but only because he has entered into a relationship with Moby Dick that makes him a becoming-whale and forms a compound of sensations that no longer needs anyone: ocean. (Deleuze and Guattari 1994, p. 169)

Affect, then, has a space and a duration:

> It is a zone of indetermination, of indiscernibility, as if things, beasts, and persons (Ahab and Moby Dick…) endlessly reach that point that immediately precedes their natural differentiation. This is what is called an *affect*. (Deleuze and Guattari 1994, p. 173, authors' italics)

An integral part of affect as defined above is its perception as process, thus the emphasis on activity, action and transition, rather than content, with the latter corresponding to inactivity, passivity and stasis. As I will discuss below, this is also key to social dreaming, where affect, in the form of dream images and associations, is allowed to flow without the potential hindrance of interruption/ interpretation by a host or participant in the matrix. In this situation of constant flow and process, an interpretation of a dream or image is likely to make concrete and definitive a meaning associated to an image, with the effect being that of turning an affect into a thing or object that can be cognitively grasped and put aside. Instead of this definition into stasis, the process continues to feed into and nurture the flow of dreams, images and associations of the continuing matrix.

Associative Thinking and Affect

The idea of process over content is, therefore, an essential feature of this kind of associative or holistic thinking, with its roots in Spinoza, its development in Deleuze and its antithesis in Descartes. This is what is meant by

> … the unit of understanding is not the form or function or organism but the composition of affective relations between individuals, together with the "plane of consistency" on which they interact, that is, their "environment" ... a field of forces whose actions await experiencing. In a human sense it can be called the unconscious, or at least the ground on which the unconscious is constructed. (Hurley in Preface to Deleuze 1988, p. ii)

This 'composition of affective relations' can be seen in the example above from Foucault's *Madness and Civilization* where it is composed of: the reader, the Abbé Desmonceaux, Foucault himself, and the split between the thinking mind and the passionate mind personified through metaphor. It is the metaphorical personification of the mind which enables the affective relations to come into play and releases the reader from, in Deleuze's terms, his or her role as a 'functioning organism', that is to say, an objectified thinking brain which in turn analyses thought as its object as we would understand it in Cartesian terms. The Spinozian term used to express this process is the 'common notion', which Deleuze links to his preferred use of the term 'composition':

> In short, a common notion is the representation of a composition between two or more bodies, and a unity of this composition. Its meaning is more biological than mathematical....' (Deleuze 1988, p. 54)

And the importance of the 'common notion' – of this 'composition' as a combination of relationships of thoughts, understandings and affects – is in the truth of its complete existence in and around itself as opposed to any existence possibly engendered through any particular cause leading to an identifiable and separate effect, what Spinoza had defined as 'self-cause':

> By that which is self-caused I mean that whose essence involves existence; or that whose nature can be conceived only as existing.' (Spinoza 1992, I, Def. 1, p. 31)

It follows that the importance of any 'cause' is not in its 'effect' but in the knowledge relationship between the two:

> The knowledge of an effect depends on, and involves, the knowledge of the cause. (Spinoza 1992, I Ax.4, p. 32)

What this suggests is that life itself, that is to say everything that exists, not just social life, should be defined by a cyclical and web-like process of relationships rather than by any linearly arranged individual features of any particular thing or object. In this way, Spinoza links all things into a process called 'life', and this is what Deleuze later calls a 'common plane of immanence' in his discussion of Spinoza:

> …the plane of immanence, the plane of Nature that distributes affects, does not make any distinction at all between things that might be called natural and things that might be called artificial. Artifice is fully part of Nature, since each thing, on the immanent plane of Nature, is defined by the arrangements of motions and affects into which it enters, whether these arrangements are artificial or natural. (Deleuze 1988, p. 124)

Thus, in Deleuze's own work on philosophy and his own idiosyncratic incursion into neuroscience, he can define life as encapsulating the inorganic and the organic as a whole life process:

> Not every organism has a brain, and not all life is organic, but everywhere there are forces that constitute microbrains, or an inorganic life of things.' (Deleuze and Guattari 1994, p. 213)

Similarly, instead of identifying brains as being the property and life-defining element of the higher species of individual organisms, and therefore by rejecting the Cartesian concept of thought as a definition of existence, Deleuze is able to talk of the life process as a whole as a 'collective brain.' (Deleuze and Guattari 1994, p. 212). The 'collective brain' is the constitution of all the 'microbrains' of everything. A 'microbrain' is anything which lends itself to 'contemplation' and 'contraction', so that a plant could have a 'microbrain':

> The plant contemplates by contracting the elements from which it originates – light, carbon, and the salts – and it fills itself with colors and odors that in each case qualify its variety, its composition: it is sensation in itself. It is as if flowers smell themselves by smelling what composes them…. (Deleuze and Guattari 1994, p. 212)

That is to say, the plant 'contracts' and synthesizes primary materials and produces a new reality. This reality becomes its 'composition' and in its 'composition' an 'affective relation' is established with another subject through the affect of pleasure experienced by the action of smell: The sensation of smell can only exist in each subject – human and plant – through the existence and collaboration of each other. The moment of affect is both the moment of the smelling action and the emission of the smelling sensation.

Although social dreaming does not delve overtly into the panorama of all the senses, so as to include, for example, the sense of smell, the Deleuzian system of affective relations described here has a close affinity to the way the matrix constructs its collage of affects that are interconnected and given existence through an on-going process of associative thinking. The eventual – but never definitive – result of this process is the collage or, in Deleuzian terms, the rhizome that leads to the creation of patterns or collages of image-affects, that pulsate in intensity according to the moment or circumstance of their relationships.

Henri Bergson and Time

Taking away linearity and emphasising a system of rhizomatic interconnectivity between image-affects, also consequently challenges conventional notions of time. If a standard narrative has a beginning, middle and an end, then the social dreaming collage is not part of that system. In social dreaming the image-affect takes precedence over the story, and the affect over the content, symbol or representation. This is more than a theoretical position, it aptly describes the sensation of reverie (Bion 1967, 1970) of the social dreaming matrix process as experienced by participants. The dream world and associated worlds of reverie appear to take place in a 'no-time' place that defies the intellectual knowledge that situates the matrix within the actual time assigned to the session.

In a Deleuzian universe of processes of affect, time becomes cyclical as well as linear, and is most aptly demonstrated in the ideas of Henri Bergson, who was enormously influential on Deleuze. Of particular interest to social dreaming is the way Bergson describes the importance and quality of memory, (which is at least partly responsible for the formation of dreams), to current time perception.

For Bergson, the concept of time in the self is related to a sense of memory which is two-tiered: the memory inside the mind, 'recollection-memory', and the memory of perception, 'contraction-memory', which is also in the mind but fed inside from an external perception of matter which is then 'contracted' into ideas of what is perceived both 'objectively' and in association to the experiences of the self, so that perception is never 'pure' but a mixture of that original objectivity of what is really there and the associations attached to perception through the action of memory. If perception is never completely 'out there', then what is within a memory, or a dream, must be tinged by affect. The perceived elements are 'contracted' in the processing of the mind so that perception becomes a relationship, or patterning, of matter and memory. This pattern of perception is at the same time linked to the 'historical' duration of the memory in the mind. In both cases, which are in constant movement and fusion, there is always a sense of the present, so that it is possible for the past to exist in the memory but be forever brought up into the present in the instance of perception and the constant state of processes of the self. Furthermore, memory is what transmits sensations to present perception, and matter is what transmits a sense of movement within that space, and therefore the possibility of future by defining the space within which future action will take place. Both of these constitute a state of 'becoming' that we define as being the 'present', and this present can, therefore, only exist through my body in space, because it is my body that feels and moves. The self exists for Bergson not as a thinking brain but as a feeling body which moves in space, and the body does not exist in isolation but is 'extended' in its connections in time and space. The 'non-extended' can only be conceived of through the possibility of a 'pure memory' which exists in Bergson only as a concept that can demonstrate its practical non-existence. That is to say, 'pure memory' must be situated in the non-extended self, the being as a separate entity as opposed to the extended self. In this state, 'pure memory' has neither action nor utility because it cannot act or interact with space and time. Memory which is brought to bear upon the present must be created in a sensorial image:

> Memory actualised in an image differs, then, profoundly from pure memory. The image is a present state, and its sole share in the past is the memory from which it arose. Memory, on the contrary, powerless as long as it remains without utility, is pure from all admixture of sensation, is without attachment to the present, and is, consequently, unextended. (Bergson 2005, p. 129)

In Bergson, therefore, we have the possibility of a time, (and a space within that time), which is both linear and patterned and relative, just like the patterns and collages of the social dreaming matrix. What is important here in our discussion of social dreaming is that linearity, if it exists in time, does not depend on cause and effect. Rather, an idea of the existence of the dynamics of cause and effect in certain circumstances is only one of many different ways we have of understanding the universe and its multiple realities. What is similar to linearity is the totality of time as we perceive it in our bringing forth our past memory to our present perception. This is what Bergson called 'duration' (Bergson 2005 p. 262), within which there are multiple layers of seamless, interconnecting time capsules. Thus, for Bergson, the future is not the effect caused by the present, and it is both a continuum and a multiple combination of interrelatedness at one and the same time:

> The future then appears as expanding the present: it was not, therefore, contained in the present in the form of a represented end. And yet, once realized, it will explain the present as much as the present explains it, and even more; it must be viewed as an end as much as, and more than, a result. (Bergson 2005, p. 192)

The idea of 'result', which I am going to equate with 'effect', in Bergson is, therefore, only part of an intellectual contraction of an understanding of the present. The continuous passing of time ensures that the 'result' can only exist in the moment 'once realized'. It is in that moment that the effect is intellectually contracted to include its cause, an illusion of cause and effect which is immediately vanquished by the passing of time. This illusory state is, however, at the same time, simultaneously instantaneous and ephemeral and continuous, as one state of the present is constantly replaced by another, in Bergson's words, 'a present ceaselessly reborn' (Bergson 2005, p. 205). This effect of timelessness can be directly applied to the experience of the social dreaming matrix. It also describes the shifts in affect towards knowledge, or from unthought towards known in the matrix, as the participants in social dreaming bring to the surface dreams and image-affects that have previously resided only in their personal unconscious which are then revealed to others in a way that creates a kind of limbo or state of reverie between the consciousness of the participants and the unconsciousness of the dreams and image-affects. In fact, in the social dreaming matrix, there is no real dividing line between the part objects of the dreams and associations, and we can never answer the question what is 'consciousness' in relation to where does 'unconsciousness' begin:

> To tell the truth, it is impossible to distinguish between the duration, however short it may be, that separates two instants and a memory that connects them, because duration is essentially a continuation of what no longer exists into what does exist. This is real time, perceived and lived. This is also any conceived time, because we cannot conceive a time without imagining it as perceived and lived. Duration therefore implies consciousness; and we place consciousness at the heart of things for the very reason that we credit them with a time that endures. (Bergson 2005, p. 208)

Bergson's Time, Foucault's History, Freud's Symbolism and Social Dreaming

Social dreaming, therefore, provides participants with an opportunity to experience another way of understanding time and history that goes beyond the linear and away from the purely personal and individual. In this, Bergson and Foucault both provide an analysis of time, memory and history that differ from clock time and which help to describe the experience of social dreaming. The meaning of 'history' for Foucault, for example, can only be grasped through an understanding of these different perceptual possibilities of the passing of time, its multiplicity of application and its naturally emergent form. Similarly, the history behind some of the dreams and image-affects in social dreaming tend to be interconnected through affective ties that are peripheral to concepts of linear time. Foucault's study and understanding of history is very close to a Bergsonian concept of time. Hence Foucault's use of the word 'archaeology' to describe history in terms of layering or patterning.

The word 'archaeology' exemplifies, for Foucault, the idea of history existing in strata, ready to be uncovered, as if the past existed in the ruins of the present waiting for a future to uncover it. 'Linear successions' are replaced by 'a set of deeper uncouplings' within 'various sedimentary strata', each of which has its own potential time scale: 'each contains a periodicity that belongs only to itself' (Foucault 2000a, p. 298). In this way, what used to be an historian's struggle to seek for the continuous in the discontinuous, that is to say trying to impose a linear and causal feel to a series of events that may just as well be viewed as discontinuous and linearly unconnected, can now be viewed as a multiplicity of strata which are linked, (or not), in many different ways, including, maybe, linearly. And the over-simplicity of the historical search for links between a pre-established series of events, (the pre-establishment being already imposed by a simplified view of sequence in time), is now replaced by what Foucault describes as

> … a series of difficult interrogations: which layers should be isolated from each other? What type and criteria of periodization need to be adopted for each of them? What system of relations, (hierarchy, dominance, inter-arrangement, univocal determination, circular causality), can be established between them? (Foucault 2000a, p. 298)

Such 'interrogations' are equally valid in an inquiry as to the nature of the social dreaming matrix, and especially to the post-matrix event or discussion: to what extent can image-affects be grouped or classified? Are some more important than others? Are some dreams self sufficient? and so on. In other words, where Foucault sees time and history as being a complex non-linear 'system of relations', so it is with social dreaming. And because history is, for Foucault, about an effort to understand mankind rather than being simply an endeavour to record events, that is to say, because history and time have to be understood from a psychological perspective of the unconscious rather than just from that of realism and consciousness, the study of history, time, memory and affect are studies of a deeper sense of knowledge than that contained in the history of facts and figures. This is why for Foucault – and obviously for social dreaming too – Freud's 'discovery' of the unconscious has had to change all our thinking:

> …one can say that, starting with Freud, all the human sciences became, in one way or another, sciences of the psyche. And the old realism à la Emile Durkheim – conceiving of society as a substance in opposition to the individual who is also a kind of substance incorporated into society – appears to me to be unthinkable now…all there is now, basically, is psychology. (Foucault 2000b, p. 252)

According to Foucault, psychology, in the discovery of the unconscious, made it possible to remove causal linearity from contemporary thought, and to replace it with layers of meaning. Once again, we can compare this to Bergson's 'psychological' view of historical evolution in time that admits the linear and the layered:

> But evolution has actually taken place through millions of individuals, on divergent lines, each ending at a crossing from which new paths radiate, and so on indefinitely. If our hypothesis is justified, if the essential causes working along these diverse roads are of psychological nature, they must keep something in common in spite of the divergence of their effects… Something of the whole, therefore, must abide in the parts…. (Bergson 2005, p. 193)

But for Freud, the conscious and rational mind could still be used to interpret unconscious symbols, so that conscious and unconscious were clearly delineated. Freud was interested in using the language of the rational conscious mind to 'decode' or 'decipher' the symbols of the unconscious language of the mind as expressed in dreams and/or free association. As Foucault pointed out 'his problem, finally, is not a problem of linguistics, it is a problem of decipherment.' (Foucault 2000b, p. 253) This observation once again makes some aspects of Freudian thought of limited use to social dreaming, since, as discussed above, social dreaming is neither concerned with repressed thoughts in the individual unconscious, nor is it given to interpretation of dreams and associations, especially not interpretations that are of a decoding nature.

Lacan: Language, the Words of Social Dreaming and the Image-Affect

Lacan was famously interested in language and believed that language reflected the structure of the unconscious. This provokes an interesting dilemma for social dreaming where precisely language is necessary and yet largely subordinated to being a tool that describes images which are themselves descriptions of affect. Since social dreaming is chiefly conducted through language (although there are examples of the use of photos and art in social dreaming too, which will be discussed below), an understanding of Lacan's position vis-à-vis language and the objects of language, the signifiers and the signified, is useful to our understanding of social dreaming. For Lacan, a turn towards the consideration of language itself was essential for the development of Freud's work in psychoanalysis: 'Bringing the psychoanalytic experience back to the Word and to Language as its grounding is of direct concern to its technique.' (Lacan 1981, p. 53) As we have seen, for Deleuze, language is a means towards creative philosophy, not a manner of translating logic. In Deleuze, and to a lesser extent in Foucault, language is engaged in the impossible expression of the ineffable.

In some respects, Lacan's study of language is quite apt as a description of the language used in social dreaming. In going beyond simple evocations of signifiers and signified, Lacan was able to emphasise the evocative nature of language as opposed to any functional properties it may have: 'For the function of language is not to inform but to evoke' (Lacan 2001, p. 94). And clearly this evocation has to do with the unconscious, the fact that the 'signifier' cannot mean any single concrete 'thing' for any length of time, before being converted and metamorphosed into another 'thing' and then another for as long as the unconscious mind continues to think and within a time scale which is recreated by that same mind, what Lacan calls 'an incessant sliding of the signified under the signifier' (Lacan 2001, p. 170). As a matter of fact, Lacan goes on to say that language is precisely anti-information, (rather than simply non-information):

> What this structure of the signifying chain discloses is the possibility I have, precisely in so far as I have this language in common with other subjects,

that is to say, in so far as it exists as a language, to use it in order to signify *something quite other* than what it says. (Lacan 2001, p. 172, author's italics)

Unlike Saussure, from whom Lacan draws for his theory of language, Lacanian thought suggests that linear time that is implied in a sentence structure does not overwhelm the potential for layers of unseen or even unintended meanings to arise in words. By comparing a sentence to music, Lacan was able to evoke the meanings attached to words in a vertical as well as a horizontal sense, as in a chord in music:

> But one has only to listen to poetry, which Saussure was no doubt in the habit of doing, for polyphony to be heard, for it to become clear that all discourse is aligned along the several staves of a score. (Lacan 2001, p. 170)

And the significant clue to how this can be so is in Lacan's concept of language as existing not in itself or in relation to a 'thing' which is 'signified' but rather in relation to 'other subjects':

> What I seek in speech is the response of the other. What constitutes me as subject is my question. In order to be recognized by the other, I utter what was only in view of what will be. (Lacan 2001, p. 94)

In this process of identifying language as only existing in a relational sense, Lacan also identifies a relationship of time between subject and object which is not that of sequential logic and is, rather, reminiscent of Bergsonian time:

> What is realized in my history is not the past definite of what was, since it is no more, or even the present perfect of what has been in what I am, but the future anterior of what I shall have been for what I am in the process of becoming. (Lacan 2001, p. 94)

We should remember here that when talking of 'time' in a Bergsonian sense, we are really talking about memory and duration, as discussed above. In this sense, there are connections between Lacan's 'temporality' and Bergson's 'duration'. For Bergson, the significant moment of perception is the instant of present duration which is always a combination of perception of the exterior reality combined with interior memory. This instant is conceptually similar to Lacan's capturing of the patient's desire in a given moment that comes from another (interior) place that exists apart from the language of (exterior) information. Language, then, for Lacan, has an exterior communication similar in concept to Bergson's exterior perception. At the same time there is a moment of fusion of languages, of interior desire and exterior information, similar to Bergson's duration that fuses past memory and actual perception. This is how Lacan puts it:

> This Language…has the universal character of a language which could make itself understood in all other languages, but at the same time, since it is the Language which seizes desire at the very moment in which it becomes human desire by making itself recognized, it is absolutely particular to the subject. (Lacan 1981, p. 57)

So language is in this sense, primarily a self discovery rather than a communication of information from one person to another. The other exists not as a recipient of information but as a link in a relationship with the subject. That is to say, the language relationship is one of a creative web between people rather than the giving of something for a purpose. For Lacan, language is not an artificial conscious thought structure, rather it has felt properties which can be experienced by the body and as a body:

> … language is not immaterial. It is a subtle body, but body it is. Words are trapped in all the corporeal images that captivate the subject. (Lacan 2001, p. 95)

Language, therefore, is not simply an abstract thought that can be separated from our being. From this perspective, the language used in social dreaming and the structures of language that are created in the collage-like fashion described above can be understood as bodies of a shared unconscious in the matrix, where even the words that are used to describe the image-affects can take on a form in themselves that is beyond the rational and logical discourse of everyday communication.

Affective States of Non-linearity

The process and relevance of social dreaming as a research method, the understanding of what social dreaming can offer in comparison to other methods can be seen in this discussion of Spinoza, Deleuze, Foucault, Bergson and Lacan. I summarise the main points below:

1. Social dreaming expresses participants' experiences in a non-linear fashion, in a way that closely resembles the Deleuzian rhizome of intensities of affect.
2. The way that the image-affects are interlinked in rhizomatic fashion is similar to Foucault's strata of history and Lacan's musical chord metaphors. That is to say, social dreaming functions according to layers of inter-connectivity as opposed to lines of thought and time. This can lead to unexpected connections between image-affects according to the affective circumstance of the social dreaming matrix at any given moment. These creative connections can reveal truths or realities that might otherwise be hidden behind a veneer of the rational in a way that is similar to Foucault's shifting lines of reality in his description of madness and sanity, or Deleuze and Guattari's attempt to reassess schizophrenia.
3. In social dreaming, knowledge is understood in terms of affect before it is defined as thought. The affect evoked in social dreaming is the same as Deleuzian affect, which derives from Spinoza.
4. The social dreaming matrix is conducted in a way that encourages a sense of reverie, so that the participants in the matrix are never either in a state of unconscious or conscious awareness, but somewhere in between, in a sense of suspended time. The combination of memory and time awareness is similar to that described by Bergson.
5. The fact that language is the normal means of communication in social dreaming does not preclude the expression of indefinite fluctuations of affect as opposed to concrete descriptions of fact or content, as described by Lacan.

References

Bergson, H. (2005). *Matter and Memory* in *Key Writings*. London: Continuum.

Bion, W.R. (1967). *Second thoughts*. London: Maresfield.

Bion, W.R. (1970). *Attention and interpretation*. London: Karnac.

Bion, W.R. (2000). *Experiences in Groups and other papers*. London: Routledge.

Capra, F. (1997). *The Web of Life. A New Synthesis of Mind and Matter*. London: Flamingo.

Damasio, A. (2003). *Looking for Spinoza*. London: William Heinemann.

Deleuze, G. (1988). *Spinoza: Practical Philosophy* (Hurley, R. Trans.). San Francisco: City Light Books.

Deleuze, G. and Guattari, F. (2004). *Anti-Oedipus. Capitalism and Schizophrenia*. London: Continuum.

Deleuze, G. and Guattari, F. (1994). *What is Philosophy?* London: Verso.

Foucault, M. (2000a). On the Archaeology of the sciences: Response to the epistemology circle. In Faubion, J.D. (Ed.), *Essential Works of Foucault 1954–1984, Volume* 2. London: Penguin.

Foucault, M. (2000b). Philosophy and psychology. In Faubion, J.D. (Ed.), *Essential Works of Foucault 1954–1984, Volume* 2. London: Penguin.

Foucault, M. (2001). *Madness and Civilization*. Abingdon: Routledge.

Lacan, J. (2001). *Écrits: A Selection*. London and New York: Routledge.

Lacan, J. (1981). *The Language of the Self*. London: John Hopkins.

Lawrence, W.G. (Ed.). (1998). *Social Dreaming @ Work*. London: Karnac.

Spinoza, B. (1992). *Ethics. Treatise on the Emendation of the Intellect and Selected Letters* (Shirley, S, Ed). Indianapolis: Hackett.

Taylor, F.W. (1911). Shop Management, The Principles of Scientific Management. Harper & Row (consulted in. www.marxists.org/reference/subject/economics/taylor/principles/index.htm).

References

Bergson, H. (2005) *Matter and Memory*, in *Art Writings*, London: Continuum.
Bion, W.R. (1967) *Second Thoughts*, London: Maresfield.
Bion, W.R. (1970) *Attention and Interpretation*, London: Karnac.
Bion, W.R. (1961) *Experiences in Groups and other papers*, London: Routledge.
Capra, F. (1997) *The Web of Life: A New Synthesis of Mind and Matter*, London: Flamingo.
Damasio, A. (2000) *Feeling of What Happens*, London: William Heinemann.
Deleuze, G. (1988) *Spinoza: Practical Philosophy* (Hurley, R., Trans.), San Francisco: City Light Books.
Deleuze, G. and Guattari, F. (2004) *Anti-Oedipus: Capitalism and Schizophrenia*, London: Continuum.
Deleuze, G. and Guattari, F. (1994) *What is Philosophy?*, London: Verso.
Foucault, M. (2006a) 'On the Archaeology of the Sciences: Response to the Epistemology Circle'. In Faubion, J.D. (Ed.), *Essential Works of Foucault 1954–1984, Volume 2*, London: Penguin.
Foucault, M. (2006b) 'Philosophy and psychology'. In Faubion, J.D. (Ed.), *Essential Works of Foucault 1954–1984, Volume 2*, London: Penguin.
Johnson, M. (2017) *Embodied Mind, Meaning, and Reason*, Abingdon: Routledge.
Lacan, J. (2001) *Écrits: A Selection*, London and New York: Routledge.
Lacan, J. (1968) *The Language of the Self*, London: John Hopkins.
Lawrence, W.G. (Ed.) (1998) *Social Dreaming @ Work*, London: Karnac.
Lyotard, J. (1984) *The Postmodern Condition: A Report on Knowledge*, [illegible] Manchester University Press.
[illegible] Managing the Dilemmas of [illegible] [illegible]

6

The Social Dreaming Collage and the Deleuzian Rhizome

What Kind of Pattern Is a Social Dreaming Collage?

To view existence as consisting of a shared, timeless, inter-connected, borderless space, which is opposed to a vision that emanates from an individual, strictly bordered, time-bound perspective, (this latter vision with its roots in Cartesian centredeness), brings the Deleuzian concept of the rhizome into the foreground, and social dreaming into a space of relevance and interest in terms of ontological awareness and epistemological pursuit. Social dreaming is, in its production and process, precisely about shared knowledge that makes most sense when each individual participant contribution, whether dream, image or association, is woven into meaning with another. It is through the sharing process of social dreaming that the dreams become 'social' and that implicit meaning can emerge through the creation of a collage of image-affects, described above. It is clear by now that social dreaming depends on this shared knowledge and diminishes the value and meaning attached to individual agency, represented in social dreaming by the dream. In other words, to reiterate one of social dreaming's favourite adages, we are interested in the dream, not the dreamer.

J. Manley, *Social Dreaming, Associative Thinking and Intensities of Affect*,
Studies in the Psychosocial, https://doi.org/10.1007/978-3-319-92555-4_6

Having said this, the nature of this sharing process and how the individual becomes subsumed into patterns of inter-connectivity with others in social dreaming needs consideration, especially in the light of recent debates about the best way to understand such patterns, whether they be part of a Gaian-type universe (Lovelock 2000), a system (Capra and Luigi Luisis 2014), a 'meshwork' of interweaving lines created by 'wayfarers' (Ingold 2007), a network of multitudinous 'actors' (Latour 2005), or a configuration of rhizomes on a plane (Deleuze and Guattari 1988). In other words, if social dreaming is focussed on the dream not the dreamer, what kind of meaning does the dream have without the dreamer and what is the relationship between the dreamer(s) and the dream(s) in the social dreaming matrix? And where does the 'social' reside?

'Imaginal Representations' and Social Dreaming Collages

The essential collage-making pattern of the dream images that emerge from each dream and are connected implicitly or explicitly by a participant or host in social dreaming define the knowledge base of the process. In my earlier studies of social dreaming, I attempted to do this process justice by creating 'imaginal representations' (Manley 2010) of the images that could be perceived at a glance rather than as a sequence. In the following example, I refrain from analysing the meaning of a sample matrix (see Manley 2010, pp. 69–103). Instead, it is my intention to use this example to illustrate the process of inter-connectivity and collage making that occurs in social dreaming.

Through the imaginal representation (Fig. 6.1), I am attempting to shift the reader's attention away from the sequential line of thought that the sentence encourages and move towards trying to 'see' what can be read in a way that closely resembles the 'seeing' mind in the experience of a social dreaming matrix. The imaginal representation is an indicative tool designed to realign perception rather than a definitive analytical tool. In this way, I am emphasising that unless we are in that state of reverie that seems to descend upon the participants of the matrix or unless we are

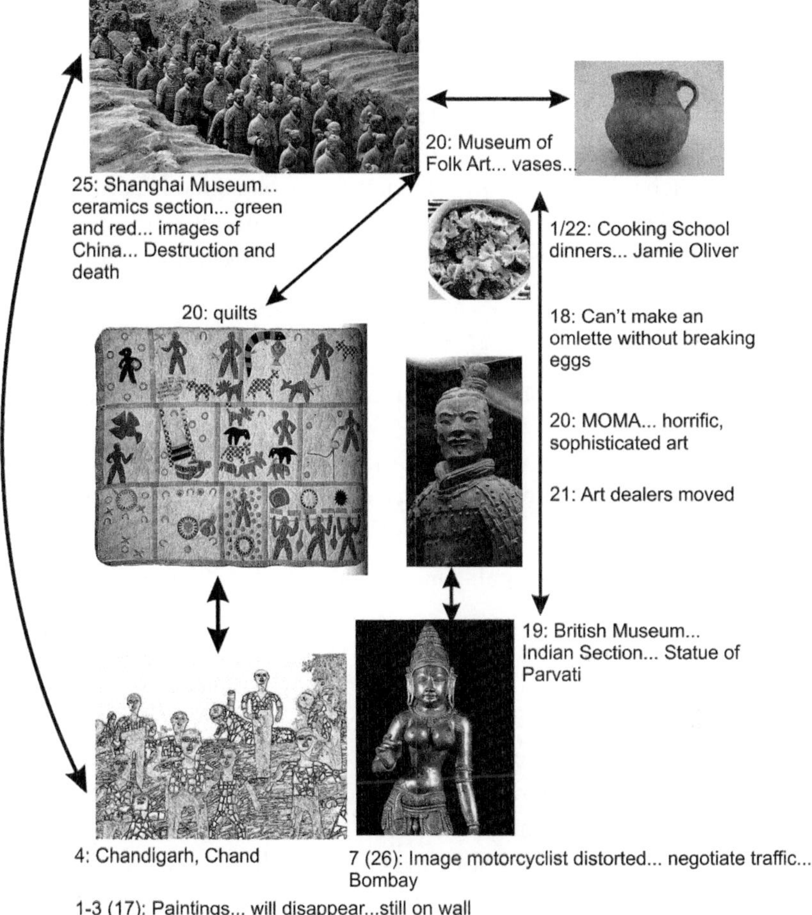

Fig. 6.1 Imaginal representation (Manley 2010, p. 80)

sufficiently aware of this difference, for example through the appreciation of metaphor in poetry, we will naturally tend to omit the visual in favour of meanings that are transmitted through our customary understanding of linguistic communication. If we omit the visual, we also omit an element of affect, as discussed above. The imaginal representation is also intended to show that these visual thoughts do not necessarily follow the same sequential line as expressed in the linguistic communication. For example, in the imaginal representation (Fig. 6.1), the sequence of language, including the images within the sequence, do not match the sequence of the transcribed matrix. So, there are three important references to museums (numbers refer to the sequence of contributions to the matrix): 19. The British Museum; 20. the MOMA, then the Museum of Folk Art; and 25. Shanghai Museum. The reference to the Shanghai Museum is visually connected to the other museums but is unconnected with what immediately precedes or follows it linguistically in the textual transcript.

> 24. in a pub in Oxford...... group of girls came – do some damage
> 25. in Shanghai museum. ceramics section.... Incredible beauty so old.... colours green and red. .... Images of China.... Destruction and death
> 26. the image of the motor cyclist distorted...... control... negotiate the traffic system in Bombay ... chaos.... Getting and navigate a cab... outside still honking
>
> (Extract from social dreaming matrix from Manley 2010, p. 79)

The Shanghai Museum is connected to the previous museum references, and these are noted in the imaginal representation. If we visualize the museum references, something different emerges: We have the pottery of the vase of the folk museum with its visual roundness connecting to the curves of the statue of Parvati; the very Indian vision of Parvati, a Goddess is linked to the very Chinese image of the soldier; we link the might of military force and that of the spiritual Goddess; this is contrasted with the somewhat cosy feel of the quilt, not the *idea* of a quilt but the *vision* of it, the powerless, artisanal, linked by museums, contrasted by artefact; and an echo of the beginning of the matrix – Chandigarh, ('Julian Schnabel – people bought the works of art, but the bits of plate kept falling off – so he employed someone to stick these plates back on.../ in Chandigarh – Chand building from these pieces' (extract from social dreaming matrix in Manley 2010, p. 72)). This reference to Chandigarh from early in the matrix – and how broken pieces of ceramics were put to creative use, unlike Julian Schnabel's contemporary western art – is a distant reference in terms of textual sequencing but close in image and affect. All of these images and their affects can be felt and visualized in the single instant, either in the mind of each participant as the collage develops, or, to a degree, through these imaginal representations. The moment of recognition of this effect and the possible dawning or emerging of a meaning through inter-connectivity is instantaneous and also complex. We 'see' the multilayered meanings simultaneously, without the need for the careful deliberation of the written word. This bears some similarity to the effect of metaphor in poetry, where the visual contains a multitude of meanings that might occur to the reader. Some of these meanings might concur with those of other readers while others might remain unique to a particular reader. The instantaneous and sophisticated effect of this event in the mind of a participant in social dreaming is extremely difficult to express, and I do not claim for a moment that my imaginal representation in Fig. 6.1 is anything other than illustrative of a process that is much richer than can be described or illustrated.

'Associology', the Collage as a Network and the 'Social' in Social Dreaming

The above examples are all visual associations rather than dreams, which illustrates the extent to which social dreaming relies upon visual associations as much as dreams. Above all, the sensation of collage depends on association, a way of inter-connecting visual images inspired by the Freudian idea of free association, which Susan Long and I have recently explored in terms of the 'associative unconscious' and 'associative thinking' (Long and Harney 2013; Long, in press; Manley, in press). These terms have become for Long and Manley a central piece of the epistemological puzzle that defines social dreaming. In my own work on associative thinking, I situate the process of association in social dreaming in the context of Latour's Actor-Network Theory (ANT) (Latour 2005). This also tells us something about the nature of the 'social' in social dreaming:

> [For Latour] the word 'social' needs to be reconfigured as "association". In trying to redefine sociology, Latour struggles with terms such as "sociology

> of associations" and wishes he could use the term "associology" (Latour 2005, p. 9). What Latour is attempting is a new, contemporary and more valid understanding of the word "social" as being equivalent to or better expressed as a network of associations that, like the associations in social dreaming, are in a constant state of flux. … In a way that reminds me of social dreaming, Latour suggests that the rigidity of "explanation" actually removes the flowing, multi-faceted layers of meaning that come with the "movement of associations". (Manley, in press)

The importance of locating this within a developing theory of sociology is to demonstrate that a value of social dreaming data for research resides in precisely the facility of the method in helping to create collages that are typical of the social dreaming experience and relevant to contemporary interpretations of society. Such a view of the social places a greater emphasis on the associations between people and people and things ('actors' in Latour's language) than on the individually centred approach to the social where all social realities emanate from the centre of a personality, as if that person were more or less a world in herself and only related to the exterior through the lens of the self.

Related to this view of the social is Latour's insistence on the need to accumulate social descriptions rather than reduce and categorise, a process he calls 'irreduction' (Latour 2005, p. 137). This idea is exactly apposite to the social dreaming process, where the collage of image-affects is in a state of ever-increasing accumulation of meaning through inter-connectivity rather than through reduction and interpretation, at least in the course of the matrix itself. This is where some difficulty may arise in people who insist on clarity and outcome, for although the sensation of the matrix is that the greater the accumulation of image-affects, the richer the meanings, it is simultaneously paradoxically true that the richer the accumulated meanings the more complicated it is to reach honed down, reduced and simplified versions of meaning that can easily be identified, clarified and discussed. This, however, should not be viewed as a defect or disadvantage. As Latour points out, 'the fact is that *no one* has the answers – this is why they have to be collectively staged, stabilized, and revised' (Latour 2005, p. 138, Latour's italics). It is such a collective revision of the collage of image-affects that occurs immediately after the matrix in a de-briefing discussion that might take place either as a debate, or as a mapping exercise on a board or flip chart, or as a mark making/ drawing session, or some other activity that enables the participants in the social dreaming matrix to unravel, as far as they can or desire, some of the meanings of the preceding matrix.

It is interesting to note how Latour himself attempts to communicate his theory of associations through images in his work with Emilie Hermant, *Paris ville invisible* (1998). In this online work (http://www.bruno-latour.fr/virtual/EN/index.html), Latour creates associations through a series of images accompanied by texts. Conceptually, these remind us of aspects of the social dreaming collage, although the work is heavily laden with theory rather than the affect of social dreaming. Nevertheless, the idea of the invisible being made visible through image association, where the enormity of the place (Paris as an urban sprawl of four million people) renders a totally encompassing vision impossible, is very reminiscent of the social dreaming process that also renders the invisible visible, or, in social dreaming speak, brings what is known but hidden into visible thought through dreams and images. The process through association also emphasises the equality of the diverse images produced in Latour's work in a way that strongly resonates with social dreaming in general. In Latour's words:

> The initial point of view doesn't count; all that counts is the movement of images. All the images are partial, of course; all the perspectives are equal: that of the baby in its pram is worth as much as that of the Mairie de Paris… (Latour and Hermant 1998, 1, plan 19)

In social dreaming, each dream image or association similarly is offered to the matrix as an equal contribution, with no precedence or hierarchy established in any way, as in the approval of the participants or host, the length or quality of the dream or image, or the status of the person giving the dream or image. The importance of any contribution can vary in the course of the matrix according to the state of the visual collage in each participant's mind, and also during the process of accumulation of image-affects as the matrix proceeds. In this way, a seemingly minor contribution may at certain moments become focussed and important as a result of the sharing process with other dreams and images that also form part of the matrix.

In many ways, therefore, the associative inter-connected collages of social dreaming may be placed within the sphere of Latour's 'associology'. Although Latour himself has little recourse to Deleuze and Guattari's work, he teasingly (maybe unconsciously) hints at the connections between ANT and the Deleuzian rhizome when discussing alternative nomenclatures for ANT, one of them being 'actant-rhyzome ontology' (Latour 2005, p. 9). A recent paper by Müller and Schurr (2016) acknowledges the closeness of ANT and the Deleuzian 'assemblage'. Of the differences that they discuss (including Deleuze and Guattari's emphasis on fluidity, affect and unpredictability compared to ANT), it seems to me that both are relevant to social dreaming. After establishing the essential similarities in the associative and relational aspects of the assemblage or network theories of Latour on the one hand and Deleuze and Guattari, on the other, the Deleuzian rhizome seems closer to the experience of social dreaming. If we consider the social dreaming collage from a Deleuzian perspective, the connections between the image-affects of the dreams and associations are primarily connections of affect, and these affects are not stable affirmations but in states of constant movement and fluidity between more than two image-affects; in fact, this complexity seems to be infinitely capable of accumulating in complexity during the course of a matrix. The strength or weakness of an associative connection between image-affects is dependent on the perceived configurations and patterns of the image-affects at any particular moment of perception, both in individual participants and in the shared perception of participants in the matrix as a whole. These are never stable. If they do become stable, then they are no longer affects, they become concrete things, named objects. Once named, they can no longer form part of the living collage of image-affects, which is why, in social dreaming, there is an imperative to refuse the interpretation that would foreclose the life of the on-going associations.

Is a Social Dreaming Collage a 'Meshwork'?

Tim Ingold is known for his definition of inter-connectivity as a 'meshwork', an idea that he specifically contrasts with Latour's ANT (Ingold 2008). Putting to one side the sense of rivalry that emerges from Ingold's refutation of ANT, the important difference, according to Ingold, between 'network' and 'meshwork' seems to reside in the idea that meshwork suggests an interconnectivity of lines without points, whereas network supposes an overlapping of lines that configure or pause at certain points in the network. Related to this difference is the affirmation that a meshwork consists of lines of agency that travel and make their mark over and/or through inorganic materials that lack agency, (such as water or air), whereas ANT makes no difference in quality between the 'actors' in the network, (whether they are organic or material, for example), (Ingold 2007). These are in part the differences between an anthropologist and a human geographer. In terms of social dreaming, the Deleuzian rhizome, with its roots in creative psychology and philosophy, is a better fit. The idea of the network being inter-connected points as opposed to inter-crossing lines is actually closer to the Deleuzian rhizome and the social dreaming collage than the concept of meshwork. In social dreaming, the image-affects are indeed points of affect that fluctuate according to moments of intensity. However, even though they are not lines, in Ingold's sense, they are nevertheless points that create fluid lines in such a way as to destabilise the rigidity of the points in question. The intensity of affect of one point forces a fluctuation of affect in the points to which it is connected, in this way reducing the rigidity of the points in a network that Ingold finds so disturbing.

The Social Dreaming Collage as a Rhizome

The complexity of the Deleuzian rhizome therefore takes in elements of the Ingold's meshwork and Latour's network, it includes both the network of points (even though these points are temporary pauses or resting points that are likely to change position at any moment) and the interweaving of lines and furthermore makes affect an integral aspect of inter-connectivity. Despite emphasising an apparently random and chaotic inter-connectedness, the Deleuzian rhizome does not entirely reject sequentialism. This is beautifully and intriguingly illustrated on the first page of *A Thousand Plateaus* (Deleuze and Guattari 1988, p. 3) with an illustration of a score by Sylvano Bussoti, where lines weave and points are connected in a way that is both vertical through the multiple staves and horizontal in time progression. That the leading and primary example chosen by Deleuze and Guattari is that of music through the illustration of a contemporary musical score (one therefore that includes lines as well as points) is a reminder of Lacan's use of the musical score to illustrate the multiple simultaneity of meanings of a signifier and Langer's focus on music as being the ultimate example of the sensation of creative affect that defies all attempt of expression in words. For Langer, music is the best example of art's expression of emotion (Deleuze's affect) and entirely non-representational, therefore ultimately impossible to express verbally:

> [Music] is pre-eminently non-representative even in its classical productions…It exhibits pure form not as an embellishment, but as its very essence… no scene, no object, no fact… There is no obvious literal content in our way. If the meaning of art belongs to the sensuous percept itself apart from what it ostensibly represents, then such purely artistic meaning should be most accessible through musical works. (Langer 1948, p. 169)

The musical score is therefore an example not just of the combination of lines and points, but also the affective quality of the rhizome, an aspect that is vital to social dreaming, where the images are affects. From a Deleuzian perspective, it also constitutes a 'de-territorialisation', the creation of new spaces that have never been travelled before, where new affects are free to travel in spaces that are 'smooth' rather than 'striated'. This too is the new territory of the social dreaming matrix, where the participants are gathered and contained within a shared space of reverie that is unlike the territory of their daily lives. And in the matrix, this new shared space is 'smooth', that is to say, the contributions of participants are allowed a freedom of expression that is uninterrupted, un-judged, un-interpreted. And finally, importantly, the rhizome also de-personalises the points and agents of inter-connectivity, reminding us, once again, of the de-personalised nature of the social dreaming matrix. As Deleuze and Guattari say in their introduction to the rhizome:

> …it is no longer of any importance whether one says I. We are no longer ourselves. Each will know his own. We have been aided, inspired, multiplied. (Deleuze and Guattari 1988, p. 3)

Creative Aspects of the Rhizome and the Ontology of Social Dreaming

The social dreaming matrix is a rhizome in process, structure and function. This is its distinguishing factor and as such it defines the kind of knowledge that it provides as research data and the epistemological stance that makes sense of this data. By approaching social dreaming in this way, the missing pieces of Gordon Lawrence's work seem to fall into place.

To begin with, Deleuze's philosophy is in itself rhizomatic in that it understands its role and purpose as being to synthesise a diversity of concepts into the creation of new concepts, and in this way philosophy for Deleuze was not necessarily ideological, rational or logical, but closer in many ways to the creativity of the arts:

> A philosophy is a kind of synthesizer of concepts, creating a concept is not at all ideological. A concept is a created thing. (Deleuze 1978, p. 8)

The source of this creativity for Deleuze is in rhizomatic thought, where logical lines are broken in favour of free-ranging affects and concepts that as a result of this freedom can produce strange joinings, sometimes paradoxical couplings or multiple inter-connections that have never before been connected:

> The rhizome connects any point to any other point, and its traits are not necessarily linked to traits of the same nature. (Deleuze and Guattari 1988, p. 21)

The creativity of the matrix as rhizome is not merely located in the dream, but in the way the dreams and associations to those dreams are shared in the matrix. That is to say, the actual rhizomatic structure is located in the physical configuration of the social dreaming matrix (the snowflake pattern) and the space that this creates for contributions from the participants in an un-guided, yet contained, proliferation of associative thoughts. These are presented as part objects that acquire temporary meanings, which come and go, through their semi-random links and connections that are suggested but not defined through free association. In this context of a temporary rhizomatic space, creativity is a spontaneous and never before conceived of synthesis of image-affects that at least in process are similar to the Deleuzian idea of creativity.

Much of this is hinted at in the literature, mostly centred around the figure of Gordon Lawrence, on social dreaming, but the vague hints and bits of ideas that have been floating around have never found a comfortable or congruent epistemological base, such as the one being pursued here. The nearest that Lawrence came to an epistemological framework for the creativity of social dreaming was to link it to Bion's thinking, especially to his theory of thinking that discussed Beta and Alpha function and elements. Bion, as has been discussed above, has provided the most interesting basis for social dreaming theory thus far, and Lawrence (with Susan Long) has directly applied this thinking to the idea of the creativity of social dreaming (Lawrence and Long 2010, pp. 224–227; 229; 231–232). However, more often than not, both Bion's ideas in this respect and other thoughts related to creativity in social dreaming remained an enigma for Lawrence, and were expressed as such:

> Yet, despite the plethora of research, the essential nature of creativity still lies beyond the grasp of scientific investigation, not quite able to encompass the combination of uniqueness of process and daring of endeavour involved. (Lawrence and Long 2010, p. 213)

If we select some of Lawrence and Long's ideas on social dreaming and creativity, we do find, however, some interesting connections to the Deleuzian rhizome, if only we exercise our powers of synthesis. The following selection illustrates this point:

1. 'We start with the essential idea that everything is connected to everything else.' (Ibid. p. 214)
2. 'The unconscious operates on infinite sets characterized by pure imagery, metaphor, and logic that is non-sequential. Images are juxtaposed asymmetrically while dreaming in an associative manner that could not be thought of while awake and conscious. It is in these bizarre, surreal juxtapositions that new thinking is heralded.' (Ibid. pp. 218–219)
3. 'What impedes intuition, and imagination, is institutionalized and sterile memory and desire; programmed thinking repeating old patterns. (Ibid. p. 228)
4. 'The infinite becomes apparent through actively imagining the object by the suspension of narcissism or auto-centric perception, whatever one knows, ridding oneself of memory or desire to be free to intuit what might be its truth'. (Ibid. p. 230)

In these observations, with their references to the 'bizarre', 'memory and desire' and the 'infinite' as an aspect of the unconscious, we see the hand of Bion. But at no stage do Lawrence and Long create a theory of creativity in social dreaming that links Bion's thoughts with the other ideas in their chapter, such as when they quote Maturana and Varela's autopoiesis, for example (Ibid. pp. 214–215).

A synthesising of these thoughts into a coherent theory, which resonates with Lawrence and Long's ideas but can also deepen and develop them further is possible through adopting the Deleuzian rhizome and applying it to social dreaming.

First, the rhizome is indeed 'everything … connected to everything else' (1. above), however, Deleuze and Guattari also emphasise that it is not rhizomatic in the sense of trees or roots. In other words, the Deleuzian rhizome is total inter-connectivity without a centre (such as a tree trunk), and the lines of the rhizome are spontaneously emitted and develop in any chaotic fashion. This corresponds to the deliberate lack of hierarchy or central force that is engendered in social dreaming, where even the host takes care to become an equal part of the matrix by contributing as a participant and refraining from interpretation, thus allowing a completely free flow of contributions to the matrix space.

The way Deleuze and Guattari describe this free flow is 'directions in motion' which are 'defined solely by a circulation of states' (Deleuze and Guattari 1988, p. 21).

Second, the Deleuzian rhizome and the social dreaming matrix are chiefly non-sequential. The rhizome 'connects any point to any other point, and its traits are not necessarily linked to traits of the same nature' (Ibid. p. 21). It is as a result of these unexpected connections, through previously unthought juxtapositions of the image-affects, that the rhizome creates new thoughts. So it is in the social dreaming matrix.

Third, the rhizome and the social dreaming matrix are free of routine, institutionalised thoughts, memories and desires. The rhizome eschews 'centred (even polycentric) systems with hierarchical modes of communication and pre-established paths' (Ibid. p. 21). In doing so, the social dreaming matrix, as a rhizome, is open to new, creative thoughts and feelings.

Fourth, the rhizome, as in social dreaming, is infinite in the sense that 'it has neither beginning nor end' (Ibid. p. 21), and it suspends autocentricity because it is 'not a multiple derived from the One, or to which One is added' (Ibid. p. 21). This is a clearly felt experience of social dreaming, where the participant is aware of substituting a sense of the I with a sense of equally shared spaces, ideas and sensations.

In all these ways, it is possible to usefully equate the Deleuzian rhizome with the social dreaming process. Furthermore, some of Lawrence's more disparate ideas related to the social dreaming matrix, such as the inclusion of autopoiesis are also easily embraced into the Deleuzian rhizome, where the self-creating aspects of Maturana and Varela's theory came close to Deleuze and Guattari's description of the rhizome as being an 'acentred, non-hierarchical, nonsignifying system without a General and without an organizing memory or central automation' (Ibid. p. 21).

In this way, the mere list of attributes that make social dreaming a creative process, according to Lawrence and Long – 'the personal unconscious, dreaming, 'negative capability', imagination, curiosity, intuition, faith, and the infinite' (Lawrence and Long 2010, p. 232) – can be assimilated into Deleuzian rhizomatic theory, providing a solid basis for interpreting and analysing the data that might be gathered from social dreaming when used as a research method. This may mean adapting social dreaming as a research method to recent general developments in using Deleuzian perspectives in research (Coleman and Ringrose 2013), or looking into inventions in qualitative research such as 'Rhizoanalysis' (Masny and Waterhouse 2011; Masny 2013), for example.

The Associative Unconscious and the Rhizome

The creation of the matrix as a rhizome depends on free association, and although Deleuze and Guattari did not discuss free association in relation to the rhizome, it is implied in the way affect and concepts are allowed to float and find their own way into connectivity, through a 'smooth space' of all directions rather than the 'striated space' governed by pre-thought out ideas. The key to how the social dreaming matrix is conducted in relation to free association and what can become a matrix resides in allowing the associations to be truly 'free', that is to be uninterrupted by interpretation (Holland 1999, p. 45).

Long and Harney (2013), Long (in press) and Manley (in press) have put forward the theory of the associative unconscious (Long and Harney 2013) and associative thinking as being key to social dreaming. Long and Harney compare the associative unconscious to a network, and although they also compare it to Jung's collective unconscious, the differences they point out in relation to Jung are important to the possibility of linking the social dreaming matrix to a Deleuzian rhizome. It is precisely the lack of fixed archetypal symbols and the possibility of individual versions of shared interpretation in the matrix that make the rhizome possible (through a 'smoothness' of space) and lead them to conclude that the associative unconscious is the 'crucible of creativity'. In all these respects, the associative unconscious can be seen as a description of the rhizomatic process of the matrix. Added to this, Manley (in press, 2018) suggests that associative thinking is equivalent to thinking in affects in ways that connect association with the Deleuzian rhizome.

The Dream Becomes Social

As important as the dream is the fact of its sharing, which is reflected in this discussion of the nature of the sharing and the proposal that this can be understood in terms of the Deleuzian rhizome. For, in social dreaming the social is not only a reference to the relevance of each dream to the social world that we inhabit, which was Charlotte Beradt's original idea (see Part I), but is also a reference to the sharing aspect of the social dreaming matrix and how the individual becomes social through the sharing collage or rhizome of the matrix. In this sense, we might even suggest that the small gathering of people that make up a matrix are in some sense a microcosm of their society. It is also remarkable to note how different the social dreaming matrix or rhizome is compared to other groups, whether these are psychodynamic groups or debating groups. In both of these cases, the position of the individual is emphasised in relation to the group where issues of power, status, role and authority, leadership and followership, as well as relational emotions based on group dynamics, such as envy, anger, shame, guilt and so on, come to the fore. In the case of the process of the social dreaming matrix, however, the way it is based on reverie as a means of sharing the associative unconscious is crucial. Just as critical is the connection between the images and the expression of affect, which is a direct result of the associative process of the matrix. The dream images, and also the associations and other visual images that become equally contributions to the social dreaming experience are all to some extent expressions of affect, coming directly from a place of feelings as opposed to a Cartesian centre located in the Cartesian brain. This shared expression of affect rather than cognitive thoughts and opinions is perhaps the primary feature of social dreaming and also situates the process within the Deleuzian paradigm. The complexity of the Deleuzian rhizome serves social dreaming well, since the matrix is indeed more than a meshwork, more than a network. The uniqueness of the process makes the matrix a singular example of Deleuzian creativity and this in turn provides social dreaming with a rich epistemological basis for further thought, analysis and development.

References

Capra, F. and Luigi Luisi, P. (2014). *The Systems View of Life*. Cambridge: CUP.

Coleman, R. and Ringrose, J. (2013). *Deleuze and Research Methodologies*. Edinburgh: Edinburgh University Press.

Deleuze, G. (1978). Lecture transcripts on Spinoza's concept of *Affect*. (https://www.gold.ac.uk/media/images-by-section/departments/research-centres-and-units/research-centres/centre-for-invention-and-social-process/deleuze_spinoza_affect.pdf) Accessed 05.03.18.

Deleuze, G. and Guattari, F. (1988). *A Thousand Plateaus*. London: Continuum.

Holland, E.W. (1999). *Deleuze and Guattari's Anti-Oedipus: Introduction to Schizoanalysis*. London: Routledge.

Ingold, T. (2007). *Lines: A brief History*. Abingdon: Routledge.

Ingold, T. (2008). When ANT meets SPIDER: Social theory for arthropods. In Knappett, C. and Malafouris, L. (Eds.), *Material Agency: Towards a Non-Anthropocentric Approach*.

Langer, S. (1948). *A Philosophy in a New Key*. NY: Mentor New American Library.

Latour, B. (2005). *Reassembling the Social*. Oxford: OUP.

Latour, B. and Hermant, E. (1998). *Paris ville invisible*. (http://www.bruno-latour.fr/virtual/EN/index.html) Accessed 05.03.18.

Lawrence, W.G. and Long, S. (2010). The creative frame of mind. In Lawrence, W.G. (Ed.), *The Creativity of Social Dreaming*. London: Karnac.

Long, S. (in press). Dreams and Dreaming: A Socioanalytic and Semiotic Perspective. In Long, S. and Manley, J. (Eds.), *Social Dreaming: Philosophy research and practice*. London: Routledge.

Long, S. and Harney, M. (2013). The associative unconscious. In Long, S. (Ed.), *Socioanalytic Methods*. London: Routledge.

Lovelock, J.E. (2000). *Gaia, a new look at life on Earth*. Oxford: OUP.

Manley, J. (2010). *Untold Communications: A holistic study of social dreaming*. Unpublished PhD thesis. Bristol: UWE.

Manley, J. (2018). 'Every human being is an artist': From social representation to creative experiences of self. In Cummins, A.M. and Williams, N. (Eds.), *Researching Beneath the Surface*, Vol. 2. London: Routledge.

Manley, J. (in press). Associative thinking: A Deleuzian perspective on social dreaming. In Long, S. and Manley, J. (Eds.), *Social Dreaming: Philosophy, research and practice*. London: Routledge.

Masny, D. and Waterhouse, M. (2011). Mapping Territories and Creating Nomadic Pathways with Multiple Literacies Theory. *Journal of Curriculum Theorizing*, 27(3), pp. 287–307. Retrieved from http://journal.jctonline.org/index.php/jct/article/viewFile/155/21MasnyWaterhouse.pdf.

Masny, D. (2013). Rhizoanalytic Pathways in Qualitative Research. *Qualitative Inquiry*, 19(5), pp. 339–348. https://doi.org/10.1177/1077800413479559.

Müller, M. and Schurr, C. (2016). Assemblage thinking and actor-network theory: Conjunctions, disjunctions, cross-fertilisations. *Transactions of the Institute of British Geographers*, 41(3), pp. 217–229.

7

Becoming Dream: The Dis-embodied/ Embodied Experience of Social Dreaming

'All Manner of "Becomings"'

Associated to the rhizome, if we are to apply this to the social dreaming collage, are suggestions of other Deleuzian concepts attached to rhizomatic thinking. One of these is the idea of 'becoming', explicitly linked to the rhizome by Deleuze and Guattari, as being part of the fluctuating pattern of intensities that creates a rhizome as 'all manner of "becomings"' (Deleuze and Guattari 1988, p. 21). This concept is all important in the Deleuzian approach and similarly, I believe, in social dreaming. Other related concepts have also been touched upon in the course of the discussions above, all of which are linked to the idea of becoming as part of the rhizomatic experience. In this chapter, I intend to delve more deeply into these concepts and show how they are intrinsically linked to the rhizomatic view and to the social dreaming collage. These concepts include the Deleuzian ideas of the Body without Organs (BwO); intensities, percepts and affects; the nomadic; smooth and striated space; and deterritorialization.

J. Manley, *Social Dreaming, Associative Thinking and Intensities of Affect*,
Studies in the Psychosocial, https://doi.org/10.1007/978-3-319-92555-4_7

Becoming Dream

The connection between the intensities of affect of the rhizome and the sense of becoming can explain both the living and holding tension of the social dreaming matrix and the strange sensation often recorded by participants in a matrix that another person's dream feels uncannily like one's own.

The Dream, Not the Dreamer and the Body Without Organs

In the first place, the reason that the matrix holds together as an entity, is because the individual in the matrix no longer feels as if she is a separate being, but rather a fragment of a 'body' that is the collection of dreams, image-affects and associations in the matrix, as if this collage of the matrix had acquired a life or 'body' of its own. Obviously, this experience is relative and subjective, and individuals participating in social dreaming will each feel it differently, however, experience shows that in a general sense, this is true. This might also help to explain why individuals persist in a task that would otherwise appear to be boring at best and a waste of time at worst, that is to say sitting among strangers recounting a personal dream to others. In the matrix, as we have already noted, the social dreaming mantra – that we are concerned with the dream, not the dreamer – holds strong because the truth is that participants are not concerned just with each of the dreams, since each of these dreams comes from an individual in the matrix and would then be identified as a personal belonging of that individual, but rather participants are concerned with the accumulation of dreams; the body of dreams; and how this body becomes part of each individual and subsumes each individual ego as part of the single body-making process. The body of dreams/image-affects/associations is quite another body to that of the individual. This other body is given life by the matrix in the Deleuzian sense of an 'inorganic life of things' (Deleuze and Guattari 1994, p. 213). It is this 'inorganic life' that Deleuze is referring to when he discusses the body without organs

(Deleuze and Guattari 1988, pp. 149–167; Deleuze and Guattari 2004, pp. 9–17; Deleuze 2004, pp. 216–222; Deleuze 2005, pp. 32–39). By taking away the body of the dreamer in social dreaming, we are left with the affect embedded in the dreams and associations, the image-affects, and the way that these image-affects combine with others in the matrix creates another body external to the individual participants; this is the body without organs (BwO). When Deleuze refers to this BwO, he describes it in terms of intensities rather than organs, 'an intense and intensive body' (Deleuze 2005, p. 32). These intensities are intensities of affect, which give this body life or an 'intensive reality' (Ibid., p. 32). What is important to the individual in her own body is not the organs within, so to speak, but the way sensation is felt and understood, the sensations that emanate from the varying intensities of affect that are pulsing at any one time in the course of the matrix or rhizome. This is how the participant in the social dreaming matrix can, in a manner of speaking, both at once embody sensation but disembody the self from the body of the matrix. This is how Deleuze describes such a peculiarity in his discussion of the painting of Francis Bacon:

> [Sensation exceeds] the bounds of organic activity. It is immediately conveyed in the flesh through the nervous wave or vital emotion... the body without organs is flesh and nerve; a wave flows through it and traces levels upon it; a sensation is produced when the wave encounters the forces acting upon the body, an "affective athleticism"... When sensation is linked to the body in this way, it ceases to be representative and becomes real. (Ibid., p. 33)

This, I contend, is what is happening in the course of a social dreaming matrix: as the image-affects become more and more intertwined, new configurations of intensities of affect are created, and become vibrant with a life of their own. Each configuration of image-affects creates its own BwO that is held together through resonating intensities of affect. Through the sharing process, which includes the active passing of sensations from a participant's 'matrix in the mind' to that of the matrix as a whole, a BwO is formed.

The Unique Quality of Dreams: Affect and Percept in Continuous Motion

The uniqueness of the qualities of dreams and the associations and images that arise as the result of the dreams in the social dreaming matrix, distinguish social dreaming from other modes of thinking and feeling. This difference in quality is the same as the distinction that Deleuze and Guattari make between affect/affection and percept/perception:

> Percepts are not perceptions, they are packets of sensations and relations that outlive those who experience them. Affects are not feelings, they are becomings that go beyond those who live through them (they become other). (Deleuze, quoted in Thrift 2008, p. 116)

The percept, in terms of social dreaming, neatly describes the nature of and the sensation given by the dream image, which is not perceived as in perception, but rather visualized as a percept, that is to say as a sensation in relation to other sensations, forming a conglomerate that I have been calling a collage of image-affects, and in this sense more than visual, more than perception. Once a percept, in this Deleuzian sense, the image-affect can be felt as affect, but this sensation is similarly more than a feeling. By connecting affect to becoming, Deleuze is describing the intensity of sensation that converts the representation of sensation into a lived, embodied sensation in a way that creates a new space of becoming. That is to say, the percept (as an image-affect) becomes a sensation that is beyond the representative possibilities of the word, (in this case it could be a dream image that is difficult to describe, even though there is no choice but to describe it in the matrix). The understanding of this image-affect resides in a kind of empathic drawing together of the percept with the affect in such a way as the felt sensation is transformed into a sensation of becoming the image-affect. The stronger the intensity of the affect the greater the sensation of becoming. In social dreaming, this effect is felt when a participant feels that another person's dream might have been her own, or that the inexplicable image of a dream becomes comprehensible through becoming the dream in the dream image. Manley and Trustram (2018) in a paper that studies the use of social dreaming in the context of a museum display about the abolition of slavery, give an example of such a becoming. In this example, they point to the use of two separate images, one of a small child being eaten by a crocodile, another of being swallowed by a whale like Jonah, and describe the affective process of becoming that emerges from their juxtapositioning:

> In our example, the fear that we associate with the image of being eaten by the crocodile is combined with the sorrow and repentance of Jonah inside the whale and the fate of the enslaved people inside the 'belly' of the slave ship. The affect is the combination of this fear, sorrow and repentance expressed in the images. In the SD sessions the participant is 'becoming-animal' as a means of expressing affect, imaginatively eaten by the crocodile and swallowed by the whale. Through imagination and felt affective experience, the participant can come closer to understanding being trapped inside the hold of the slave ship, which might otherwise be difficult to conceptualise. This sense of 'becoming' is what enables the disparate combinations or image-affects to be experienced by each participant in SD. (Manley and Trustram 2018, pp. 13–14)

In this example, the becoming also demonstrates the effect of the rhizome in joining together disparate elements, including relating to things as opposed to being limited to organic entities. Through the social dreaming matrix in the museum, the participants were, for an instant, able to 'become-slave'. Importantly, as Manley and Trustram go on to discuss, this unconscious process can have a significant effect on the participants' conscious views about the realities of slavery and how one can become more empathic and knowledgeable about the subject of slavery in more than cognitive terms. This is the process that Deleuze and Guattari describe when they say that 'affect is not the passage from one lived state to another but from man's nonhuman becoming' (Deleuze and Guattari 1994, p. 173). In other words, the rhizome of the social dreaming matrix has created a nonhuman BwO that is nevertheless alive and that has enabled the participants to understand realities that did not have to emanate from their own bodies/persons, but rather were created through the flows and movements of the rhizomatic connections created in the course of the matrix. The matrix has become 'a zone in which we no longer know which is animal and which human, because something like the triumph or monument of their nondistinction rises up' (Ibid., p. 173).

The Matrix as the Smooth Space of the Nomad

The BwO of social dreaming is only made possible by the containing space of the matrix being made openly available for dreams and associations by being, in Deleuzian terms, a 'smooth space', not 'striated'. As I have already noted above, 'striated' implies that movements are restricted, limited or channelled, and direction is from one point to another. The 'smooth space' in the work of Deleuze and Guattari is that of the 'nomad', where travel, like process, is an end in itself rather than a destination. The nomad has no fixed destination, is defined by constant movement marked by temporary pauses, and is open, by the very nature of nomadism, to new and unexpected/planned for experiences. The rhizome can only be created through smoothness, where all the inter-connected concepts – or image-affects in the case of social dreaming – can move and create unexpected links without any kind of hindrance. In social dreaming, this means that the image-affects need to be given the maximum facility for their creation and inter-connection without the interference of cognition, memory, desire or interpretation, precisely the space created by the experienced host in a social dreaming session. The practice of nomadism is achieved along territories that are smooth and free to flow in unchartered directions.

The Deleuzian smooth space exactly corresponds to the conditions necessary for the creation of the rhizome, which is, as discussed above, neither a meshwork of lines without point, nor a network of interconnected points:

> In striated space, lines or trajectories tend to be subordinated to points: one goes from one point to another. In the smooth, it is the opposite: the points are subordinated to the trajectory. (Deleuze and Guattari 1988, p. 478)

In the social dreaming matrix, this is equivalent to the sensation of free flowing dreams, image-affects, and associations, unimpeded by comments or interpretations. In some examples of social dreaming, where participants make extended comments or attempt interpretation, this effect is lessened. However, when social dreaming is working well, the temporary points in the smooth space are the image-affects that are allowed to gently rest in the matrix, without being fixed into rigid points by any undue attention or importance given to them at the expense of other image-affects, so that the BwO of the matrix can continue to grow and develop in un-predetermined ways that lead to a sensation of shared creativity, which has already been identified as a defining feature of social dreaming. An important feature of the smooth space of the rhizome is the fortuitous encounter of affects, as described in the following extract from Deleuze and Guattari, and which can easily be applied to the chance (because free associative) encounter of image-affects in a social dreaming session:

> Smooth space is filled by events or haecceities, far more than by formed and perceived things. It is a space of affects, more than one of properties. (Deleuze and Guattari 1988, p. 479)

The 'Deterritorialized' Space of the Social Dreaming Matrix

Finally, the rhizome/matrix can be understood as a 'deterritorialized' space (Deleuze and Guattari 1988, pp. 174–91), that is to say a space (or territory) within another space where something different to the initial space can be created. The snowflake pattern seating arrangement of the social dreaming matrix actually creates a new physical space that is different from the room where it is created, and it is within this physical new territory (created through the deterritorialization of the room) that a new virtual smooth space leading to the rhizome can be created and developed. There are instances in social dreaming where this is remarked upon, as sounds or thoughts from the original space of the room become interruptions or additional material for the social dreaming within the snowflake pattern territory. The idea of the creation of a new territory is more than a concept, it actually leads to the sensation of inhabiting a different world, where, therefore, things can be thought about differently. What is especially significant about this difference is the participant sensation that the thought processes of the new territory are experienced within rather than represented outwith, which is what Deleuze means when referring to non-representational art in the following extract from his book on Francis Bacon:

> It is like the emergence of another world. For these marks, these traits, are irrational, involuntary, accidental, free, random. They are nonrepresentative, nonillustrative, nonnarrative. They are no longer either significant or signifiers: they are asignifying traits. They are traits of sensation… (Deleuze 2005, p. 71)

The Reality of the Virtual

In his work on Bergson, Deleuze discusses how Bergsonian time provides a scenario of flux between the virtual and the real. The reality of time is that it is a unified whole of all time past and present, a 'gigantic memory' and a 'single Time' (Deleuze 1988, p. 100), and yet the virtual reality of perception understands it only as fragments, 'virtual multiplicities' (Ibid., p. 100). The timeless quality of the matrix discussed above is such a virtual world of fragments, these fragments being the dream part objects that form the collage or rhizome of the matrix. Through the rhizome, a new world is created where dream images, image-affects and associations can cross, meet and depart once more, creating new virtual possibilities that have never been thought of before. Such is the '*reality of this virtual*' (Ibid., p. 100, Deleuze's italics), and such is the unthought known of the matrix. The matrix, therefore, creates a virtual world of dreams, image-affects and associations that is also the real world, a strata or layer of the external world, just as real, despite its virtuality. The same can be said of the BwO of the created collage of image-affects of the matrix. The BwO is unreal in a sense, but vital, alive and real, in the sense of the virtual reality of the matrix. The sensation of participating in the matrix is that for a temporary moment of the experience, the shared BwO of the matrix is the lived reality of the participants. This reality is not an external reality in the sense of perceptions, but rather another reality of percept and affect and made into reality through sensations of intensity. The intensity of the affects bring them to life, so to speak, and this is what allows the 'knowns' to become 'thought', to return to Bollas' idea of the unthought known once more. The virtual reality of the affective rhizome is also a space that is smooth, in the Deleuzian sense. It is perhaps the smoothest of possible spaces through its virtual, unconscious design and as a result of the practice of social dreaming as a method that refuses the Deleuzian striated space through its deliberate non-interpretive, non-discursive, and non-hierarchical practice. A new territory is created and further strata of our shared world are discovered.

References

Deleuze, G. (1988). *Bergsonism*. New York: Zone Books.

Deleuze, G. (2004). *Difference and Repetition*. London: Continuum.

Deleuze, G. (2005). *Francis Bacon*. London: Bloomsbury.

Deleuze, G. and Guattari, F. (1988). *A Thousand Plateaus*. London: Continuum.

Deleuze, G. and Guattari, F. (1994). *What is Philosophy?* London: Verso.

Deleuze, G. and Guattari, F. (2004). *Anti-Oedipus. Capitalism and Schizophrenia*. London: Continuum.

Manley, J. and Trustram, M. (2018). 'Such endings that are not over': The slave trade, social dreaming and affect in a museum. *Psychoanalysis, Culture and Society*, 23(1), pp. 77–96.

Thrift, N. (2008). *Non-Representational Theory*. London: Routledge.

Part III

From Data to New Thinking

8

Processing Social Dreaming Material as Data

In this chapter, I will use the data from a social dreaming matrix to illustrate in greater depth the approach to the social dreaming materials and how they can be viewed from a Deleuzian perspective, as discussed above. This is a study of process, design and structure rather than a complete study of the image-affects and general content and meanings of the social dreaming matrix that is used to illustrate the points made in this chapter. In Chap. 9, I will present an example of an actual case study of the interpretation of a social dreaming matrix using this approach.

In order to reflect upon the process, I will use extracts from the transcript of one of a series of social dreaming matrices that were hosted by Gordon Lawrence at the Working Men's Club in Camden, London, UK, and also some of the material that emerged from post-matrix activities. The transcript is not a verbatim record of the matrix, because it was written down from notes rather than transcribed from a recording.[1]

---

[1] In some cases, such as this one, there was a reluctance by some of the participants to consent to an audio recording of the matrix. However, this reluctance did not extend to the recording of hand written notes.

J. Manley, *Social Dreaming, Associative Thinking and Intensities of Affect*,
Studies in the Psychosocial, https://doi.org/10.1007/978-3-319-92555-4_8

Living in Contemporary Times

The sample social dreaming matrix under discussion here was a day event programmed for the 14th April 2005, under the heading 'Living in Contemporary Times', held at the Working Men's College in Camden, north London. The following is an extract of the information published to advertise the intention of the Social dreaming matrix:

> Contemporary times are suffused by tragedy. Natural tragedies, like tsunami, cannot be avoided, but human tragedies can. AIDS, poverty, genocide, ethnic cleansing, terrorism, threats to democracy, totalitarian-states-of-mind, Holocausts, Gulags, corruption, wherever they occur in the world, are now part of our conscious awareness because of mass communication. They cannot be denied, or wished away. And there is the unintended, silent, looming tragedy of global warming, which may end all civilization. Will the human spirit allow us to survive? (Lawrence, event information sheet, 14 April 2005)

Structures of the Matrix

Each quoted contribution from the transcript has been given an order number from 1 to 35. 'D' at the beginning of a contribution signifies 'Dream', while an 'A' means that the contribution was of another kind, an 'Association', for example. This simple separation of the dream material from all other contributions demonstrates the extent to which the social dreaming matrix is as much about associations and other material triggered by the dreams as it is about the dreams themselves. In terms of the rhizomatic quality of the matrix, this also emphasises the different aspects of the collage and how the lines of and between affects are in themselves of different intensities and how in some cases they are conduits of intensity and flow. A matrix with nothing but dream contributions would soon become rather static because of the similar emotional tone between the dream images and the consequent difficulty of creating a trace of intensity between them. Between similar affective intensities, there can be little movement; movement occurs between contributions that have different intensities, rather like a pair of old fashioned scales, which instead of remaining equally weighted and poised in equilibrium, shift up or down according to the different weights at either end of the scale. Having said this, it is still true that these other, differently weighted contributions, are still presented within the state and containing norms of reverie of the matrix. In other words they continue to encourage seamless flow between affects rather than provide stops and starts to the flow through participants' and host's conscious, rational interpretation of the material.

I have provided further subdivisions by bringing together the contributions into clusters of images, (labelled 'paragraphs' below), like fractals that seem to belong to a rhizomatic whole – both complete in themselves and also forming part of the larger collage – as far as the unconscious thought images are concerned. These are the multiplicities of part objects referred to earlier. Each part object can complete a cluster but still remain a part object, never quite reaching resolution as a definitive whole. Although I am going to discuss mainly the beginning and end of this matrix, these subdivisions are as follows:

1. Paragraphs 1–4 (122 words)
2. Paragraphs 5–13 (368 words)
3. Paragraphs 14–16 (59 words)
4. Paragraphs 17–28 (260 words)
5. Paragraphs 29–31 (34 words)
6. Paragraphs 32–35 (126 words)

From this, it can be seen that a particular shape or form for the way that images are clustered seems to emerge and suggest itself: We have the introductory images in a section of 122 words that appear to create a frame with the concluding images in a section of 126 words. Then, there are two more substantial middle sections, (368 and 260 words respectively); each of these is 'punctuated' by a brief hiatus, (59 and 34 words for each).

The 'shape' of the matrix, illustrated below in Fig. 8.1, will be seen to form part of our understanding of the whole.

Figure 8.1 shows how although there is obviously a linear sequence that governs the matrix in terms of clock time, the way that the image-affects link

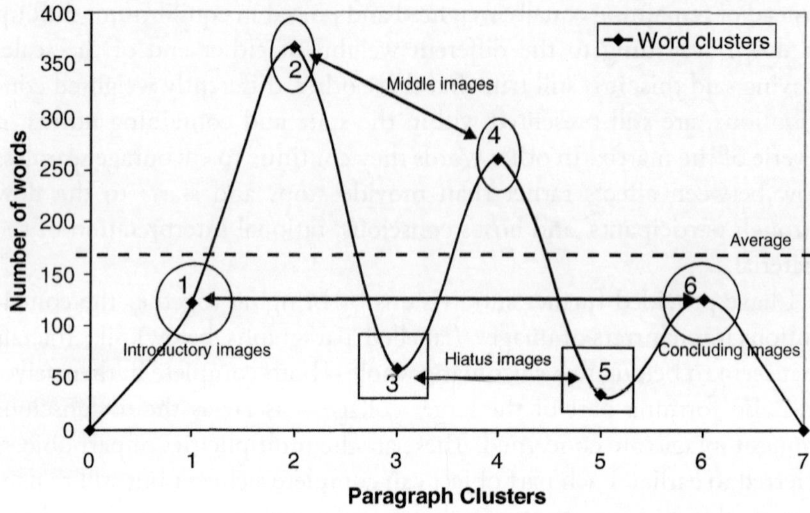

Fig. 8.1 Clusters of image-affects forming in the course of the matrix

together is not necessarily or not uniquely sequential. Therefore, many of the images in 1 link through to 6; and the images in cluster 2 are connected to those in 4. The latter clusters consist of the greatest number of words; the former of less and similar number of words. In terms of the overall structure, this would suggest a kind of framing or balance of the whole matrix in clusters 1 and 6. Viewed as clusters, the time sequence dissolves, as in Fig. 8.2 below, where the connecting clusters are defined by colour.

In Fig. 8.2, therefore, the clusters of images are true to themselves and also linked to other clusters but not in sequential fashion. In this sense the clusters are inter-connected with each other in a rhizomatic fashion as described in the previous chapter. What Fig. 8.1 cannot display, however, is the sense of changing intensities of affect that pulse at different moments, which is also an integral part of the rhizome. For example, a link between clusters 1 and 6 will become evident through the connection made through intensity, since the sequential link has been lost. One way of understanding this would be by suggesting that a memory of an image-affect in cluster 1 was reignited in cluster 6 due to a mutual image-affect connection between the two. However, following a Bergsonian line of thought within the Deleuzian paradigm, this memory is more than a recollection of a past event (which would locate it back into the sequence).

Fig. 8.2 Non-sequential relationship of clusters

It becomes, instead, an indissoluble combination of past and present, and in this way forms a new present. According to Deleuze, as influenced by Bergson, what links the past with the present in this way is not sequence but movement. The memory-image and the image produced in the present become one and the same:

> What is the framework common to recollection in the process of actualization (the recollection-becoming-image) and the perception-image? This common framework is movement. (Deleuze 1988, p. 67)

It is in the dream that this fusion is at its most absolute, because the mind is completely relaxed between all pasts and presents:

> For what happens in a creature that confines itself to dreaming? Since sleep is like a present situation requiring nothing but rest, with no interest other than "disinterest", it is as if the contraction [JM note: meaning the 'contracting' of the past into the present] were missing, as if the extremely expanded (*détendu*)[2] relationship of the recollection with the present reproduced the most expanded *(détendu)* level of the past itself. (Deleuze 1988, pp. 66–67)

[2] The italics are the translator's in the original. In my opinion, 'expanded' is not such a good translation as 'relaxed', which immediately evokes the opposite of 'contracted', which is Deleuze's point.

The quality of the intensities of the image-affects in the collage or rhizome of the social dreaming matrix is special and particular compared to other modes of debate or group work. In social dreaming, the image-affects move together in this way and as a result produce intensities that resonate with the shared affect of the matrix.

Clusters of Intensity

In the following commentary, I will quote the extracts from the social dreaming matrix in question, in the pattern determined by intensities of affect, as described above. Although I will be primarily discussing the extracts I have bonded together for this purpose, by looking particularly at extracts 1 and 6 together (the framing extracts at the beginning and end of this social dreaming matrix), I will also be making reference to other moments in the matrix that further emphasise the rhizome-like pattern of the collage of image-affects as they resonate from different moments in the matrix.

Extract summaries 1 and 6 (with reference to the matrix structure depicted in Fig. 6.1)

Extract 1 (Aligned to Extract 6)

D1 – remember final part… cook something… invent recipe….. seafood... fish... veg… I woke up with thought of creating new recipe…
D2 – in a large house… new… sea… like a David Hockney painting… framed in a rectangular shape… green grass… saw workmen throwing brightly coloured plates on this patch of grass… One I collected for refuse collection… I thought of retrieving these plates and making a collage…artistic composition… need lots of time and experiment for this… arrange in a spiral pattern…
A – Julian Schnabel – people bought the works of art, but the bits of plate kept falling off – so he employed someone to stick these plates back on…
A – in Chandigarh – Chand building from these pieces.

Extract 6 (Aligned to Extract 1)

A – The idea of framing … thinking about power of defining what is important and what effects it has on theirs
A – Chinese using power to destroy
A – image which frames the book… Indian girl going to sacred rock… throwing the flowers, the petals to the rock in the sea... when the tide is low… When the sea rises, the collage disappears… creation of sacred picture which is transformed… Communication with nature
A – A cemetery in Nairobi… We scattered them on the petals of the grave… On one grave a teacher and small boy who was drowned… after my mother died... did the same with my sisters… I am in touched with the mother of the boy… She is moved… Now it is not safe… Get police escort.

Commentary to Extracts 1 and 6

As is often the case in social dreaming, the opening dream images are especially clear and appear to give shape to the images that follow. Lawrence referred to this effect as a fractal system:

> Each dream is a fractal of the other, for dreaming is revealed in repeating patterns: one dream is part of a whole sequence of dreams in a matrix. (Lawrence 2005, p. 15)

The opening dream begins with the end of a dream. There is no attempt or need, from the beginning of the matrix, to ensure any kind of linear continuity. This beginning that begins with an end could be anywhere, demonstrating how the important aspect of the opening dream is in the image-affects rather than the narrative. We are presented with an image of creation expressed through cooking and seafood. The juxtaposing of the seafood and the cooking is more important than the story behind it, what for and for whom the cooking was being prepared, or why the seafood was chosen, and so on. In other words, the aspects of story telling that include purpose, action and characterisation are largely absent.[3] Instead, the person who offers the dream suggests the importance of a concept arising from the images, i.e. that of invention or creativity. This suggestion is succinctly and directly expressed through the images, without a need for further thought and explanation. In this case too, because of the presence of the images shorn of narrative, the participants in the matrix are allowed to be stimulated by the affect rather than any cognitive reaction. The affects associated with the images might vary from person to person, but are still likely to resonate with others. Affects arising from the opening dream might include excitement (at the idea of creation or invention); a yearning (associated with hunger or imagined smell); curiosity (about how the recipe will turn out), and so on. Whatever the affect, it is important to note the lack of any need to think through or provide an opinion about any of the contributions. The images simply exist. In their existence as such, and by bypassing further thought or discourse, in the free associative manner described above, the participants in the matrix are free to associate to the image-affects by contributing further dreams and associations.

At first, the mention of cooking appears to stimulate a dream memory that includes the mention of plates and the idea of artistic creation, ideas that seem connected somehow to the first dream, but are in no way a continuation of it. They are two part objects that share an affinity without ever forming part of a definitive whole. As the associations begin, a clear link is made between the two opening dreams and the two following associations, developing the idea of the value of creativity, but using the image-affects of the artists' work and the use of plates, which though broken appear to lend themselves more easily to creative use.

In sum, central themes of creation are expressed in the images of cooking and artistic composition. The cooking is creative because the recipe has to be invented. It comes from the sea, often a representation of the unconscious and therefore especially important as an indication of the source of creativity in this matrix.[4] The creation is there to 'feed' us and

[3] See Fig. 6.1 in Chap. 6 for a representation of this kind of juxtapositioning.

[4] Even though social dreaming is not concerned with Jung and his collective unconscious and ideas around the archetypes, the following quotation demonstrates the typical idea of the depths of the

therefore to be 'served' on plates. These plates are used in the creation of an actual piece of art, as is illustrated in the dream of the plates being thrown onto the grass in a David Hockney scene, also by the sea, and the association of this to the Julian Schnabel paintings that consist of plates stuck to the canvases, food for the spirit, as it were. In both Dream 2 and the first Association, workers or an employee have to contribute to the making or remaking of a collage of plates, as if the single figure of the artist as an especially gifted giver of creativity is insufficient unless supported by another, more ordinary participant. Here we have the introduction of the theme of leaders and individuals and the followers or the collective. This immediately brings up the association of the use of plates in an art form that is more clearly participatory and collective and three-dimensional, even though initiated by a single artist, the building of the figures and architecture of Chandigarh in India, by the artist Nek Chand.[5] The figures mentioned in these contributions are well known and relevant to the development of the concepts of the matrix, but it is not necessary to have in-depth or even any knowledge of them to participate in the images and affects. Sometimes factual details about some of the figures or events of the dreams, (as in this case, information about the artist Nek Chand), are provided in the post-matrix discussion. However, in the course of the matrix itself, such information is not normally forthcoming or encouraged. This emphasises the ethos and working culture of the matrix, that nobody is explicitly more expert or has a greater validity in opinion or thought to any other person who is participating in the social dreaming matrix. If a member of the matrix does not, at the stage of utterance, know what Chandigarh refers to, it is not crucial to that person's overall understanding, since there are many more image-affects available to the participants apart from this one. Furthermore, the matrix is able to move seamlessly from image to image, instead of being interrupted and broken up by deliberations and cognitive explanations that might threaten to disrupt the state of reverie of the matrix. In the example above, the most important connections that are being made are

sea representing the unconscious: 'The sea is the symbol of the Collective unconscious, because unfathomed depths lie concealed beneath its reflecting surface', (Jung 2004, p. 122).

[5] Nek Chand was an Indian artist, known for building the Rock Garden of Chandigarh, a sculpture garden of ceramic figures in the city of Chandigarh, India.

between the creativity of cooking and art and the possible suggestion that creativity 'feeds us'. Since the focus is on the image-affects, the exact nature of the content, of the facts, is not of primary importance.

By the time we reach extract 6 at the end of the matrix, the participants will already have accumulated their own personal collages of dreams, associations and image-affects. By this stage of the matrix, the contributions tend to be associations rather than dreams. The scattering of the petals in extract 6 resonates with the throwing of the plates of the opening extract 1. In extract 6, these are distributed creatively, first as a ritual that emphasises human connectivity to nature and secondly as a link to the inevitability of death. The resonating effect is emphasised by the mention of a novel (a work of art) and the Indian girl, possibly reminding us culturally of Nek Chand. In this way, the main elements both resonate and develop the opening image-affects. The initial creativity of the recipes, plates and art works become, in extract 6, a participative ritual that connects the participants of the matrix to the more mystical aspects of creativity and imagination, i.e. how these might be linked to developing a relationship between human beings and nature and eliciting the mystery of death, which also includes an ambivalence between the beauty of the petals (and a hint of the afterlife) and the constant presence of a more negative death that might be felt to pervade life.

Although extracts 1 and 6 resonate with each other in this way, by this time the matrix has already fed in a multiplicity of dreams and associations that are all potentially open to resonate with the image-affects evoked at this final stage of the matrix. For example, the presence and mystery of death, and its connection and disconnection with religion (represented in extract 6 by the cemetery) also elicits a resonating memory from earlier in the matrix, as in this example from extract 2:

> The Pope was dying… his frailty… Tears in my eyes… death of my father… dream broke up on me… in Paris visiting Sacre Coeur. There were two figures… Pope and Wolfowitz…in the body of basilica. … Two figures came out of the ceiling and machine gunned everybody… Contrast between Pope…tyranny and spiritual… end of war of communism… Whole idea of nation state ending and the world we live in…

Once again, it is not necessary to know who Wolfowitz is[6] in order to feel the strange horror of the two figures descending from the dome of the Sacre Coeur to machine gun the spectators inside the church. The image of death coming down from the artistic and religious creation of the Sacre Coeur, resonates by the time we reach the end of extract 6, with the beauty of the petals and the haunting feeling of the presence of danger in a cemetery, a place of supposed peace and faith that, nevertheless requires an escort of protection.

The reference to the 'Chinese using power to destroy' similarly resonates with previous iterations in the matrix. This is an example of a contribution in extract 6 that would otherwise be almost meaningless without the rhizomatic, resonating connections between image-affects that have previously referred to China. Previously, the references to China have linked to the feeling of danger of the growth of China and a contrast between what the matrix presents as the spirituality of India and the military might of China. This was expressed through an association previously in the matrix citing the terracotta army[7] as being both beautiful and miraculous but symbolising, too, the military might and danger of an emergent China. At the same time, this was contrasted with the ceramic figures in Chandigarh, like a peaceful, spiritual army that is similar in terms of sculpture (enabling the comparison) but different in terms of affective message. In the Chandigarh image, the spirituality of India is further bolstered through additional associations that brought up the figures of Parvati and Shiva[8] in the course of a visit to the British Museum.

Finally, the conclusion presents two balanced images that demonstrate how the same image can be both positive and negative: In the first, the Indian girl performs a living ritual on a rock, where a collage of petals is formed, only to be washed away by the tide. The image is of a 'sacred picture' that is connected to nature and more 'sacred' than the 'sacred

---

[6] Former President of the World bank, and therefore the leader, so to speak, of the material world who, in the matrix, is paired and contrasted with the Pope as spiritual leader.

[7] The Terracotta Army is a collection of terracotta sculptures depicting the armies of Qin Shi Huang, the first Emperor of China. It was buried with the emperor in 210–209 BCE to protect the emperor in the afterlife.

[8] Parvati is the Hindu goddess of fertility, love and devotion; as well as of divine strength and power. Shiva is the third god in the Hindu triumvirate who are responsible for the creation, upkeep and destruction of the world.

heart' ('Sacre Coeur' in a previous dream image). In the second, the same action of throwing the petals becomes an action that commemorates death. We are reminded that not everywhere has the sacred possibilities of India, and that places like Nairobi face a more uncertain future.

Sporadic and Rhizomatic Intensities of Affect

The mention of the Chinese danger expressed in extract 6 above is a good example of the way the rhizome works in the matrix. The mention has no direct link to the contributions immediately before or after it, but instead resonates with an earlier contribution to the matrix. In terms of the rhizome, this particular contribution – that of the Chinese danger – builds its own inter-connectivity through another branching out of the rhizomatic pattern that is not at its most intense within extract 6, where it is located in terms of its linear sequencing. However, neither is it irrelevant to the extract, because it resonates in contrast with the example from India (as described above) and contributes to the feeling of danger associated with the final contribution that brings up an affect based around fear and danger of death. It is important to emphasize, once again, that these rhizomatic branchings are in evidence throughout the matrix and they serve to maintain the sense of the living whole of the collage being created, in a constant sense of 'becoming'. It is in a state of becoming because the themes and affects that appear at any given moment are never guaranteed to be finalised or definitive, and there is always a potential for further development at any moment in the matrix. Even the moments denominated 'hiatus' images (i.e. in extracts 3 and 5 in Fig. 8.1 above), where there appears to be a pause in the development of images in the matrix, there is still some rhizomatic interweaving occurring. For example, in extract 3 there are mentions of 'green grass', 'throwing plates' and 'Hockney pictures', where the development of these aspects from their first mention in extract 1 is not so clear, but the effect is to bring back these particular image-affects into the collective memory of the matrix and in this way make this memory present again, so that the opening of the matrix is neither forgotten nor completed.

Process and Processing

The analysis and interpretation of a social dreaming transcript is therefore intimately linked to the nature of its rhizomatic form. The structure of the shared contributions of the participants are formulated in terms of intuitive and spontaneous contributions that emerge as guided by the impetus provided by the dreams. The dreams and associations that follow are, in this configuration, only partly linear in their presentation and mostly rhizomatic in structure. This is essential information to bear in mind when processing the material as data, with the researcher having to maintain an expansive and abductive (see Long and Harney 2013) frame of mind that is open to surprising links and connections between disparate elements of the social dreaming transcript. This attitude and the Deleuzian context that supports such an approach will be adopted in the next case study chapter.

References

Deleuze, G. (1988). *Bergsonism*. New York: Zone Books.

Jung, C.G. (2004). *Dreams*. London and New York: Routledge.

Lawrence, W.G. (2005). *Introduction to Social Dreaming. Transforming Thinking*. London: Karnac.

Long, S. and Harney, M. (2013). The associative unconscious. In Long, S. (Ed.), *Socioanalytic Methods*. London: Karnac.

9

A Case Study. Slow Violence: Art, Climate Change and Social Dreaming

Slow Violence was the title given to an exhibition held at the University of Hertfordshire, 29 November 2017–20 January 2018. In this exhibition, eight UK-based artists exhibited works that depicted some aspect of the threat of climate change. There were examples of film, photography, print and installation. Of these works, the following were specifically referred to by participants in the social dreaming matrix:

> Emma Critchley's 'Frontiers' film (2015), which takes the viewer on a journey over water and through 'a seemingly apocalyptic landscape encountering what may appear to be detritus from the aftermath of a disaster or perhaps boats carrying those fleeing crisis'.
>
> Michael Pinsky's 'Pollution Pods' (2017), which recreated the pollution that a person can typically encounter in various different cities around the world by entering specially constructed 'pods', 'represented in the exhibition through working drawings, models and a documentary film.'
>
> Ackroyd & Harvey's 'Seeing Red…Overdrawn' (2016) a large canvas which lists species in extreme risk of extinction that exhibition visitors are invited to overdraw with indelible pens in order to 'memorialize individual endangered species.'

J. Manley, *Social Dreaming, Associative Thinking and Intensities of Affect*, Studies in the Psychosocial, https://doi.org/10.1007/978-3-319-92555-4_9

Adam Chodzko's film 'Deep Above' (2015), which 'attempts to reprogramme our psychological responses to climate change so that we can push through a passive intellectual acceptance in order to produce deep behavioural change.'[1]

The title of the exhibition was taken from a book by Rob Nixon, *Slow Violence and the Environmentalism of the Poor* (2011). According to Nixon, slow violence is 'a violence that occurs gradually and out of sight, a violence of delayed destruction that is dispersed across time and space, an attritional violence that is typically not viewed as violence at all.' Among the examples of slow violence, Nixon names 'climate change, the thawing cryosphere, toxic drift, biomagnification, deforestation, the radioactive aftermaths of wars, acidifying oceans, and hosts of other slowly unfolding environmental catastrophes…' (Nixon 2011, p. 2).

The idea of using art to help communicate or understand the human dilemmas arising as a result of the need to face up to climate change, arose from a general hypothesis that art would better be able to communicate and therefore to lead people to an understanding of the nature and imminent danger that climate change presents humanity, and, therefore, to lead to meaningful action that might mitigate or reverse this change. In this sense, the use of images and other aesthetic experiences of art as a primary communicator related to climate change, bears some similarities with the use of social dreaming as a means of gaining knowledge through the experience of interchanging dreams, images, affect and associations in a way that prioritises a non-verbal and pre-cognitive way of thinking and feeling. A series of social dreaming matrices were therefore organised to accompany the Slow Violence exhibition. These followed on from a similar endeavour that used art and social dreaming in the context of climate change organised by Cape Farewell (http://www.capefarewell.com) a few months beforehand, where the social dreaming was conducted in the context of a brief exhibition in a farmhouse in Dorset and directed at artists and climate change activists and experts (Manley and Hollway 2018 forthcoming).

[1] All quotations from the exhibition leaflet.

Practical Arrangements

A total of 10 participants in the social dreaming matrix event were recruited from staff at the University of Hertfordshire and the general public who had already visited the exhibition. The matrix was conducted for 50 minutes, and the post-matrix session lasted 30 minutes. Time before the matrix started was also allocated to an introduction to the method, the distribution of information sheets and the signing of consent forms for the recording of the sessions and the use of the data.[2] The purpose of the social dreaming event was to provide a space for the expression of the understanding and feedback of the reactions of participants in the matrix to the exhibition and, as a result of that, their attitudes to climate change, especially attitudes and feelings that in other contexts may not have been expressed, in other words image-affects from the shared associative unconscious of the space of the matrix.

Let Us Not Begin

Let me begin with the least obvious, or let me not begin with the obvious. If social dreaming evolves as part of a rhizome, then we can expect the unexpected and follow the spaces between paths as yet untrodden, the path of the Deleuzian nomad. In this presumed rhizome, there is no good place to start, no theoretical structure to act as guide. I do not, therefore, intend to begin by homing in and identifying themes that seem to have arisen and occurred with greater frequency than others and in this way laying claims to a greater relative importance of such frequently cited themes or ideas compared to other less mentioned themes. This would be to begin an accustomed thinking process of classifying, cataloguing, placing and ranging ideas in order of importance or greater value, creating structures, hierarchies or a pyramid of straight lines that pass through clearly identified stages and lead to satisfying conclusions for all to see, and especially designed above all for my own satisfaction. In mostly rejecting

[2] Ethics approval for the project was granted by the University of Central Lancashire's Ethics Committee, Number PSYSOC 405

this way of working, through an intuition honed by experience, Lawrence was right in his rejection of the ego implied in interpretation and his insistence, again and again, on the idea of creating a working hypothesis instead of an interpretation, and such a hypothesis would never end or conclude, and even less be proven. The impossibility of proving or defining evidence in the social dreaming process arises from the inherent qualities of the rhizomatic nature of the matrix, in particular that of the rhizome's constant movement and flux, the intensities of affect. In a working hypothesis, this means that a structure of meaning once set, defined and concluded is open to its immediate destruction in favour of another set of definitions and conclusions as the relative intensities of the affect within the images shift in relation to each other and with others, existing and yet hitherto unignited, to produce further and different directions and senses. Similarly, the same may occur with this new working hypothesis as structured into a collage of image-affects, and so on, potentially forever. Even if this process has stopped and settled in my own mind as a participant in the matrix, it may be continuing or developing elsewhere in another participant's mind, or even in another part of my own mind, as yet undiscovered, waiting to be drawn out by some other suggested configuration of image-affects. This is the rhizome, the ever-expanding background of knowledge that continues to fill the ever-expansive mind of the matrix, that Body without Organs, the 'body' of free flowing thought and affect in the matrix, without impediments against such expansion, allowing for a sensation of gliding, sliding freedom of directionless directions of pure creativity, a 'bloc of sensations' like a work of art that becomes a thing in itself, separate from its creator:

> What about the creator? It is independent of the creator through the self-positing of the created, which is preserved in itself. What is preserved – the thing or the work of art – is *a bloc of sensations, that is to say, a compound of percepts and affects.* (Deleuze and Guattari 1994, p. 164, authors' italics)

Similarly, the dreamer in social dreaming is separated from the rhizome of dreams that becomes a compound of internal and external vision and sensations with an existence of its own. The release from channelled, striated thinking to an abandonment to the smooth, is expressed in this extract from the Slow Violence social dreaming session:

> I was pushing [NAME] across, as if he couldn't swim, you know when you learn to swim as a child, your mum or your dad are holding you in the water and they're guiding you and that feels a really safe place in a way when you are being held in the water, and I was doing that with [NAME], I was helping him across, and there was one bit when I was shooting him across, like a missile, actually it wasn't that fast but he kind of glided away almost magically...

Distant-near and Then Near-distant Again

A programme note for the exhibition acknowledges another Slow Violence exhibition, a show elsewhere that by chance, apparently, has opted for the same title:

> Coincidentally UHArt's exhibition follows a group exhibition of the same name and similar premise Slow Violence (18 June – 13 August 2017) at Kunsthal Charlottenborg, Copenhagen – there is no official connection between the exhibitions... (https://kunsthalcharlottenborg.dk/en/exhibitions/charlottenborg-art-research-slow-violence/)

This is an example of the unexpected, unplanned extension of the rhizome in geographical space. The 'prophetic' examples of dreams that inspired Gordon Lawrence in Charlotte Beradt's book *The Third Reich of Dreams* illustrate the rhizome's extension in time. Whether in time or space, these are not examples of actual magic, rather they are 'almost magic', as in the participant quotation above from the social dreaming matrix. That is to say, they demonstrate the working of the associative unconscious that is shared by all, but can often lie fallow until provided with a space of expression, such as the sharing of dreams. The 'magic' resides only in the sensation of unexpectedness of their revelation and the uncanny resonating pulses that attract the disparate together. The affect triggered by the title and/or the reading of the book Slow Violence, makes a connection that was unthought or unplanned and yet functions with some 'almost magical' logic. Similarly, the artworks in the UH Slow Violence exhibition are relevant to the social dreaming session not only through their direct mention, as indeed was the case in the social dreaming matrix, but through indirect resonance enabling a hitherto unexpected and unsuspected mutual attraction that becomes part of the rhizomatic whole. For example, the following striking line from Adam Chodzko's work 'Deep Above' which we hear intonated as part of the film soundtrack, was never directly mentioned in the social dreaming session:

> If you stay under water for long enough, you will find a way to breathe...

Yet, it is totally relevant to the matrix which became intensely involved with images and feelings of drowning, the sensation of panic and fear associated with being under water and breathing. This is evident in the following examples taken from the matrix, where the overwhelming sense of the feeling of fear and panic associated with drowning, and therefore death, become an intense affect in the created rhizome; associated feelings are transmitted through the image and the empathically felt affect of drowning in water, which in turn, or in parallel, rather, (because in the rhizomatic structure affective events happen spontaneously and simultaneously rather than in succession), become part of the matrix's reflection on climate change. That is to say, the evolution of a different planet through climate change, the possible difficulty of breathing in this new environment and the fear and panic of death are associations related to these image-affects of change. The following examples occur as a sequence in the matrix:

> - A memory of swimming, my dad taught me to swim, and I was very small, and I remember initially he taught me how to swim with armbands, I must have been four, I suppose, and we were doing it for ages, and I was really proud of myself because I was actually swimming, but I had the armbands on, and then, playing around, I got out of the pool, took the armbands off, and then there was someone else, I guess it must have been mum and I wanted to show her that I could swim, but I forgot to put the armbands on, so I jumped back in the pool and I just went straight under, and I remember that panic as well.

- A memory of a holiday, being in the ocean and we had lilos and I fell off of mine and as I fell my brother's skidded over the top, and I got stuck underneath my lilo and I remember that kind of panic feeling, not being able to see, not being able to get out of the water. It was only probably a few seconds but it felt like it went on for ages.

- On holiday, and being attached to a bodyboard, huge waves and I was pulled under, I was trying to get out of the water and the bodyboard kept pulling me under, and that felt like an eternity, so…

- When I was young and just learned to swim and there was this outdoor pool, and I was kind of showing off, trying to get out of the side of the pool, you know, you think you can pull yourself up, I nearly got there and fell backwards, and went really right under, and really panicked. It reminded me of the exhibition piece that [NAME] and I were just looking at, the Emma Critchley piece, that kind of panic of not knowing which way was up, and which way to go to get out, and that kind of panic of being in deep water (well not that deep but as a child it felt very deep), and going backwards all the time and that kind of floating the wrong way, not knowing where to go…

- That's it, isn't it? You know there's a way out… and it should be up… but which way is up?

- A friend of mine lived on a longboat, like a barge, and fell off between two boats, and she ended up underneath a boat, and she had to make a decision about which was the width and which was the length, and she told this really graphic story that she had to feel her way under the boat, and I think that every time now, if I see a film where people, because quite often you see in films where people are drowning, I really feel viscerally, like really you feel it don't you, when you see that idea of… it's almost unbearable to me… watching people drown on … you know, it's probably the worst horror for me, watching people drowning. I think about how she made the right decision, but she might have made the wrong decision, she had no idea, it was pitch black underneath this boat…

Eventually, there is a sense of possibility in adapting to the change, when in the following contribution, the children are able to adapt to life on and in the water in ways that are necessary for survival, echoing the line quoted above from Chodzko's film, creating an unspoken echo or a rhizomatic attraction that exists between the film and the expression of the following contribution from the social dreaming matrix. In this way all possible aspects of the experience between the visit to the exhibition and the new space of thought and affect of the matrix are potentially existing as an all-encompassing whole experience, even if tacit and implicit, even without direct utterance:

> - It's [a book] about how climate change happens very quickly and places start flooding very quickly, and about how some particular people are somehow rescued and put on those big ships that have been set up by government for private companies that knew that this was kind of gonna happen. And very few people were able to actually escape. And the flood literally takes over the world so there is no land mass anymore. And all that's left is these people on these boats, there's no food apart from what they've already stored, too many people have got on the boats so it's not going to last enough, and there's a struggle with human nature of who is going to be able to survive, who deserves to survive, should doctors survive, should children survive? Who shouldn't? To try to make it last longer… The young children – this goes on for quite a period of time – almost start adapting to the new world, they become really good at swimming, because the food is from the sea, and all this waste product that's coming up, you know where everything's been washed over, and how these children start surviving and becoming better at surviving in that situation.

I have quoted these examples at length (and they are not the only examples in the matrix) to provide a sense of how through the repeated and yet different examples of images associated to drowning – and the affect associated to that image – the sense of implicit meaning and importance of this image-affect is given prominence and layered richness. The repeated sharing of similar-yet-different images provides a sensation of consensus among the participants (further evidenced in the post-matrix discussion), which creates a pulsing intensity of affect that can be tacitly acknowledged as belonging to the shared containing space of the matrix formed as a 'body without organs'. In terms of the rhizomatic nature of the matrix, this series of image-affects then becomes an intensity of affect that at these moments of expression grows in intensity; at other moments in the matrix this original intensity may diminish without ever disappearing from a participant's or many participants' inner view or locus of affect. For example, these quotations occur in the first half of the matrix. They then lie dormant, so to speak, and are tacitly associated with other image-affects expressed in the second half of the matrix. In this developed state, much later in the matrix, when the initial images might have been forgotten, the opening series of images related to drowning becomes implicitly alluded to and therefore connected in affect through a further image that is explicitly associated to climate change and a sense of a human connection to other life on the planet:

> - Reminds me of a snippet from Blue Planet II, it was the elephant seals, a mother and a young baby swimming, and the babies need to come out of the water to rest, and all the icebergs were melting, not so many icebergs as before, and all the mothers were trying to get themselves and their babies onto these icebergs that were breaking up; and that kind of struggle, and the thing that really touched me emotionally was this mother was desperately trying to get her child, her baby out of the water and there was no space and so she was holding it in part of her arms, her flipper, she was trying to hold it up, and I just thought I know nothing about these particular animals but I had that emotional connection, … it was just seeing that, they caught that on camera, and that really kind of touched me, did anybody else see it? Eventually they all got on one and it all broke up, didn't it? And then eventually she found one and they rested. That emotional attachment…

In this striking further image-affect, the speaker personifies the seals and evokes the fear of drowning, which reignites the affect of the previous images and therefore becomes reconnected to them in rhizomatic fashion (since their connection is not expected, logical or sequential). In this way, the BwO is the affective mass of these multiple image-affects that no longer belong to the individual speaker, nor even to the shared space of the speakers. Instead, the new 'body' or BwO takes on a life of its own, so that even the participants who have not offered any of these images can feel a connection and link to this new 'body' of thought and affect. This BwO is now an existing entity in and of itself, observable and 'feelable' as an object made up of part objects, moving parts, ephemeral, temporary part objects, where – to use an oft cited idea from complexity theory – the whole expresses something more than the sum of the parts. This is why the questions that the speaker asks in the above extract are unanswerable. They are not even rhetorical questions. Whether anyone did or did not see the extract from Blue Planet II that is being referred to here is irrelevant to the new 'body' that has been created, or rather that has somehow created itself. To explain the intensity of this moment in the matrix, it is now possible to understand what is meant by the speaker's own attempts to describe the relevance of this recollection of a scene from television; the 'emotional connection' that 'kind of touched me' and the tailing off comment at the end 'that emotional attachment…', all despite knowing 'nothing about these particular animals'. It is through the intensity of affect, built up not in this extract in isolation but in the combination of the extracts in rhizomatic connection, that the participants in the matrix, for an instant become seal, in a Deleuzian sense of becoming. This is not due to any factual knowledge of the seal 'these particular animals', but to an overwhelming sense of affective empathy that the speaker struggles to explain, and asks for affirmation and consent from others, but is clearly strikingly felt and identified in a merging fashion that bypasses cognitive thought and allows for a complete expression of affect and a losing of the self in this affect of becoming. Such a melting away of barriers between the cognitive and the sensual, described in this process of rhizomatic intensities of becoming is a principle feature of the social dreaming matrix.

Prior to the preceding extract quoted above, one of the participants has made a direct reference to the Chodzko film, which provides a direct link to the unspoken in the film and its connection to the image-affects of the matrix, and uses the experience of the film to bring this sense of becoming to mind, but in an affective rather than cognitive fashion:

> - …I was just thinking about seeing with your hands, a kind of strange thing, but you suddenly can feel the animals. It was this really strange – if you guys haven't seen the film – dip in and out, it's quite a long film, it's about an hour – but some really kind of moving parts like that, you suddenly then can feel the animal. Some connection with empathy. I was thinking it's a different way of connecting with the idea of the other animals in the world…

The participants in the matrix are thus brought to stretch their ideas of how to acquire knowledge, how to 'feel' knowledge, and the expressed sensation that this might be a way of connecting with 'the other animals in the world'. This is surely the 'new thinking' or the 'transforming thinking' that Lawrence was intuitively suggesting in his work on social dreaming (Lawrence 2005).

Eventually, the images of drowning re-emerge towards the end in a combination of the drowning theme with the sense of a lack of breathing connected to Michael Pinsky's Pollution Pods. In Pinsky's work in the exhibition, it is the physical sensation, the sensual knowledge that is emphasised. The speaker wonders how the sensual can be extended outwards to everybody, since any strength of change is no longer identified in the matrix with individualism but rather with some form of collectivity:

> - Made me straightaway think of the exhibition, the Michael Pinsky work, the pods, the idea of walking in and feeling, what does it feel like to breath in Shanghai? Or what is it like to breath in, I don't know, Beijing? That could be enough for me to say ok, I'm going to run around, I'm going to say stop. But I will then get squashed. So I think I'm not going to do that because I think I don't want to get squashed, so do we need these pods? In every art gallery, in every city all over the world? And everyone goes into them at the same time and then we can all go, ok we'll stop that. How do you do that?

Pinsky's work is in itself a rhizome of interconnected pollution pods. In Pinsky's piece, each pollution pod is an entity in itself but connected to the next pod through a tunnel. Here, the actual geographical distance between cities – London, New Delhi, São Paulo and Beijing – where in reality distance disconnects them in a direct physical sense, is artificially brought together to a new geographic space that is nevertheless an invented, imagined mental space, and the 'real' lack of connectivity between the cities is thus redefined inside the pods. These cities are now brought closer to each other and shown to be interconnected through varying examples of pollution as part of the artwork. In this way, the configuration of Pinsky's work resembles the BwO of the new thought of the social dreaming matrix. Once again, there is no answer to the question 'how do you do that [put a pollution pod in every gallery of the world]?' And once again, this demonstrates the efficacy of the social dreaming process in enabling the participants to creatively bring together new ideas and sensations of interconnectivity through associative and rhizomatic thinking to create thoughts through affect that could not otherwise exist. It is only in the shared space of the matrix or in the resonating space of the artwork that the pods can be brought to every city. It is only in the social dreaming matrix that the intensity of affect associated to the decline and death implied in being unable to breathe, which has been built up through multiple image-affects in collage of the matrix (here linked to the artwork), that some comprehension of the complex reality of climate change can be contemplated by and reflected upon by participants in the matrix.

This theme in its complexity is not resolved –as in social dreaming, the images are allowed to float and become connected to each other rather than discussed and defined – but further explored through the following extract that combines time and the elements of air and water, so that the drowning in water of the images expressed until this point in the social dreaming matrix are now confabulated with an image of 'drowning' through asphyxiation, in an event that is created neither by water nor pollution but in a self-inflicted dying through lack of air combined with a sense of the absurdity of self-inflicted disaster that resonates with the impending doom of climate change.

> - When someone mentioned about being unable to breath and the pods in the exhibition I immediately had that image of Salvador Dalí in his underwater suit. He was doing one of his shows and he was wearing an underwater diving outfit but what he didn't realise was that the oxygen inside the helmet was limited, and suddenly he started waving his arms around because he couldn't breath and at first people thought it was a joke, thought it was part of his surreal acting. It was only when he got really desperate that people realised that they had to unscrew the helmet from him so that he could breath.

In this example, an artist from the past (compared to the artists of the present in the Slow Violence exhibition), Dalí, is wearing an underwater suit but he is not underwater. Ironically, even though he is not underwater, he starts to 'drown' because his suit runs out of air, and in this image, therefore, there is a combination of being unable to breath on earth with the ideas of drowning expressed previously and the connection to art through a past artist and one of the contemporary artists of the exhibition. This image-affect, therefore, in terms of the rhizome, is particularly intense and leads directly to the following key moment in the matrix:

> - Reminds me of the poem by Stevie Smith 'Not Waving but Drowning'. It's the same thing about everybody thinks it's somebody having fun and people not realising that a drowning person is actually drowning and they think he is waving.

This moment horrifyingly combines the false joy associated to a friend's wave with the real truth of the drowning. In terms of affect, the intensity is doubled through this gruesome juxtaposition. At this moment, the matrix falls silent for an extended period of 34 seconds. This testifies to how the social dreaming matrix as a BwO is able to see how the participants together, and by extension humanity or society at large, (in the sense that all is rhizomatically interconnected), might be waving happily in an enjoyment of a life that steadfastly ignores the reality of climate change, and such a realisation almost seems to stun the matrix into silence. This was identified by the participants themselves in the post-matrix session, in their choice of the word 'disorientation' as a principal starting word to describe the meaning of the matrix to the participants in the matrix. The social dreaming matrix had brought out a sense of disturbance in the face of the reality of the effects of climate change that is not normally faced, and this was identified as such in the word 'disorientation'.

Disorientation and Conclusion

The word 'disorientation' was mentioned at various points in the matrix as well as featuring as an important expression of affect in the post-matrix discussion. As an experience of affect, it has no single application to a specific meaning, but becomes part of the rhizomatic affective experience of the participants in the matrix, as a BwO. The sensation of the social dreaming matrix that the 'body' of the matrix is where the affect belongs, (the BwO), is a sensation that disorientates each individual from the habit and custom of the Self, (i.e. the body *with* organs).

I mentioned previously how the Chodzko film was able to resonate rhizomatically. By returning to Chodzko's film, we can capture another instance of this sensation. There is a moment in the film, as the viewer looks into the eyes of an ape behind bars, when we are told:

> This you will just need to watch, without guidance, there is no sound here. Watch what that does to you, how it brings you back to the body, not your body but someone else's body, turned inside out.

In a similar evocation of the rhizome, this utterance in the film and the emphasis on the embodied, yet out-of-body experience expressed as a silent contemplation of the image of an ape's face, brings about an 'inside-out' sensation of disorientation which is at once a realisation of the quality and value of that affect. Once again, although this particular line of Chodzko's film was not mentioned in the social dreaming matrix, it demonstrates a rhizomatic resonance that nevertheless exists in relation to the transforming body of the matrix. It is as a result of this affect that we have a resonating silence, in film and in the social dreaming matrix. In the matrix, it is after the 34 second silent pause that the participants are led to a sense of learning from the 'inside-out' sensation of the body of the matrix, a place where an apparently happy wave is simultaneously a wave of death. After this pause in the matrix, the idea of disorientation is qualified and becomes a learning:

> - There was something you guys were saying that gave me the sense of so, a lot of this kind of session, this thing I'm feeling disorientation, but there was a certain point where I thought actually, I got an image of the Arab Spring and all those people meeting and Tahrir Square in Cairo and thinking that was social media. I can remember all those people coming together. It's dark but there's loads of fireworks going off, there's loads of lights, kind of mixing it with images, more recent images of demonstrations in northern Spain. I can see flags, but people get together through social media. I'm thinking there's a bit of hope there. That with enough, if there's enough

> pressure, we go away from being, feeling sorry for the innocent thing and being annoyed with ourselves, but coming together and, and "come on we can fight this, we can run round, stop the ball." I really love those images. I really would love to be in the middle of those kinds of demonstrations, there's a real crackle in that. Lots of people coming together. The anonymous masks in America. The mask itself is just from a comic, but I really like the idea that it has an image, it has a logo, unified as one, as opposed to individuals. It's very nicely wrapped up. In a single logo, I'm one of them. There is a hope in seeing a big group of people that's... I mean in the U.K., when do we do it? Festivals in the summer. And actually we just wander around, watch bands and move a bit, be quite disorientated, usually on purpose. But there's a common goal... A flag...

In this reflection that comes at the very end of the matrix, the individual is subsumed into the collective (just as in the social dreaming matrix, the individuality of participants occupy a secondary place compared to the matrix as a whole and the 'body' that is created) and hope in the face of climate change is described as the taking away of the ego through individuals becoming anonymous (as in social dreaming) and creating strength in numbers rather than 'being annoyed with ourselves'.

What is clear, however, is that this apparent solution or idea does not embrace the affective power of the accumulation of the whole matrix, and that there is always something more remaining in the air after a social dreaming matrix session. The very last contribution of this matrix makes reference to a radical activist movement called the Zeitgeist movement. As the matrix moves to a close, the contributions become more cognitive and reflective:

> There is this movement called the Zeitgast movement, which is people that believe that society shouldn't be based around money, it should be based around trade, so that nobody should actually own their own things...

Even at this stage, however, the idea of the Zeitgeist movement is presented as an interesting phenomenon rather than a persuasive course of action or a specific idea, and it is the excitement or affect of such a movement that predominates. It draws on the theme of collectivity, as explored in the matrix, as more important than the movement itself:

…thousands of people meeting in London and they do all these talks and marches and workshops all around this kind of ideal of changing the way that we are as a society and how we might be moving forward. Interesting how it pulls people together.

That 'something more' that remains is affect that is difficult to define (for example 'becoming seal', or a complexity of rhizomatic connections that are difficult to explain). The post-matrix session is important in order to give the participants a chance to move out of 'matrix mode' and back into 'reality mode', and also to give people a chance to somehow reframe the image-affects of the matrix into a framework and structure that is more familiar and in a sense comforting after the high intensity of the matrix. In this way, participants are able to re-engage with the external world to where they will return. Nevertheless, the participants do not return to their familiar worlds unaffected by the experience, and although the post-matrix sessions appear somewhat dry and significantly less exciting than the matrix itself, the exercise still demonstrates a sense of wonder at some of the newly identified ideas that emerged in the matrix and that will be taken away by the participants, to a greater or lesser degree. An example of the way this works emerged in the post-matrix discussion of the lack of leaders in the world to guide nations and the planet, even, through the crisis of climate change. The matrix expressed its frustration by comparing this lack of leadership to David Attenborough:

- Reminds me of what you said about the Blue Planet thing. David Attenborough spoke at the end and said that it's up to us as humans to make sure that these animals don't lose their habitats, don't become extinct etc etc. And I was listening and I was really kind of thinking right… I was waiting for him to tell us what to do. And he doesn't. And it's kind of frustrating that feeling of yes we know, we want to… you're David Attenborough… tell us what to do…

In this extract from the matrix, which was discussed in the post-matrix session, the figure of Attenborough takes on a 'Wise Old Man' or 'Sage', almost a Jungian archetype. Nobody is suggesting that Attenborough should in reality take on a pro-active leadership role. Interestingly, however, it is not the archetype that is discussed in the post-matrix discussion, but rather the frustration at the realisation that there is no Sage 'out there' who is going to save the planet. Instead, and as a result of the complexities of the process of the matrix, the participants become involved in a discussion of the multiple emotions behind frustration, and by allowing this frustration to be named, the post-matrix discussion was able to acknowledge such an affect as belonging to them. This, while it may not be a specific tool or decision, is a significant addition to the maturity and completeness of understanding required to eventually take better decisions in the face of this complex and potentially apocalyptic global problem.

References

Deleuze, G. and Guattari, F. (1994). *What is Philosophy?* London: Verso.

Lawrence, W.G. (2005). *Introduction to Social Dreaming. Transforming Thinking.* London: Karnac.

Manley, J. and Hollway, W. (2018 forthcoming). The Unthought Known of Climate Change: How Social Dreaming and Art can be used to think the unthinkable. In Hoggett, P. (Ed.), *Climate Psychology: Psycho-Social Research on Human/Nature Relations in the Age of Climate Change.* Basingstoke: Palgrave Macmillan.

Nixon, R. (2011). *Slow Violence and the Environmentalism of the Poor.* Harvard: Harvard University Press.

[illegible]

References

[illegible]

10

Combining the Internal Virtual of the Matrix Dream Space with External Reality: Lessons of Chaos and Complexity

Difference, Repetition and the Rhizomatic

One of the issues behind concluding that a Deleuzian approach is helpful for an understanding of social dreaming – that social dreaming is a rhizomatic pattern of intensities of affect and a combination of the virtual and the real – is how to make this apparently unique research method and way of perceiving the world relevant to everyday existence. This was a struggle that Gordon Lawrence himself never managed to resolve. For Lawrence, the way to promote social dreaming into daily life was through presenting it as an advanced organisational consultancy tool for the world of work, hence the title of his first compendium on social dreaming, *Social Dreaming @ Work* (1998). However, although social dreaming has been gaining ground in acceptance and practice since its inception in 1982, it certainly has not found its way into the general practice of companies, organisations or businesses.

This chapter seeks to explore these questions by showing that social dreaming is potentially relevant to our everyday thinking, discussion and decision-making because it provides us with a method that has been tested over a number of years and is capable of bringing to the fore a more

J. Manley, *Social Dreaming, Associative Thinking and Intensities of Affect*, Studies in the Psychosocial, https://doi.org/10.1007/978-3-319-92555-4_10

complete and rounded means of thinking that often seems to encourage a form of inter-relational cooperation and understanding, sometimes set against a background of enhanced creativity.

Among the many problems that a Deleuzian social dreaming brings up as a challenge to thought (a 'shock' to thought, according to Massumi (2002)) is that of its place in a framework of knowledge which is difficult to locate within a scientific or positivist paradigm. This is why it is easier to place it somewhere in the psychosocial. But even here it sits uneasily. The 'father' of psychoanalysis, Freud, was only interested in dreams in a dyadic relationship and as evidence of repressed desires in the individual unconscious, neither of these approaches to dreams being helpful to social dreaming. Although Bion was working with group psychodynamics, he did not work with dreams in groups. His theory of thinking did include concepts related to dreaming and reverie, but this was not systematically applied to dreaming in the group space.

In this chapter I will make reference to the wider inter-relational possibilities of subject-to-environment as opposed to subject-to-subject relationships because I think that social dreaming has something to offer in this respect. I shall also be taking seriously the Deleuzian vision of existence as being a system of relatedness and based on relationships between 'bodies without organs', in other words beyond but including the human subject. In doing so, I shall be picking up the network and systems themes of Chap. 6 and developing these to include social dreaming as a 'holistic' contribution that can make this thinking part of our existence in the context of systems of life as expressed in our integral relationship to our environment. By holistic, I mean inclusive with the possibility of expansion. At no stage, however, will I be attempting to clarify the ambiguity of working with dreams. As I will show below, ambiguity in social dreaming is also richness and nuance.

The Complex Knowledge of Social Dreaming

Social Dreaming as Mystery, Not Puzzle

The sense of the ambiguous usefulness/uselessness of social dreaming that concludes the previous chapter is both its fascination and its difficulty. When I say 'ambiguous' I mean this according to the forms and structures we often demand of knowledge, an epistemology that demonstrates itself, that clarifies the obscure, and creates lines of thought that even if they begin in an undefinable 'somewhere' will eventually lead to a 'this-where', an end goal and outcome upon which further thoughts can build and proceed, what Kuhn called a 'scientific paradigm' (Kuhn 1996). Within this Kuhnian paradigm, that in varying degrees is accepted by the traditional social sciences, scientific problems are *puzzles* with a specific end result. The end result is the hypothesis that is proved. The purpose of (social) science is to reach this end, that is to say to provide proof. The existence of a hypothesis is already an established end; in other words, there is no *mystery* to be discovered in science. Instead of mystery, Kuhn describes this process as the 'puzzle' that drives the scientist as a person to search for a solution, one that is framed according to the knowledge of the paradigm, which is itself embraced within the initial hypothesis. The solving of the puzzle is an affirmation, therefore, of the paradigm, which is already known. As Kuhn points out, what is most striking about 'normal research problems' is 'how little they aim to produce major novelties, conceptual or phenomenal' (Kuhn 1996, p. 35). He continues to say that a project that does not find itself in a 'narrower range' which is 'always small compared with the range that imagination can conceive' is perceived by the scientific community as a 'research failure, one which reflects not on nature but on the scientist' (Kuhn 1996, p. 35). This is the crux of the matter in considering social dreaming as being a valid or useful source of data in social scientific research. The question 'what do the dreams in the social dreaming matrix mean?' is the wrong question to ask, but what kind of answer is there to an unasked question? The limitations of the puzzle (question) with a preordained outcome (answer) cannot be applied to social dreaming. Kuhn's own example of a puzzle – the jigsaw puzzle – that he uses to illustrate his point is particularly interesting for understanding how social dreaming is precisely not this kind of puzzle. As Kuhn says, the jigsaw puzzle has a known end and rules to follow: there can be no forcing of pieces together and the lines and colours of each piece need to properly connect. The less complexity in the puzzle, the more likely we are to reach the known outcome. If one adds and mixes two puzzles together at random, the problem becomes almost impossible to solve:

> In any usual sense, it is not a puzzle at all. Though intrinsic value is no criterion for a puzzle, the assured existence of a solution is. (Kuhn 1996, p. 37)

In social dreaming, however, our sensation of being able to grasp knowledge is paradoxically increased rather than diminished, by the addition of 'pieces' to the matrix, despite the fact that with each additional dream or association, any interpretation of meaning in a clearly bounded way – as if the pieces could be pieced together in order to illuminate our knowledge with a clearly defined picture with meaning attached – becomes more and more difficult. Yet as we move away from clarity of meaning understood in this interpretive manner, as the dreams and associations begin to accumulate, participants in the matrix appear to gain another kind of knowledge, which is not that as defined by a thinking position that Kuhn shows to be the scientific position.

Difference Instead of Generalisations

As already indicated by evoking Latour earlier in this book, and by Tarde, quoted as the basis of Latour's theories, an understanding of how social dreaming works is greatly enhanced by taking the object away from the social and seeing sociology as what Latour refers to as a network of associations, although for reasons that should become apparent in this book on social dreaming, the Deleuzian concept of rhizome is a closer match to the process in social dreaming than network. An important aspect of this paradigm shift is to turn reductionism and positivism on its head and emphasise the validity of subjectivity, intersubjectivity, the imagination and creativity; and the conceptualising of the macro as a vast collection of details and differences that should not be reduced through the elimination of that same detail and difference in favour of providing a supposed and mistaken generalised truth. Tarde's description of this way of conceptualising the complexity of the macro resonates with social dreaming as a complex rhizome of interconnected image-affects that complement each other as differences in detail that would lose their inherent ability to retain nuances of affect through any process of reductionism and normalising into simplified strands and categories:

> … the error of believing that, in order to see a gradual dawn of regularity, order and logic in social phenomena, we must go outside of the details, which are essentially irregular, and rise high enough to obtain a panoramic view of general effect; that the source and foundation of every social coordination is some general fact from which it descends gradually to particular facts, though always diminishing in strength. (Gabriel Tarde quoted in Latour 2005, p. 14)

Within the Deleuzian position that this study of social dreaming largely embraces, a theme such as 'drowning' that was studied in the previous chapter may appear to repeat itself, but we should beware of falling into the trap of imagining that this repetition can lead us to some general idea; because each repetition of the theme is also different in itself, and to generalise and forget this difference would be to falsify the experience and the qualitative nature of the affect therein as knowledge. This is precisely Deleuze's point in the opening pages of *Difference and Repetition*, that resonates with Tarde's comments above:

> Repetition is not generality. Repetition and generality must be distinguished in several ways. Every formula which implies their confusion is regrettable: for example, when we say that two things are as alike as two drops of water; or when we identify "there is only a science of the general". Repetition and resemblance are different in kind – extremely so. (Deleuze 2004, p. 1)

In other words, to generalise in our analysis of the knowledge imparted through the image-affect of social dreaming is to erroneously assume that the repetition of a theme or subject matter indicates a general truth, which it can only do by stripping each example of its specific detail. By simplifying into representation or symbolisim the content of a dream through an interpretation that presupposes knowledge, the thinker (by which I mean all the participants in the matrix) would also be presupposing and imposing a condition of 'everybody knows, no one can deny' which, says Deleuze, 'is the form of representation and the discourse of the representative' (Deleuze 2004, p. 165). This position is identified by Deleuze as being essentially Cartesian and can be contrasted with another philosophical position that aims to begin 'without presupposition' (Deleuze 2004, p. 165). This reminds me of Bion's advice for the consultant in psychodynamic groupwork, to approach the group 'without memory or desire'.

The importance of this position for social dreaming cannot be overstated. It is the reason that dreams are not interpreted: interpretation of one dream would presuppose knowledge of or given to the next, eliminating the next dream's idiosyncratic differences in an attempt to make sense through bringing it towards the previous dream. It is why social knowledge in social dreaming can only be hinted at through working hypotheses that do not presuppose an outcome or a paradigm to be worked towards. It is precisely the richness of the nuances that are in fact *nuances of affect* that distinguish this work from puzzle work, from any attempt at 'decoding' the dreams. The decoding of dreams is a puzzle that attracts the popular imagination, as demonstrated by the plethora of dream dictionaries and the like on the market today, but even Freud, who was a great decoder of dreams himself, warned against equivalence of meaning and repeating interpretations from one dream to the next:

> My procedure is not so convenient as the popular decoding method which translates any given piece of a dream's content by a fixed key. I, on the contrary, am prepared to find that the piece of content may conceal a different meaning when it occurs in various people or in different contexts. (Freud 1991 [1900], p. 179)

Affect in its multiplicity must exist in multiplicity, and any attempt to reduce it to the general and deny or ignore the differences that each dream delivers would be to take away the very specific element of the experience of social dreaming that makes particpation worthwhile. These nuances of affect are expressed in the pulses of intensity as described in the previous chapter and above, that emerge through perceptions of difference that are exactly described by Deleuze and completely relevant to social dreaming, even though his writing had no practical examples – such as social dreaming – to draw from:

> For it is not figures already mediated and related to representation that are capable of carrying the faculties to their respective limits but, on the con-

trary, free or untamed states of difference in itself; not qualitative opposition within the sensible, but an element which is in itself difference, and creates at once both the quality in the sensible and the transcendent exercise within sensibility. This element is intensity, understood as pure difference in itself, as that which is at once both imperceptible for empirical sensibility which grasps intensity only already covered or mediated by the quality to which it gives rise, and at the same time that which can be perceived only from the point of view of transcendental sensibility which apprehends it immediately in the encounter. (Deleuze 2004, p. 181)

Not Representation; Not Symbolism

Deleuze's discomfort with representation and symbolisation comes in part from the idea that if something is represented or given a symbolic attribute by someone or through the idea that 'everybody knows', then this symbol or representation is always the same despite the nuances of difference that might exist from different manifestations of the similar (repeated but different). In the previous chapter this is the difference between interpreting David Attenborough as a symbol or archetype – Senex, the Sage – and viewing the mention of his figure in the context of the matrix as a means of engaging with the nuances of affect around the affect of frustration.

Invoking Wittgenstein's 'possibilities of fact' to describe the execution of Francis Bacon's non-representative, non-figurative art, Deleuze suggests that the figurative that is seen with the optical eye can be reinvented as a 'visual' that can be seen through an alternative view that creates an object that is not figurative (Deleuze 2005, pp. 71–72). In a similar fashion, the dream images in a social dreaming matrix are not visual in the sense of optical representation, although they are still 'visual' in this other alternative, non-figurative fashion as described by Deleuze. This 'visual' is the image-affect in its rhizomatic, interconnected and intersubjective collage of intensities.

As indicated here, such a rhizome is also intersubjective because the participant in the matrix is 'seeing' both subjectively and in relationship with all the other subjects in the matrix. In a way, there is nothing to 'see'. Nothing objective, that is. What follows is not intended to be an account or analysis of intersubjectivity in its various manifestations from the philosophical of, say Habermas, to the psycho-analytical of, say Jessica Benjamin. Rather, I wish to make connections between the concept of intersubjectivity and the processes of relatedness of social dreaming that I have discussed previously.

Bateson and Relatedness as a Precursor to the Rhizome

One of the great advantages of the social dreaming experience is that it provides the participant with practical experience of a reality of thinking complexity that is not at all easy to describe in words. Gregory Bateson, cited by Deleuze and Guattari as the inventor of the idea of the 'plateau' in *A Thousand Plateaus* (Deleuze and Guattari 1988, pp. 21–22), is one of those thinkers who has concerned himself with what appears to me to be a perception of thought that came very close indeed to this felt experience of the participant in a social dreaming matrix. As a precursor of one of the essential ideas in Deleuzian thinking, Bateson's discussion of relatedness provides helpful insights into the nature of relatedness to knowledge.

In talking about thinking, Bateson identifies unconscious thought with what he calls 'primary process', 'secondary' process being 'normal' conscious thought. Thus far his definition is, of course, Freudian, (Freud 1991 [1900], pp. 745–770). Where Bateson diverges from Freud and comes closer to the social dreaming effect is in his intuition that the main feature of primary processes is not only metaphor, 'lacking negatives, lacking tense, lacking in any identification of linguistic mood … and metaphoric' but also that metaphor is relational:

> In primary process the things or persons are usually not identified, and the focus of the discourse is upon the *relationships* which are asserted to obtain between them. This is really only another way of saying that the discourse of primary process is metaphoric. (Bateson 2000, p. 139, Bateson's italics)

For Freud the primary process is not metaphorically relational in this sense, although it is 'perceptual' and establishes a 'perceptual identity'. (Freud 1991 [1900], p. 761) In joining the metaphor to the relational, Bateson links the dream process to connectivity, patterns and systems:

> The subject matter of dream and other primary-process material is, in fact, relationship in the more narrow sense of relationship between self and other persons or between self and the environment. (Bateson 2000, p. 140)

Furthermore, Bateson was able to point out that these 'relationships' were actually feelings, just as in the dream image, the feeling *is* the image:

> ...the relationship between self and others, and the relationship between self and the environment, are, in fact, the subject matter of what are called "feelings" .... (Bateson 2000, p. 140)

Freud had already associated the primary process with something akin to 'feelings' which he called 'intensities' or 'affect' (Freud 1991 [1900], p. 762) but these tended to be negative features of the mind that had to be repressed by the mind in secondary process and they were not relational in any sense. It seems to me that what Bateson, on the other hand, is trying to describe in words is this union of the metaphor and the relational of the primary process in a way that closely mirrors what the participant in the social dreaming matrix actually experiences.

Bateson's descriptions here are strikingly close to what I understand intersubjectivity to mean in a social dreaming context. In particular, he cannot be satisfied only with the fact of the thought process of the dreaming and free associative mind as having clearly identifiable characteristics that are true of the dream world as an individual thought process, but insists on the idea of *relationships* and that these are equivalent to *feelings* which, in turn, can be the fruit of relationships between subjects as both people and the 'environment'. He called the nature of the communication that engenders this relationship 'iconic communication', that is to say a communication that is not based on the linguistic signs that constitute 'language' in a 'secondary process' way.

The thinking that Bateson represents is the kind of systems thinking that I proposed as being relevant to a non-linear, non-Cartesian frame of thought in Chap. 5 and has been implied throughout the discussion of the social dream in the preceding chapters. The link between social dreaming and this way of thinking is that social dreaming comes closest to giving us a practical example of what it really means to experience thinking in this way. It helps to provide a felt example of what so much theory is attempting to demonstrate and this is useful to us because this theory is sometimes perceived as being maybe overly complex, or impossible to understand and therefore verging on the mystical and/or spiritual, (as in some of the Australian aboriginal world views I will be discussing below).

In terms of the nature of the communication that goes on in social dreaming, I find Bateson's willingness to embrace the 'environment' as 'subject' in intersubjectivity and his comment that in the 'primary process' 'the things or persons are usually not identified' particularly interesting. In social dreaming, as we have seen, the individual participants have their individuality deliberately suppressed by means of the 'snowflake' pattern of the seating plan discussed in Chap. 1 along with the avoidance of direct commentary or interpretation of the participant's contribution(s), and this clearly resonates with this idea of the lack of identification of things or persons. It is, indeed, the relationship between the various dreams of various persons that makes for the rhizomatic 'collage' of understanding that is so characteristic of social dreaming. And it is also truly a central characteristic of social dreaming that this understanding is 'social' and maybe this is what Bateson means by 'environmental', although I want to discuss exactly what we do mean by that in a little more detail below.

Chaos and Dissipative Structures in Social Dreaming

Before I move on to discussing Bateson's 'environment', I want to delve a little further into the idea of thought emerging from 'relationships' or patterns, (i.e. not from the confines of the self in Cartesian fashion).

There is a sense whereby the patterns of the rhizome in social dreaming are mirroring and mirrored by structures of patterns in the environment.

Prigogine's Dissipative Structures

There is implicit in this idea of relationships a sense of movement that has connections with the scientist Prigogine's work on science and chaos (Prigogine and Stengers 1984). Prigogine, who influenced Guattari's thinking on ecology, (see the final chapter of this book), showed how order can emerge from chaos in the formation of dissipative structures, such as vortices that are structures in movement, far from passive equilibrium and become order emerging from chaotic organization:

> When you take, for example, a layer of liquid and you heat it from below you observe a thermal disorder, which is chaotic. But when you heat it more and more, when the layer is not very thick you observe that there comes a point when vortices are built. (Prigogine 2003, p. 72)

In this chemical observation, it is the relationship between the heat source and the liquid that creates movement that eventually leads to order through chaos. The liquid on its own is inert equilibrium. There are interesting parallels between this observation and the understanding of the emergence of some form of orderly meaning from the 'chaos' of images offered in a social dreaming matrix as observed in the preceding chapters. As applied to human systems, this is what Bateson means when he says 'The unchanging is imperceptible unless we are willing to move relative to it' (Bateson 2002, p. 90). That is to say, in the context of Prigogine's observation, the 'unchanging' is the state of liquid before its relationship with a heat source and the movement is that which is provoked by that source. In the social dreaming matrix, the image is offered within the matrix as a container and it 'moves' in relation to the other images that are offered, so that it is forever renewing itself in relation to the other images and vice versa in a movement of ever-increasing complexity. The more complex this movement becomes the greater the sense of meaning that emerges. This is a similar apparent paradox as in Prigogine's example where heat creates chaos but more heat creates order. In the social dreaming matrix, the first images, dreams and associations make very little sense, but the more images, dreams and associations are added, the clearer the meanings seem to become. Furthermore, these understandings are in constant movement, just like a dissipative structure or in the movements of intensity in the Deleuzian rhizome, and these movements create greater understandings, or order, as the matrix becomes more complex. Interestingly, this may also account for the feeling that is sometimes expressed during a post-matrix event, for example a 'Dream Reflection Group' or post-matrix discussion, that the meanings are *less* clear than they were during the matrix itself. This is despite the best efforts of the group to settle into a rational analysis of the meanings of the matrix. Possibly, following the line of thought of this section, this is because the images, dreams and associations have found their way out of the complexity of the dream matrix and into the passive equilibrium of the conscious and rational reflection of the post-matrix dialogue group.

Social Dreaming and Bateson's Environment or Guattari's Ecology

If it is possible to apply the idea of dissipative structures to our understanding of the thinking processes that occur in the social dreaming matrix, then we are in a position to consider this process in the context of the 'environment'; because if the nature and quality of the structures and patterns of our inter-relationships in terms of interchanges of dreams and associations in a social dreaming matrix are essential to its process, then it is also an interesting proposition to consider these in the light of our inter-relationships with our inter-related environment. This is the kind of work that Margaret Wheatley attempts in her consultancy work with organizations through holistic and environmental parallelisms.

For Wheatley, patterns of human relationships must parallel those of the environment. For example, in talking about dissipative structures, she draws a direct parallel between an organizational system and the theories of Prigogine. A living system, she says, will be in a state of non-equilibrium, where it is constantly fed and provoked by the outside 'environment'. At some stage in this process, the system becomes overloaded and collapses. But, she continues:

> ...this disintegration does not signal the death of the system. If a living system can maintain its identity, it can self-organize to a higher level of complexity, a new form of itself that can deal better with the present. (Wheatley 2006, p. 21)

Applied to social dreaming, it seems to me that similarly the thinking system of the matrix is in a state of constant movement of ideas, images, associations, thoughts and feelings, where the danger of overload and collapse is felt as being the possible conscious recognition of the 'unthought known'. By maintaining the (dissipative) flow of thought and affect in the matrix, we are able to see what had been hidden from our conscious thinking. The feeling we have in the matrix is that these primary process thoughts are somehow not belonging to us but are, in a sense, imported from outside, from the 'environment', 'dreams in search of a dreamer' (Lawrence 2005, p. 87), or the body without organs. In this way, we can interpret the matrix as being similar to a structural reorganization of our thinking state, to a 'higher level of complexity' where it seems possible to the participants that the dreams do not, in fact, emerge solely from the participants themselves but from elsewhere. This is akin to the idea that the unconscious-like state of mind of the social dreaming matrix as opposed to the conscious state of mind in 'normal' reality can be compared to a fundamental change of structure in our relationships. As Jan Zwicky says in her discussion of Freudian definitions of the conscious and unconscious:

> ...in Freud's conception, the *fundamental* distinction between what he calls 'conscious' and 'unconscious' thought is a *structural* one. There is not an on-off attention-switch involved in the transition from one to the other, but something more like a change of state. (Zwicky 2002, p. 127 (author's italics))

This 'change of state' is what I am incorporating to my understanding of 'states of thinking' so as to understand what social dreaming has to offer us in the holistic fashion mentioned above. Since this approach encompasses the non-human and human subject, the processes that we engage with in the social dreaming matrix must be part of that greater, holistic context.

Intersubjectivity and the Environment

Fractals

Bearing this in mind, in talking about the social dreaming matrix, I am taking 'environment' to mean 'all that is around us' and 'intersubjectivity' to mean all the non-binary relationships in this 'environment'. The environment would, therefore, include all the interconnected 'mini' environments, such as the 'environment' of the matrix as a psychological container, the room where the matrix takes place, the building and institution, the street, the town and so on in ever increasing outward and inward resonating patterns. Thinking about social dreaming in this way can also lead to considering how structures of fractals in the environment might resonate with Gordon Lawrence's idea that the first dream of the social dreaming matrix is a 'fractal' of the rest of the matrix, (Lawrence 2007a, p. 11), the whole structure being, therefore, ever greater dimensions of the original 'fractal' dream. These ever-increasing dimensions give sense to the ambiguous idea of the 'infinite' in social dreaming, that Lawrence sometimes enunciated (Lawrence 2007a, b, c).

Intersubjectivity

In terms of intersubjectivity, I am reaching further than the original feminist requirement to go beyond the duality of the dyadic relationship implied in Freudian analysis in the analyst-analysand relationship that begins with 'Freud's polarization of sex along the fault line of active/masculine vs. passive/feminine' (Kimble Wrye 1999, p. 1456). For Jessica

Benjamin, (1988, 1995, 1998, 2018), who is an essential voice of the feminist intersubjective approach, it has been important to replace the masculine/feminine polarity with a theory of pluralities of gender for men and women. Beyond feminism, however, there is a lot to be learnt which is applicable to the idea of intersubjectivity in a group and/or societal process such as social dreaming. If you take away the dyadic pressure to split male and female in a one-to-one relationship and you replace this with a group situation, especially a 'group' such as a matrix, intersubjectivity becomes easier to assume. This is partly why Jung emphasized the qualities of the hermaphrodite when discussing dream archetypes (Jung 1972, p. 31), (that is to say dream symbols that could be relevant to all, to the 'collective' rather than simply to the analyst/analysand), so that by having male and female qualities recognized in each individual, s/he can be freed as a subject with no need to seek for the 'other'. So, if we move to the idea of intersubjectivity in collectives, I believe we find similar lines of thought as expressed by feminist intersubjectivity but with a special power and resonance. In particular, what connects Benjamin's theories of intersubjectivity and intersubjectivity in a social dreaming context are the theories of Winnicott concerning the created space of play between children that takes away object identity and replaces it with subjectively accepted identities:

> Winnicott's spatial metaphors which emphasize playful encounters between two selves are vital to Benjamin's exploration of non-coercive acts of recognition. (Driver 2005, p. 8)

Intersubjectivity and the Ecology of Social Dreaming

Intersubjectivity, then, in the context of social dreaming begins with the recognition of the subject through the denial of the existence of the 'other' as object. This happens in the space of the matrix conceived of as a space of 'play' (or creativity) in a Winnicottian sense. Combined with the Lawrencian idea of dreams as fractals of each other, whatever is exchanged in this inter-subjective space is a fractal of the social environment. Whatever the meanings or understandings the communicative interchanges of the matrix offer, these are interconnected like fractals to the whole of our interior/exterior interconnected social environments. This 'exterior', in the context of social dreaming, is naturally 'interior' too; that is to say, it belongs to an unconscious aspect of the psyche. This emphasis on ever-increasing fractal reverberations of intersubjectivity must eventually leave the containing confines of the social dreaming matrix and become intertwined with the social environment, and eventually as part of an ecological system. This is where human intersubjectivity combines with the environment and ecology. In considering this, I take even further de Quincey's view of interconnectivity between all organisms – 'I prefer to remain open to the Whiteheadian possibility that all organisms are centres of subjectivity' (de Quincey 2005, p. 204) – and consider intersubjectivity as taking on Gaian, or ecological systemic proportions. Lynn Margulis has discussed this interconnectivity (which must also be inter-subjective if all things are considered 'alive') in terms of Gaia theory and fractals in her book *The Symbiotic Planet* (2001):

> Life produces fascinating 'designs' in a similar way [similar to fractal geometry] by repeating the chemical cycles of its cellular growth and reproduction … Gaia, as the interweaving network of all life, is alive, aware, and conscious to various degrees in all its cells, bodies, and societies. (Margulis 2001, p. 158)

In social dreaming, there is a sense of such a Gaia-like design in the process, as the smallest dream fractal expands outwards, potentially infinitely. In Chap. 13 of this book, I relate the social dreaming process to the ability to 'see' the unseen and give the example of grasping the nature of the hyperobject, (an object of immense complexity), through the social dreaming process.

Similarly, the 'designs' or patterns that are created in the rhizomatic collage of images of a social dreaming matrix combine a repetition of process through the constant evocation of images, dreams and associations that provoke unsolicited feedback loops that simultaneously look backwards and forwards within the same social dreaming process and eventually lead to meanings or understandings that seem to emerge or crystallize from the mass of apparently unconnected and disconnected figures, in a way that reminds me of Margulis' 'interweaving network'.

Social Dreaming and Living Systems

Some writers, (Maturana and Varela 1998; Wheatley 2006; Capra 2003; Capra and Luigi Luisi 2014), have attempted to identify human communications systems as parallel to living systems through comparing both systems' processes to autopoiesis:

> Auto, of course, means "self" and refers to the autonomy of self-organizing systems; and poiesis (which shares the same Greek root as the word "poetry") means "making". (Capra and Luigi Luisi 2014, p. 129)

The concept has bridged the biological and the social, and the connection to a broader, social interpretation of the term was first made by Maturana and Varela, the biologists who originated the theory. For Maturana, for example, the human system is autopoietic when it is both interconnected and also functions like a biological system that self-organises, self-produces and self regenerates. Maturana explains that this is not automatically true of a human system. For example, if the human beings are connected through a system that does nothing more than produce things that could also be equally well produced by machines or robots, then that is not an autopoietic system. The definition of what it is to be human within a living system is that there is a flow from within the system outwards, and back again in such a way that allows the system to self-organize and continue. In attempting to differentiate between living human systems of this kind and inorganic systems that are not autopoietic, Maturana, without meaning to, points to how the element of children's phantasy in play is able to create a living system out of a non-living one, in ways that remind me of Winnicott's (1991) *Playing and Reality*:

> The microphone that we use to record our conversation cannot simply be regarded as an autopietic system even if we were very much tempted to do so. Only children can do that sometimes. In their play, the non-living may appear to be living. (Maturana and Poerksen 2004, p. 100)

For Luhmann, it is the interweaving links of communications in a human system that make it autopoietic:

> Social systems use communication as their particular mode of autopoietic reproduction. Their elements are communications that are recursively produced and reproduced by a network of communications …. (Luhmann, quoted in Capra 2003, p. 72)

Certainly, if this is so, nowhere is this more obvious than in social dreaming as a communication system, and one that can create something living through phantasy and play, or creativity; if it is possible to conceive of 'normal' conscious human communication in this way, then the social dreaming process is even closer to living systems: social dreaming seems to create a life of its own; it is relatively unimpeded by rules and norms of discourse; it weaves and intertwines and accumulates in a non-linear fashion; it works, so to speak, 'naturally'. That is to say, the unconscious images flow unsolicited and in free association – with minimal interruption from the conscious applications of the mind – in a self-creating fashion. The images, dreams and associations that have been offered, in turn create or provoke further images, dreams and associations; this then continues in a further process of created associations that may stimulate further association or provoke the memory of a dream, and so on. In this way, the whole system is self-creating in an autopoietic fashion. Meaning self-emerges from this self-generating, autonomous system thus creating a structure of shared understanding that becomes stronger and more convincing than the mere physical structure of the configuration of chairs that the matrix began with. In this way, a permeable boundary of meaning and understanding is created and the social dreaming matrix becomes a bounded system with its own life and self-generating creativity. The fractals of dreams that began with the pattern of the first dream are built up within this boundary so that the whole process of recursive generation is able to create a fractal design that illustrates this meaning and understanding through what I have called rhizomatic collage. In this way we 'bring forth a world' (Maturana and Varela 1998, p. 234) but not so much linguistically, in the sense that Maturana and Varela meant when they coined this phrase in their book *The Tree of Knowledge*, (1998), but rather iconically in the social dreaming matrix, where language tends to be a tool for the evocation of image rather than a code for conscious communication.

In terms of 'intersubjectivity', clearly none of the participants in the matrix is expressing a linguistic communication to an 'other' as object. Instead of this, we have a situation where all the participants share in expression, understanding and meaning simultaneously between subjects. The container for this shared understanding is the social dreaming matrix that began as a physical construction of chairs and was reinforced by the imaginal construction of the thinking process. Now this container, as we have seen, can be conceived of as a living structure in its own right, a body without organs, and also as a 'mini-environment' within a bigger 'environment', itself nesting within another 'environment' and so on, theoretically to infinity. If we look at intersubjectivity as a process in the social dreaming matrix in this light, then it is the same as saying that intersubjective relationships function to create an environment – the social dreaming matrix – that is as a fractal of other living processes that both occupy and create our environments and environments within environments.

Social Dreaming as a Process in Context: From Naess to Deleuze and Guattari

The ultimate example of an attempt to combine an environmental system with a system of thought comes to us in the philosophy, or 'ecosophy' called Deep Ecology as developed by Arne Naess, whose philosophy emerged from his study and knowledge of Spinoza and who resonates with some of Deleuze and Guattari's later work on philosophy and ecology. There is a linking strand of thought that connects Deleuze, Guattari, Naess and Spinoza to ways of understanding the system of thought and affect that governs social dreaming and ecological systems and attitudes. This works through an understanding of the social dreaming process as an ecology, a rhizome, a system of intersubjectivity, and fractals that contribute to knowledge through the way that affect is created and expressed as part of this system.

The position of Deep Ecology is expressed by Arne Naess in the need for intersubjectivity to be extended beyond the sphere of living to that of intersubjectivity among everything. The human subject, for Naess, is not 'a thing in an environment, but a juncture in a relational system without determined boundaries in time and space' (Naess 1990, p. 79). Naess' philosophy that tries to make the human being part of the natural environment in order to save nature from the destruction of man has its philosophical and psychological roots in Spinoza and Gestalt theory:

> *Gestalts bind the I and the not-I together in a whole.* Joy becomes, not *my* joy, but *something joyful* of which the I and something else are interdependent, non-isolatable fragments. (Naess 1990, pp. 60–61, (Naess' italics))

The 'relational system' is the Deleuzian rhizome with its connections in Spinoza. It envisages joy as a thing out of the self, just as in social dreaming the affect is out of the individual and belonging to the matrix. It is also the governing feature of social dreaming and Naess' ecosophy, which later we shall see is close to that of Guattari. In the following example from Naess' book *Ecology, Community and Lifestyle,* (1990) the conservationist is Spinozian and the developer is Cartesian:

> Confrontations between developers and conservers reveal difficulties in experiencing what is *real.* What a conservationist *sees* and experiences *as reality,* the developer typically does not see – and vice versa. A conservationist sees and experiences a forest as a unity, a gestalt, and when speaking of the *heart of the forest,* he or she does not speak about the geometrical centre. A developer sees quantities of trees and argues that a road through the forest covers very few square kilometres compared to the whole area of trees … And if the conservers insist, he will propose that the road does not touch the *centre* of the forest. (Naess 1990, p. 66, (Naess' italics))

There is a struggle here that does not seem so very different from the Cartesian versus Spinozian positions. I do believe, however, that in this description of these differences we can find the relevance of social dreaming. In social dreaming all the participants are invited to share what comes to us naturally – images, dreams and associations, 'unthought knowns'. It is in this context that the 'developer' in Naess' example might be able to share the image of the 'heart in the forest' which is therefore 'of the forest'. What needs to be changed are not our modes of argument, not our ability to express 'strong, clear expressions of values and norms' (Naess 1990, p. 65) but our containers (environments) for thinking. What Naess refers to as 'gestalt' thinking requires a considerable leap of the imagination for the conscious mind, but in the context of social dreaming, this kind of perception is both natural and normal. The reason for pointing this out in this context is because it seems to me that social dreaming is a process of thinking that through its affinity with life processes is particularly apt in the environment of systems thinking that is becoming more and more prevalent in our world today and that is especially applicable to the networked web of life that constitutes ecological concerns. In this sense, social dreaming is ecology. By this, I mean that our naturally shared thoughts in their totality as expressed in the social dreaming matrix work in parallel process to the workings of nature.

Why Social Dreaming and Deep Ecology?

The reason for comparing social dreaming and Naess's Deep Ecology is to emphasise how the processes and systems, the prerequisites, suppositions and expectations for both are so similar that it suggests that social dreaming is a knowledge generating system that is waiting to be applied to problems and challenges that we are currently facing. It may be that in order to confront issues of ecology, climate change and sustainability, we are in need of new systems of knowledge. I am suggesting that the knowledge created and experienced in social dreaming may provide such insight as we have need of and may also make social dreaming an appropriate way of reflecting upon the biggest systemic issues of our lifetimes, those related to climate change and the sustainable survival of the species.

References

Bateson, G. (2000). *Steps to an Ecology of Mind*. Chicago: University Press of Chicago.

Bateson, G. (2002). *Mind and Nature*. New Jersey: Hampton Press.

Benjamin, J. (1988). *The Bonds of Love*. New York: Pantheon.

Benjamin, J. (1995). *Like Subjects, Love Objects.* New Haven and London: Yale University Press.
Benjamin, J. (1998). *Shadow of the Other*. London and NY: Routledge.
Benjamin, J. (2018). *Beyond Doer and Done to.* London and NY: Routledge.
Capra, F. (2003). *The Hidden Connections.* London: Flamingo.
Capra, F. and Luigi Luisi, P. (2014). *The Systems View of Life*. Cambridge: CUP.
de Quincey, C. (2005). *Radical Knowing*. Vermont: Park Street Press.
Deleuze, G. (2004). *Difference and Repetition*. London: Continuum.
Deleuze, G. (2005). *Francis Bacon*. London: Bloomsbury.
Deleuze, G. and Guattari, F. (1988). *A Thousand Plateaus*. London: Continuum.
Driver, S. (2005). Intersubjective openings: Rethinking feminist psychoanalytics of desire beyond heteronormative ambivalence. *Feminist Theory* 6 (1): 5–24.
Freud, S. (Strachey, J. (Trans.). (1991 [1900]). *The Interpretation of Dreams.* London: Penguin.
Jung, C.G. (1972). *Man and his Symbols*. London: Aldus.
Kimble Wrye, H. (1999). The Shadow of the Other: Intersubjectivity and Gender in Psychoanalysis. By Jessica Benjamin. *Journal of the American Psychoanalytic Association*, 47, pp. 1455–1461.
Kuhn, T.S. (1996). *The Structure of Scientific Revolutions*. Chicago: Chicago University Press.
Latour, B. (2005). *Reassembling the Social.* Oxford: OUP.
Lawrence, W.G. (Ed.). (1998). *Social Dreaming @ Work*. London: Karnac.
Lawrence, W.G. (2005). *Introduction to Social Dreaming. Transforming Thinking*. London: Karnac.
Lawrence, W.G. (Ed.). (2007a). *Infinite Possibilities of Social Dreaming*. London: Karnac.
Lawrence, W.G. (2007b). Dream Reflection Group. In Lawrence, W.G. (Ed.), (2007). *Infinite Possibilities of Social Dreaming*. London: Karnac.
Lawrence, W.G. (2007c). Creative Role Synthesis. In Lawrence, W.G. (Ed.), (2007). *Infinite Possibilities of Social Dreaming*. London: Karnac.
Margulis, L. (2001). *The Symbiotic Planet*. London: Phoenix.
Masssumi, B. (Ed.). (2002). *A Shock to Thought*. London: Routledge.
Maturana, H.R. and Varela, F.J. (1998). *The Tree of Knowledge: The Biological Roots of Human Understanding*. Boston: Shambhala.
Maturana, H.R. and Poerksen, B. (2004). *From being to Doing*. Heidelberg: Carl-Auer.
Naess, A. (1990). *Ecology, Community and Lifestyle*. Cambridge: CUP.
Prigogine, I. (2003). *Is Future Given?* New Jersey: World Scientific.

Prigogine, I. and Stengers, I. (1984). *Order out of Chaos*. London: Fontana.
Winnicott, D.W. (1991). *Playing and Reality*. London: Routledge.
Wheatley, M.J. (2006). *Leadership and the New Science*. San Francisco: Berret-Koehler.
Zwicky, J. (2002). Dream logic and the politics of interpretation. In Lilburn, Tim (Ed.), *Thinking and Singing, Poetry and the Practice of Philosophy*. Cormorant Books.

11

Expressing the Virtual and the Image-Affect: The Problem of Language

The reason why the Slow Violence social dreaming event, used as an example in Chap. 9 above, was such an appropriate area of investigation for the use of social dreaming as a method of exploration is partly because of the ineffable and complex content of the session, climate change, including a 'slowness' of destruction towards extinction in ways that are almost impossible to see, understand or conceive of in any normal or routine sense or mode of thinking. Climate change – the fact that it is human-made in ways that are made manifest in the natural world, its long-term change that is difficult to physically perceive or sense and is unlikely to be understood personally in its most apocalyptic form by anyone alive today – is a topic that is by its very nature indescribable. It is part of the Gaia system discussed above. Social dreaming, using as it does, images through dreams and associations, attempts to avoid the issue of the inherent inefficacy of words to transmit the knowledge of climate change. And yet, language is still its vehicle, if not its driver. This chapter addresses the problems of language in social dreaming and considers to what extent the method enables a certain bypassing of these problems.

J. Manley, *Social Dreaming, Associative Thinking and Intensities of Affect*,
Studies in the Psychosocial, https://doi.org/10.1007/978-3-319-92555-4_11

Words and the Nature of Dreams

The language of dreams is very unlike standard discourse, and in social dreaming, even the associations, comments, ideas and feelings that are not a direct recounting of dreams acquire a dream-like mode of expression. The ethereal and ephemeral feelings that accompany dreamwork as well as the idea that dreams are somehow very personal and intimate are not only specific features of social dreaming, they are also ways of expression that can cause suspicion and distrust in speakers and listeners who are attuned to the language of the rational and the discursive as a means to reach knowledge claims for action and decision making. Furthermore, the expression of these features in social dreaming is weighted towards the viewing of images in the mind as a priority over 'rational' thought expressed in words. In social dreaming the words attempt to convey the pictures. In this sense, the process is inevitably unusual and potentially unsettling and, in a sense, bound to never completely succeed, since the word can never fully express the picture. This is simply but effectively expressed by Steven Pinker in his distinction between the array and the propositional model, with the 'array' being a sketch, picture or image, and the 'propositional model' being a schematic diagram of inter-linked descriptions of that image (Pinker 1999, p. 290). The diagram in Pinker's book is like a mind map and resonates with the kind of inter-connected schema of words and sentences that are created by the host of the social dreaming matrix when she takes on the role of facilitator in the post-matrix discussion and all the contributions of the participants in the discussion are noted on a flipchart or whiteboard or similar, immediately after the matrix. What is immediately apparent is the difference between the images that have been expressed in the matrix (albeit images expressed in words), and the ideas that emerge from these images in this schematic fashion. The 'array' is spontaneously captured in an instant, as are associated emotions (Pinker's example is a picture of a teddy bear, which therefore combines the picture of a bear with the affect attached to the image which might be slightly different for each participant but at the same time is likely to be some form or nuance of affect associated with a childhood toy). The pattern of words, on the other hand, provokes cognitive reflections and a sequentialisation of these words as they are patterned in the form of a mind map. During this post-matrix process, the facilitator deliberately limits the words to single or small clusters and links these together with lines and arrows to try to avoid the sequentialisation of sentence structures, yet there is no getting away from a certain sense of one idea leading to the next, unlike the array. In contrast to the rhizome of the matrix, this post-matrix mind map follows an interconnectivity that Deleuze and Guattari defined as more like a pattern produced by a tree, with its central trunk and branchings out from the centrepiece (Deleuze and Guattari 1988, p. 21). The rhizome of the matrix is different to this, in that it has no centre and no principal focus, or at least no central fixed focus. Given a casual glance, both patterns might appear superficially similar, but the essential difference of the rhizome – that it has no governing centre – is crucial to the Deleuzian theory and also to the way the dreams and associations work in the matrix.

Having said this, it is also true that language is probably not as uniquely different to the visual as it may seem at first sight. I believe that by understanding the richer nature of language, the way that the visual is potentially within language, we can become more open to the visual in social dreaming. My purpose here, therefore, is to show how a more complex understanding of the nature of language as used in social dreaming can encourage the use of a process such as social dreaming in an everyday human context, such as in the world of work, for example. In most everyday contexts that are not cultural events or experiences, the idea of objectivity as an especially laudable goal is represented by what this world recognises as facts and figures, charts and results, profits and loss and other measurable targets and results. In this space there is little room for emotions and their associated images as expressed in a social dreaming matrix. In fact, there may be a case for claiming that 'feelings' and 'pictures' might interfere with objectivity and logical reasoning. Maybe this is especially so in the workplace, which is why emotions are frequently banned in such a context, at least when actually doing the work. This is based on the idea – an idea not restricted to the workplace but prevalent in all situations where 'rationality' is understood as being the key to progress – that emotions are potentially damaging to practical progress due to their irrationality. There is now a slow moving away from this limited view of the use of words at work and in organisational theory, (see, for example, Morgan's work in this field (Morgan 2006, 2016)). Indeed, the whole idea of cognition and language as being more logical than emotion and visual imagery may now be dying away. As the neurologist Joseph LeDoux says, 'If cognition is not just logic, and is sometimes illogical, then emotion might not be as far afield from cognition as it was initially thought.' (LeDoux 1999, p. 36).

In order to help us manage that situation, there is a whole working language that is employed to help us ensure dry objectivity in the workplace and the idea behind this use of language is that we are able to speak a language of facts and figures, the 'familiar verbal and math abilities', a language that is able to exclude all other impractical connotations (Goleman 1999, p. 375). Language, therefore, is part and parcel of the Cartesian logic of our rational and logical world of production and consumption. Essential to this endeavour is the idea that language is a simple code for our thoughts, that it can 'translate', as it were, our 'pure and rational' thoughts into active communication in cause-and-effect fashion. However, language is far from being only this; in fact, it could well be argued that the nature of language is greater in scope and more closely approximates the nature of our thoughts and feelings in the human and affective sense evinced in social dreaming. If we can understand this, then social dreaming no longer remains a strangeness of communication that can only be approached under rarefied circumstances but becomes a channel of communication that can be opened up to help us in our total participation in the creative thinking process that acknowledges the nature of our beings.

Emotions, the Word and the Image

The idea of the worth of emotions in the workplace has maybe come to be popularly identified with Daniel Goleman's 'emotional intelligence' (Goleman 1999), but this popular account of the use and value of emotions is very instrumental in its approach. Rather than this superficial recognition of emotions in the workplace, Armstrong suggests that an understanding of emotion in the organization is fundamental and intrinsic to its existence, its meaning 'as a system in context', so that we 'move from emotional intelligence to the intelligence (as in "military intelligence") afforded by emotion' (Armstrong 2004, p. 13). I am proposing that social dreaming can help us to become more deeply aware and participative in this emotional world through the expression of this affect as images in the context of a social dreaming matrix. In proposing this, however, I want to avoid the idea that because social dreaming works as a rhizome and uses visual 'collages' we have to find some sort of purely visual language of dreams or a means of transmitting the visual of our minds to the 'real' world as represented in the rational communication of language. There are instances of social dreaming that use physical drawings or objects as part of the process (La Nave 2010; La Nave, in press; Berman and Manley 2018), and these have often formed part of social dreaming applications in the context of art therapy; but the long and extensive experiences of the use of social dreaming since 1982 demonstrate that there is specific value in the internalisation of the image and associated affects, the image in the mind, to allude to David Armstrong's work in this domain (Armstrong 2005).

Language was in the beginning and remains today infused with multiple visual meanings that keep our 'rational' minds in touch and in tune with our 'irrational' minds. The pictorial origins and relevance of the visual in language are discussed in a section in David Abram's (1996) book *The Spell of the Sensuous*, where he traces the visual in writing to the perceived in nature: 'Our first writing, clearly, was our own tracks, our footprints, our handprints in mud or ash pressed upon the rock' (Abram 1996, p. 96). This is why figurative language is both natural, due to the pictorial origins of language, and also conflictive, due to the scientific desire for a pure language free of other connotations as opposed to a clear relationship between signifier and signified.

Within language, then, we cannot escape elements of 'irrationality' or 'absurdity' and their expression in metaphor should be accepted as an important part of linguistic communication in social dreaming. Indeed, the dream often seems to come close to a poetic use of language that Freud saw as being close to the use of language in free association, long before Breton and the surrealists had made that same connection (Freud 1991 [1900], p. 177). This means accepting the absurdity of the 'language' of dreams as having an important sense and meaning, just as Freud himself suggested in *The Interpretation of Dreams*: 'It is quite true that we have described dreams as absurd; but examples have taught us how sensible a dream can be even when it appears to be absurd.' (Freud 1991 [1900], p. 748) In this chapter, I aim to show how it is in this 'irrational' expression that emotions are transmitted and how it is often the metaphors and absurdities of ordinary language that communicate important realities in everyday life.

Language and 'Objective' Meaning

The assumption that language can be an objective transmitter of truth through the careful use of words, or what Lacan, from Saussure, (Lacan 2001) calls 'signifiers', pieced together by an 'objective' writer or speaker for the benefit of a passive, recipient reader or listener is certainly doubtful if not untenable. And yet this belief, or something like it, continues to exert a powerful influence on all of us today. How often, for example, do articles and books begin with the writer 'objectively' defining a key word for his or her argument by quoting from a dictionary, as if this were irrefutable 'proof' of the meaning of a definition? It has become common practice to use the definition of a word to seek out its original meaning, maybe through its Latin root or similar, as if this original meaning somehow held the key to its real meaning today. The idea is that we can somehow reach out for the absolutely objective truth of this word. What psychology and contemporary philosophy have revealed to us, however, is that words can never be defined.

As a reductio ad absurdum, let's take the definition of the word 'cat', for example and use a prestigious and famous dictionary compiled in 1755 by Samuel Johnson:

> CAT: A domestick animal that catches mice, commonly reckoned by naturalists the lowest order of the leonine species.

Let us compare this to a definition from my aging copy of the Concise Oxford Dictionary:

> CAT: Small furry domesticated carnivorous quadruped…

Which is objectively the more correct? Clearly, mice were a big problem in 1755 and the first thing a householder would associate with a cat was a mouse, which had to be caught. The modern definition, on the other hand, could be mistaken for a dog, a 'small furry domesticated carnivorous quadruped.' Parts of the definition are not clear: What does 'small' mean? The same dictionary defines 'dog' as a 'Carnivorous quadruped of genus Canis ...' and there we have our Latin root. There is no doubt, however, that Johnson's definition must surely be a cat, not because of its clearer definition in an 'objective' sense but because of its unequivocal association to mice. In other words, we understand 'cat' through association rather than definition, in the same way as meaning emerges through association in the social dreaming matrix. And if I go back to my aging Oxford Dictionary, published in 1979, I see that the next definition of 'cat' is a 'spiteful or malicious woman', and then a 'person, esp. jazz enthusiast...' and I have to think a little before I understand the former as a male-orientated definition of woman which I cannot remember being used in conversation, and the latter as being a reference to the slang use of 'cat' as in 'cool cat', which I cannot remember ever having heard either. In other words, the definition of 'cat' is subject, despite its apparent simplicity and unchanging nature, to different definitions according to contexts, subjectivities and time. The inexorable and irreversible movement of time contributes to the multiple and ever-increasing possibilities of definition that a word might accumulate. One definition never stops developing its future possible definitions. The 'signified' is never sufficiently defined. The 'signifier' is not absolutely bound to the 'signified', and yet is never entirely freed of it. The signifier-signified-signifier process ad infinitum continues to develop through time. Meanwhile, the process simultaneously feeds back into itself, multiplying the complexity of meanings of words and associations as they move through time. The signifier becomes self-amplifying, assigning ever more complexity of meaning to the signified.

Language, especially as used in social dreaming, is also subject to self-amplifying feedback; it, too, is ever-increasing in complexity. The seeking of the original and/or Latin meaning of a word in a dictionary is an attempt to reverse the clock by peeling away layers of acquired meaning over time. In the social dreaming matrix the opposite happens: multiple meanings are celebrated.

Language, then, has a life of its own. If its meanings were ever to be objective and definitive, then it would die, just like a living organism dies as soon as it stops its autopoietic development through time. I would venture to say that the Newtonian physical world of cause and effect and reversibility, and the association that is made between this way of thinking and rational logical thinking, has been, and is still today, applied to our use of language, especially professional language: the simple 'signifier' means the specific 'signified' and vice versa. This way of thinking denies the possibility, or at least the usefulness, of the irrational and the unconscious in language.

The Unconscious as Language

However, not only is unconscious thought present in language, the unconscious *is* itself a language. According to Freud and Lacan, the unconscious has a language-like structure. The unconscious is an integral part of our being and cannot be separated from any attempt to rationalize. The meanings of words change in time because of their connection with the subjective mind, a mind which is, in Rafael Nuñez's words in *Reclaiming Cognition*, (1999), 'situated, decentralized, real-time constrained, everyday experience orientated, culture-dependent, contextualized, and closely related to biological principles – in one word, embodied', as opposed to the kind of thinking many would associate with academic thought: 'rational, abstract, culture-free, centralized, non-biological, ahistorical, unemotional, asocial and disembodied' (p. 55). The latter sounds rather like the 'objectivity' which is sought after in any rational and professional use of language, while the former, with its 'embodied mind' accepts the value of subjectivity.

The legitimate study of the irrational, the emotional and the unconscious is often recognized as belonging to psychology but I am arguing that it is also a feature of social dreaming and accessible to all. By reaching out for an understanding of this area of our minds we may be empowered to a creative understanding of what might otherwise be rejected as irrational or subjective and therefore unacceptable. Subjectivity can become a valuable tool for thought; and intersubjectivity can create its own shared and created objectivity, the inter-subjective objectivity of a created truth rather than a reality, where reality is not equivalent to truth. In some cases, language used 'objectively' is uncreative and destructive. We can see an example of this in one of the conversations Fritjof Capra transcribes in his (1989) book *Uncommon Wisdom*, where Antonio Dimalanta talks about his clinical practice:

> In my practice, I am very aware of the limitations of language. The only way I can communicate something beyond rational thought is when I use metaphor, sometimes even what I call metaphoric absurdity. Now, when I communicate with a family, the clearer I become, the better they understand me, the less it helps. This is because I am describing a reality which is an abstraction. (Capra 1989, p. 310)

That is to say, the reality being described is not the emotional truth. There is a clue here to how we can understand some of Deleuze and Guattari's work where the rational basis for what should be the most rational of expressions, philosophy, seems often to give way to an expression spiced with metaphor and subjective irrationality. By using a visual approach that is reminiscent of a visual collage of the social dreaming matrix, we can begin to make sense of the following from *A Thousand Plateaus*, both in text and image:

> Metallurgical India. Transpierce the mountains instead of scaling them, excavate the land instead of striating it, bore holes in space instead of keeping it smooth, turn the earth into Swiss cheese. An image from the film Strike presents a holey space where a disturbing group of people are rising, each emerging from his or her hole as if from a field mined in all directions. (Deleuze and Guattari 1988, pp. 413–414)

This sounds like a dream, or madness maybe. Here, Deleuze is linking the idea of the metal-workers, the smiths, with his theory of 'immanence', that space which is between the form of expression, (Deleuze's 'smooth space'), and form of content, (Deleuze's 'striated space'). For Deleuze, striated space is the world of controlled society and organization, whereas 'smooth space' is the world of the 'nomad' who is free to roam the land without restrictions and directives. The images can be decoded and represented in the language of the rational. However, just as we have seen how the social dreaming host avoids interpretation in the social dreaming matrix, in saying this we have already said too much, because the truth of the communication is in the raw power of the accumulated images – as in the matrix – which, in this extract, actually culminates in a real image, a still from Eisenstein's film *Strike*. Is there anything more distant than Eisenstein's Soviet film and the description of India as Swiss cheese? And if the reader is to be 'objective' and 'rational', the writing must be dismissed. If, however, the reader enters into a relationship, as it were, with the writers, then an understanding can be built upon another premise, a potential space. Instead of deciphering the rational in the text, the reader can attempt to make sense of the irrational.

To understand Deleuze we need to look beyond the rational and towards the world of sense of imagery within the words. This is not what Foucault describes Freud as doing:

> I would say that Freud… decodes, which is to say, he recognizes that there is a message there. He doesn't know what the message means; he doesn't know the laws according to which the signs can mean what they mean. So he has to discover at one go both what the message means and what the laws are by which the message means what it means. In other words, the unconscious must convey not only what it says but the key to what it says. (Foucault 2000, p. 253)

It is the decoding and eventually, therefore, the naming of the image that takes away its independence and autonomy and converts it into the property of the decoder or namer. This is well expressed by Brian Massumi in his introduction to the collection of essays *A Shock to Thought*, where the natural force of a flash of lightning, which is the result of an intensity in nature, is captured by the human eye and converted into Zeus: 'A creator now owns the deed' (Massumi 2002, p. xxv) and a link can be made which tells us that Zeus is 'like' the lightning:

> He is as decisive and unforgiving as his thunderbolt. They share properties. They conform and correspond. Properties: the flash has gone from the expressive to the possessive. (Massumi 2002, p. xxv)

Eventually, when Zeus throws his thunderbolt, it is representative of his anger, his affect. The lightning of nature has become the anger of a god, it has become part of the conscious mind: we own it. The more we own it, the tamer it becomes. Eventually it may become a commonplace, a cliché, but before doing so, it will have travelled through a process of multiple change in meaning and adaptation to context. As Massumi says, 'The violence of the flash has been domesticated to serve the functioning of the system operating according to its own rules of formation, at a certain level of reality,' (Massumi 2002, p. xxvi). The affect produced in the flash of lightning has come from the 'smooth space', through the 'holes' of the being to form part of the 'striated space' of the 'real' world. The language of Deleuze and Guattari is frequently probing our unconscious understanding, as if it were pure expression rather than content. Each reader is free to 'own' the text because Deleuze and Guattari have, by not naming, so to speak, never really 'owned' it and this is reminiscent of the social dreamer who does not 'own' his or her 'own' dream. The meaning is not theirs, or at least not theirs alone. The account of transpiercing the mountains, boring holes in space, Swiss cheese and Eisenstein's *Strike* have a metaphorical quality, they are evocative rather than explicative, and this is how they have to be understood. This description of an emerging meaning in our understanding of Deleuze and Guatttari could easily be applied to the process of emergent meaning in the social dreaming matrix. By making this parallel, we give an almost philosophical value to the matrix and sense to the idea that the social dreaming matrix is about thinking new thoughts.

And Lacan...

The unconscious thought processes being described here are very much along the lines of Lacan's descriptions of the function of language. For Lacan, the words, or 'signifiers' do not simply have a single signified object attached to them, but they have their own life and they develop in the mind of the subject as a chain of signifiers, like the string of images of a dream. It is in this sense that the dream has a language-like structure, a chain of signifiers. In this way we can understand Deleuze's 'transpiercing', 'boring holes', 'Swiss cheese', the holes in *Strike*, and finally the concept of 'holey space' as a chain of images, where the sense emerges through the reader's sharing the development of the 'holes' metaphor with the writer. The 'holes' mean more than one thing. Thus we have Deleuze's 'transpiercing' becoming 'Swiss cheese' and eventually becoming an actual image in the film still from Eisenstein's film. It is significant that the nature of the meanings is progressively more visual: Deleuze is writing in metaphors, the language of dreams. Clearly, the experience of psychology, in theory and practice, can help us to understand such a text. Anyone who has shared the dreams of others will have learnt to be patient with emerging meaning through listening and feeling, through transference and counter transference. We can learn that the speech of the rational, the 'real', so to speak, can be put to one side in favour of the understandings of the irrational, with its own laws, waiting to be discovered. And so we can learn to be patient with Deleuze and in ourselves, letting the figurative language have its effects on us as readers, storing the effects and affects, and building the meanings in process through time. The reader of Deleuze can ask herself 'What does 'Swiss cheese' suggest to me?' and whatever it suggests is as valid as any another association. Its 'objective' meaning is not actively sought. Any feelings or associations are there to be felt and stored. The text is not lending itself to 'objective' analysis. I could suggest that the cheese is 'Swiss' because Deleuze is talking about mountains, as in Swiss Alps, but by doing so I have already started to take away the strength of the image, its possible multiple meanings by naming it. And I have made it mine, so that others cannot participate except by accepting or denying the naming of it. That is to say, by suggesting some meaning to the image, I have interrupted the unconscious quality and norms of the dream language and replaced them with the conscious norms of everyday language. The price we have to pay for such a rationalizing of the text is the taking away of the multiple possible meanings of a chain of images to be substituted for a single, simplified, rationalized explanation. It is my contention that Deleuze's writing is no more than an amplified expression of everyday language. That is to say, it is still our language, rich in visual meaning and multiple associations and not so far removed from the experience of pictorial language that often seems to emerge during the social dreaming experience.

The Metaphorical Nature of Language

Even if this is true, many will argue that this use of metaphorical language is to be reserved for unusual situations, for poetry and suchlike, including events such as a social dreaming matrix, that this is fine for the analysand and therapy but irrelevant for research purposes or indeed for the real world. This, however, would be to ignore the reality of our minds and the nature of language. It would be to deny the very essence of what it is to be human. Our minds are not separate machines of rationality, where the experience of the unconscious can be conveniently cut off. The human mind is not a machine manufactured by scientific knowledge and Artificial Intelligence is unlikely to replace it. The human mind is embodied: all experiences pass through the whole body, including, but not exclusively, the brain, all the time. Nothing is clear cut in the human mind, everything merges and flows, constantly. That is why the dictionary definition will never be definitive, and if a dictionary definition cannot be definitive, then what hope is there for objective argument?

Gregory Bateson was fond of pointing out the difficulty of using the human mind as if it were a machine. I quote an episode described in conversation with Fritjof Capra:

> (The) whole fabric of living things is not put together by logic. You see, when you get circular trains of causation, as you always do in the living world, the use of logic will make you walk into paradoxes. Just like a thermostat, a simple sense organ, yes?
>
> 'If it's on, it's off; if it's off, it's on. If yes, then no; if no, then yes.' With that he stopped to let me puzzle about what he had said. His last sentence reminded me of the classical paradoxes of Aristotelian logic, which was, of course, intended. So I risked a jump.

'You mean, do thermostats lie?'

Bateson's eyes lit up: 'Yes-no-yes-no-yes-no. You see, the cybernetic equivalent of logic is oscillation.

Bateson continues by referring to

'…the trees over there. Logic won't do for them.'

'So what do they use instead?'

'Metaphor.'

'Metaphor?'

'Yes, metaphor. That's how this whole fabric of mental interconnections holds together. Metaphor is right at the bottom of being alive.'

(Capra 1989, pp. 78–79)

Metaphor, then, for Bateson is the key to understanding. What the thermostat does not do is measure the subtle movements in temperature between the 'yes' and the 'no'. This difference is similar to Foucault's discussion of the definition of 'prison' in *Discipline and Punish*, (1991), where the logic of (1) This person is guilty, (2) This person must go to prison, can be questioned by the debate on delinquency, as conceptual, non-concrete, and prejudiced, influenced by fear and other emotions. Between the two logical actions, there is an expression which can shift and move according to context. It is the debate on delinquency, in this case, which defines human thought and language. In the case of Foucault, there is a preoccupation with madness as a crime: if the language of the mad is not acceptable, then it is a crime, then the mad should be locked away. Deleuze and others can be similarly locked away from the rational world of debate through the denial of the sanity of their language. Similarly, in the case of social dreaming, we can see how rarefied it seems to appear to the world of 'rational' space.

Preconceived notions of the need for a rational use of language and a consequent logic in argument have militated against introducing the apparent 'irrationality' of social dreaming practice into the work space:

> I have often found it difficult to justify to an organizational client why we should be doing Social Dreaming. Often there is perplexity ... What is often unspoken is why "we" – organization – should do Social Dreaming when our task is ABC. The implication has been that Social Dreaming belongs somewhere else. (Bain 2007, p. 154)

From this perspective, if we are not careful, the whole idea of social dreaming might well be considered anything from eccentric to insane, depending on your self-perceived and understood level of 'rationality'.

'Signifier' and 'Signified'

There are, nevertheless, good reasons for thinking otherwise, even for a 'rational' thinker. Interestingly, for example, Bateson's metaphor-for-trees idea finds an echo in Lacan, where the signifier, the word 'tree', is placed, like an equation, over the signified pictorial representation of a tree (Fig. 11.1):

At first sight, the logic is clear: (1) The word 'tree' means (2) This image of a tree. But the line that separates the signifier and the signified is not as impermeable as it looks. Its permeability is emphasized by Lacan with a play on the word for this line separating the signifier and the signified: in French, 'barre' is an anagram of 'arbre', through which meanings

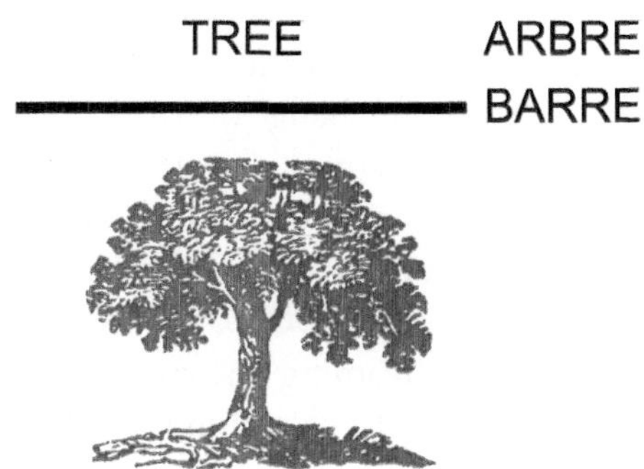

Fig. 11.1 Signifier/signified. (After Lacan 2001, p. 166)

filter and the clarity of the original logic is blurred. Lacan goes on to produce a chain of meanings inspired by 'tree', talking about the

> significations it takes on, in the context of our flora, of strength and majesty. Drawing on all the symbolic contexts suggested in the Hebrew of the Bible, it erects on a barren hill the shadow of the cross. Then reduces to the capital Y, the sign of dichotomy … Circulatory tree, tree of life … tree of Saturn, tree of Diana…. (Lacan 2001, pp. 170–171)

The meaning, then, is the '*something quite other*' than what is apparently stated in the words as they stand. This is the meaning that emerges out of the unconscious and the 'unthought known' of the social dreaming matrix. It is the area of the line separating the signified image from the signifier. It is the movement through this barrier from the unconscious to the conscious, where the signified is converted into metaphor. As Lacan says, 'We see, then that, metaphor occurs at the precise point at which sense emerges from non-sense' (Lacan 2001, p. 175). It is the same logic, with its own laws, that we find in Bateson's idea of the metaphor, quoted above, which holds together what he called a 'fabric of mental interconnections.'

To be able to see these interconnections, to be able to make sense of the metaphor in the text or the image in the matrix, the reader or listener must accept an intersubjective relationship with the writer(s) or speaker(s). This intersubjectivity is what happens when 'memory' and 'desire', in Bion's sense of the terms, are removed, so that we become more 'elastic' in our understanding of communications. 'Memory' and 'desire' are extinguished in favour of an interchange of parity that is the baseline for intersubjectivity. As human collectives, we can become open to potential, possibility and intersubjective interconnections through a 'readiness to hold in suspension the memory or desire of our organizational inheritance' (Lawrence and Armstrong 1998, p. 68). Similarly, the hosts and the participants of a social dreaming matrix need to 'democratically' accept and allow for all contributions within the frame of the practice so that these free flowing mental interconnections can be made and a space created for eventual meaning to emerge.

Language and Computers

The effect of the taking away of 'memory' and 'desire' is amusingly illustrated in an experiment in AI with a computer programme called 'ELIZA' (named after Eliza Doolittle in George Bernard Shaw's *Pygmalion*). ELIZA was programmed, in the programmer's words, to 'parody the responses of a nondirective psychotherapist in an initial psychiatric interview' (Weizenbaum 1993, p. 188). This role was chosen because the programmer would not have to fill the database with real-world knowledge. The programmer, Joseph Weizenbaum, goes on to explain 'After all, I reasoned, a psychiatrist can reflect the patient's remark, "My mommy took my teddy bear away from me", by saying, "Tell me more about your parents", without really having to know anything about teddy bears, for example' (Weizenbaum 1993, p. 189). Although this playing with a patient's unconscious mind might sound unethical, the result of this conversation between the computer and 'patients' was that the 'patients' tended to think that they were, indeed, being understood by the machine. Apparently, says Weizenbaum:

> They would often demand to be permitted to converse with the system in private, and would, after conversing with it for a time, insist, in spite of my explanations, that the machine really understood them. (Weizenbaum 1993, p. 189)

The situation would be, of course, unsustainable, but it is interesting to see how the no-memory, non-desiring machine can begin to produce a reflection of the 'patient's' self. Similarly, the text is non feeling and does not interfere with memories of a past encounter, but it can still provoke an interchange of thoughts and feelings with the reading subject, and in particular if the text is dealing with a language approximate to the dream through metaphor, because, as we have seen, the text does not state, explain or own meaning, it merely evokes what the reader is capable of responding to. The text, of course, is limited. It cannot change itself, adapt or shift meanings without the reader's cooperation. This, on another level, was the limitation for ELIZA: the 'patient' was instructed to provide the computer with the kinds of statements one would normally be expected to make in this kind of interview. It could not have responded to questions outside this field. The cynic might simply have finished the interview immediately by asking the computer my question at the beginning of this chapter, 'How do you define a cat?' to which the computer may have responded along the lines of 'How often have you defined cats?' The benefit of this conversation would certainly have been limited. Similarly, a text which is presented to the reader with certain expectations, for example, the Deleuze text we have been looking at, or the communication of a social dreaming process, has to be approached in a certain way for the 'conversation' or interchange to continue and become fruitful.

It is precisely this same lack of intervention as seen in the ELIZA experiment that ensures the accumulation of the web of images in the social dreaming matrix that I have been calling a 'visual collage' or rhizome. The nature of an associative comment from a matrix participant is such that each participant is presented with an open opportunity to think further, to expand her own 'matrix in the mind' in a non-judgmental way that encourages 'democratic' participation. As this participation becomes evermore complex with the passing of time during a matrix session, it often seems that the accumulated visual collage acquires a life of its own, as it were. It is not an expression that belongs to or is owned by any of the participant members of the matrix. Participants are dis-identified, (we should recall here that this has been one of the purposes of the seating plan arranged in 'snowflake' pattern), and the images join, un-join and re-join in constant and vibrantly shifting configurations in autopoietic rather than belonging fashion, as discussed above.

The Non-Human Reality of Language

This idea of the non-belonging of language is expressed in the essential interchangeability of doctor-patient roles implied in reading a Deleuzian text as suggested by Deleuze himself in the following statement from *Essays Critical and Clinical:*

> The writer as such is not a patient but a doctor, doctor of herself and of the world. The world is the whole set of symptoms in which sickness is confounded with humankind. (quoted in Ettinger 2002, p. 215)

The therapy, he continues, is fashioned through, as it were, a foreign language within a language, by a 'becoming-other of language' that opens 'an outside or flipside consisting of Visions and Hearings ... These visions are not phantasies, but veritable ideas constituted by the passage of life into language' (quoted in Ettinger 2002, p. 215). So, Deleuze himself identifies the key to the approach to his own texts which we have been discussing:

1. The understanding of the nature of the language used,
2. The nature of the relationship and attitude of the reader to the text (for if the writer is her own doctor, then she is the patient too, and so the reader).

It should be pointed out here that the nature of language used, and the consequent relationship established between reader and text might often be associated with literature as an art rather than philosophy as an academic argument. But this is precisely why the reader's approach has to adapt itself to writing which will not limit itself to a narrowly confined genre. This is why what Ettinger (2002) has to say about art is also relevant to the texts we are considering:

> The intrapsychic trans-subjective doctor-and-patient sphere with-in the artist is transported onto inter-psychic trans-individual relations between the artist and the viewer with/through the artwork.... (Ettinger 2002, p. 215)

In literature, or in texts that use literary modes of expression, language takes on its own life through intensity and through this intensity the mind of the reader is engaged in its own creation. This is what, according to Bourassa, Walter Benjamin called 'magic', when language takes on a power of its own. In Bourassa's words:

> If language is itself a force, if it is language that opens a space of being, or language in which all of nature rests, then it is far more than an instrument. (Bourassa 2002, p. 63)

According to Deleuze, the writer 'twists language, makes it vibrate, seizes hold of it, and rends it in order to wrest the percepts from perceptions, the affect from affections, the sensations from opinion.' (Deleuze and Guattari 1994, p. 176).

Language, then, for Deleuze, can include the non-human, meaning the world outside human rationality. Language is neither independent nor just a fabrication of the brain. It is not just about human perception, but percepts too, that is to say, it is the object of perception itself; it is not just an account of human affections but it is affect itself; language can be more than human opinion, it can be pure sensation. This is because language is not the product of a detached human brain, rather it exists with and within the non-human in a multitude of different manifestations, flowing through the embodied mind, to consciousness and back again, in a constantly flowing feedback cycle. Language is alive because of this. We are alive because of this. Again, in the words of Alan Bourassa:

> When it is caught up by a modality of the non-human, a force, and an event, language is not other than that force, that event. It maintains no autonomy. And indeed, if we ask whether there is a 'pure' language, a language free of the intensive possession by the non-human, we must answer that such a language could neither refer, express, or in fact even appear. (Bourassa 2002, p. 75)

Language, then, depends on our existence in relation to our world, what Massumi calls the 'nature-culture continuum' (Massumi 2002, p. xxxviii). The ideas that surface in our conscious minds in the social dreaming matrix, for example, need to return to their origins, through the unconscious. By bringing out these thoughts in the form of associations into the container of the matrix, participants in social dreaming do just this. Thoughts through associations and dreams are returned to their origins to be recycled once more back to our being, so that an idea is never identical to the next.

According to Walter Freeman (1999):

> There are no fixed representations (in brains), as there are in computers; there are only meanings … A sensory stimulus from an object does indeed

> induce the formation of a pattern in the brain, but when it is given repeatedly it does not induce precisely the same patterns in the same brain.... (Freeman 1999, pp. 29–30)

So, the participant in the matrix, in constant interchange with the world will similarly be in constant inter-communication with the matrix itself, the meaning of which will be constantly adjusting itself in a Lacanian sense, according to a constantly shifting context. And the context, therefore, is not a mere backdrop to language, it is the source of our 'becoming'. Deleuze puts it like this: 'Everything is vision, becoming. We become universes. Becoming animal, plant, molecular, becoming zero' (Deleuze and Guattari 1994, p. 169). In the social dreaming matrix, it is this moment of becoming which is true, even if it may not be 'real'. It is the truth of the moment rather than the 'reality' that is important. This is the distinction that was made by Dimalanta earlier in this chapter, and by Lacan when he says:

> One is never happy making way for a new truth, for it always means making our way into it. We are used to the real. The truth is always disturbing. We cannot even manage to get used to it. We are used to the real. The truth we repress. (Lacan 2001, p. 187)

Finally, then, it seems that language is bound to the universe in an intimately unbreakable way. When Deleuze says 'We become universes' he acknowledges our truths as opposed to any reality external to our beings. And our truths must be created in languages, languages conscious and unconscious.

The Artificiality of Language According to Jung

Jung was particularly interested – over-interested, some would say – in man's relationship with his environmental universes. With reference to languages, Jung points out the problem of making language part of the universe, the non-human:

> I must resort to artificial means to determine what things are like apart from myself. Then I discover that tone is a vibration of the air … or that colour is a wavelength of light. We are in all truth so enclosed by psychic images that we cannot penetrate to the essence of things external to ourselves. (quoted in Ryan 2002, p. 19)

Jung's archetypes and his collective unconscious are part of this relationship to the outside, of how our being identifies or becomes at one with the external world, part of Deleuze's 'becoming animal, becoming plant…' This relationship with the world was, for Jung, most obvious in primitive man, where nature and language fused: '(Primitive man's) knowledge of nature is essentially the language and outer dress of an unconscious psychic process' (Jung 1991, p. 6). This reminds me of Abram's identification of language with nature briefly discussed above. Without going into the differences between the 'collective unconscious' and the processes of the social dreaming matrix, that I have also discussed above, the interesting aspect of Jung's perception here is in his description of the relationship between man and nature that is such that the individual is as much an inter-subjective part of his/her environment as s/he is that individual. This is similar to the use of language in Deleuze's relationship to the external world, the non-human and perhaps is why we sometimes feel that communication using the language of a Deleuzian text is a contact with nature, a created universe, a truth rather than a reality, a thinking in primordial images. Jung believed that the human psyche was a product of evolution, as much as the body, and what remains of that evolutionary process forms part of our psyche, and, therefore, of our language. Jung was able to say of his relationship with his patients: 'Together the patient and I address ourselves to the 2,000,000-year-old man who is in all of us' (quoted in Ryan 2002, p. 24). Just as primitive man could subjectively identify himself with his surroundings, be at one with the environment, attribute life to the inanimate, so could Deleuze contemplate an 'inorganic life of things' and a 'collective brain' (Deleuze and Guattari 1994, p. 212). Deleuze and Guattari's 'holey mountain', discussed above, begins as inorganic but becomes, through metaphor, the embodied mind through which a new man or idea may emerge at the end of a sequence of images which have created their own language and understandings, just like a sequence of dream images may create a language of understanding between the analysand and the analyst or a shared visual collage in the social dreaming matrix.

The Language of Social Dreaming

It seems, then, that the very nature of language itself – its irrationality, absurdity, its multiple meanings and tendency to express a plethora of visual images – is an indication of how poorly language lends itself to any kind of simple and/or purely rational end, despite our best efforts to use it so. If this is indeed the nature of language, as I have been suggesting, then the use of a means of communication, such as a social dreaming matrix, where the absurdity of language is accepted as being part of the process of emerging communication through shared imagery and association, makes powerful sense. By understanding the multiple richness and potential of verbal communication, we come some way towards accepting that we might be able to share our thinking with others in a social dreaming way. Thus, we can use language to express what often seems to be purely visual or pictorial, without having recourse to other methods of visual support. This is, of course, because the human mind and our whole expression in communication is complex too.

References

Abram, D. (1996). *The Spell of the Sensuous.* New York: Vintage Books.

Armstrong, D. (2004). Emotions in organizations: Disturbance or intelligence? In Huffington, Clare, et al., (Eds.), *Working Below the Surface. The Emotional Life of Contemporary Organizations.* London: Karnac.

Armstrong, D. (2005). *Organization in the Mind.* London: Karnac.

Bain, A. (2007). The organization as a container for dreams. In Lawrence, W. Gordon (Ed.), *Infinite Possibilities of Social Dreaming.* London: Karnac.

Berman, H. and Manley, J. (2018). Social Dreaming and creativity in South Africa: Imagi(ni)ng the unthought known. In Adlam, J., Gilligan, J., Kluttig, T., and Lee, B.X. (Eds.), *Creative States: Overcoming Violence*. Vol 1, Part 4, Ch. 2, pp. 221–237. London: Jessica Kingsley.

Bourassa, A. (2002). Literature, language and the non-human. In Massumi, B. (Ed.), *A Shock to Thought*, pp. 60–77. London: Routledge.

Capra, F. (1989). *Uncommon Wisdom. Conversations With Remarkable People*. London: Flamingo.

Deleuze, G. and Guattari, F. (1988). *A Thousand Plateaus*. London: Continuum.

Deleuze, G. and Guattari, F. (1994). *What is Philosophy?* London: Verso.

Ettinger, B.L. (2002). Trans-subjective transferential borderspace. In Massumi, B. (Ed.), *A Shock to Thought*, pp. 215–240. London: Routledge.

Foucault, M. (1991). *Discipline and Punish*. London: Penguin.

Foucault, M. (2000). On the Archaeology of the sciences: Response to the epistemology circle. In Faubion, J.D. (Ed.), *Essential Works of Foucault 1954–1984, Volume* 2. London: Penguin.

Freeman, W. (1999). *How Brains Make up their Minds*. London: Phoenix.

Freud, S. (Strachey, J. (Trans.). (1991 [1900]). *The Interpretation of Dreams*. London: Penguin.

Goleman, D. (1999). *Working With Emotional Intelligence*. New York: Bantam.

Johnson, S. (1755). Dictionary. (https://johnsonsdictionaryonline.com/search-johnsons-dictionary/?SearchValue=cat)

Jung, C.G. (1991). *The Archetypes and the Collective Unconscious (Collected Works of C. G. Jung)*. London: Routledge.

La Nave, F. (2010). Image: Reflections on the treatment of images and dreams in art psychotherapy groups. *International Journal of Art Therapy*, 15(1), pp. 13–24.

La Nave, F. (in press). Looking for Treasure in Dream Water. In Long, S. and Manley, J. (Eds.), *Social Dreaming: Philosophy research and practice*. London: Karnac.

Lacan, J. (2001). *Écrits: A Selection*. London and New York: Routledge.

Lawrence, W.G. and Armstrong, D. (1998). Destructiveness and creativity in organizational life: Experiencing the psychotic edge. In Bion Talamo, Parthenope, et al. (Eds.), *Bion's Legacy to Groups*. London: Karnac.

LeDoux, J. (1999). *The Emotional Brain*. London: Phoenix.

Masssumi, B. (Ed.). (2002). *A Shock to Thought*. London: Routledge.

Morgan, G. (2006). *Images of Organization*. Thousand Oaks, CA: Sage.

Morgan, G. (2016). Commentary: Beyond Morgan's eight metaphors. *Human Relations*, 69(4), pp. 1029–1042.
Nuñez, R. (1999). Could the Future Taste Purple? Reclaiming Mind, Body and Cognition. In Nuñez, R., and Freeman, W.J. (Eds.), *Reclaiming Cognition. The Primacy of Action, Intention and Emotion*, pp. 41–61. Thorverton: Imprint Academic.
Pinker, S. (1999). *How the Mind Works*. London: Penguin.
Ryan, R.E. (2002). *Shamanism and The Psychology of C.G.Jung*. London: Vega.
Weizenbaum, J. (1993). *Computer Power and Human Reason*. London: Penguin.

12

Disembodiment, Embodiment and the Image-Affect

The problem of language and communication, and the relationship between these and the visual experiences of the participants in the matrix, resonates with other 'problems' in the process of social dreaming which are baseline onto-epistemological questions that have been the subject of much of this book. Other problems include the following:

- the idea of the rhizome of intensities of affect as a definition of process that emphasises a non-sequential, non-logical presentation of ideas;
- the unnerving sense of each individual being dispossessed of ownership of dreams and associations that she may have offered, and the consequent idea of the Body without Organs (BwO) of the resulting collage of image-affects;
- the primacy of affect over intellectual cognition as a source of knowledge;
- the rejection of hypothesis in favour of a constant reiteration of working hypotheses that specifically delay or even deny any sense of concrete outcome;
- the embracing of creativity and imagination as chief sources of knowledge as opposed to logic and argument;

J. Manley, *Social Dreaming, Associative Thinking and Intensities of Affect*, Studies in the Psychosocial, https://doi.org/10.1007/978-3-319-92555-4_12

- the suppression of the validity of discussion and opinion in favour of this creativity.

All of these aspects of social dreaming are challenges to the way many of us are used to expressing, gathering and sharing information, whether for research or any other purpose for which social dreaming has been employed. They demand of us openness to new possibilities in being and understandings of knowledge.

This chapter will delve into one of the most difficult of these problems, the idea of the BwO and the disembodiment of the self in favour of the BwO. In doing so, I will also bring in an apparent contradiction that suggests that there is something embodied about the process of cognition that goes on in the social dreaming matrix, which is how the knowledge of the dreams and associations is communicated, since, as the previous chapter describes, language as a rational communicator of generated knowledge is not a tool or feature of social dreaming.

Visual Art, the Mental Image and Our Shared Dreams

As has been made clear throughout this study of social dreaming, the communication in the matrix is visual and affective as opposed to linguistic and cognitive. This does not mean that there are not moments of a tendency to give opinions or think more intellectually in social dreaming (a tendency that was demonstrated at the end of the Slow Violence social dreaming matrix in a previous chapter), but it does mean that the overall feel of the social dreaming matrix is one of the accumulation of image-affects presented in a waking state of reverie. This is an essential general norm of the matrix. Indeed, one of the few guiding tasks of the person hosting the matrix is to ensure that if a participant does attempt to contribute in a more discursive mode that is not in keeping with the spirit of the matrix, the host intervenes either with a direct comment to this effect or through a process of modelling responses. The dream images, image-affects and associations are, therefore, the essence of the matrix.

Not only is the 'language' of the matrix heavily weighted towards the visual, but the content is also weighted towards the expression of affect, and the whole is both presented and experienced as new knowledge. The nature and value of this content and its means of communication have been usefully understood from a Deleuzian perspective. Ironically, for a philosopher, Deleuze was interested in the creativity of developing new concepts before the idea of following the reason and logic of philosophy. This in part explains the highly condensed and poetic use of language of much of his work, both alone and with Félix Guattari. Occasionally, Deleuze referred directly to art and the visual (especially in his monograph on Francis Bacon, and his volumes on cinema, and finally in his seminal work with Guattari, *What is Philosophy?*) and in these references he is keen to point to the idea that the value of art and the visual resides not in what might be represented but in what is directly experienced as affect; what is not perception but percept:

> Percepts are no longer perceptions; they are independent of a state of those who experience them. Affects are no longer feelings or affections; they go beyond the strength of those who undergo them. Sensations, percepts and affects are beings whose validity lies in themselves and exceeds any lived. (Deleuze and Guattari 1994, p. 164)

This indicates a mode of thinking that I believe comes close to that of social dreaming. It is worth being reminded again that although social dreaming is working with image-affects, it is still a way of thinking. Gordon Lawrence always insisted on this, and I think he was right. The only thing we have to remember is that the nature of this thinking differs from the discursive. In Deleuze and Guattari's words, 'Art thinks no less than philosophy, but it thinks through affects and percepts' (Deleuze and Guattari 1994, p. 66). And so it is with social dreaming, where the visual is perceived as a mental image, as a percept rather than a perception; and knowledge is transmitted as affect embedded within the image, rather than intellectually. The nature of the percept is to 'see' something invisible, which Deleuze and Guattari call 'forces':

> Is this not the definition of the percept itself – to make perceptible the imperceptible forces that populate the world, affect us, and make us become? (Deleuze and Guattari 1994, p. 182)

In social dreaming 'percept' is equivalent to the mental seeing of the images in the dreams and associations of the matrix. Percept in the matrix describes the sight of the dream that is never an objective image but exists for the dreamer and the teller as a mental image, and even more so for the listeners, i.e. the other participants in the matrix. The 'force' of the image is in the associated affect that comes with it (hence the term 'image-affect'). And this force becomes intensity in this image-affect that pulses to a greater or lesser degree depending on the way it interacts with other image-affects in the created rhizome of the matrix. Furthermore, it is such intensities of affect that 'make us become', and since the process is continuous, in the sense that the image-affects keep emerging and making further connections with the other already existing image-affects, this 'become' is 'becoming'. An example of this was the 'becoming seal' of the Slow Violence matrix as suggested in the personification of the mother seal and the empathy thus created. In this example, the affects associated with the human becoming seal is indicated by the personification but has more than the effect of a figure of speech; this is more than an intellectual agreement that compares the action of the seal to the love a human may feel for a baby, because by the time the matrix has proceeded and the participants have developed the rhizome of image-affects in the matrix, the sensations are all interconnected into what Deleuze would have called a 'bloc of sensations' (Deleuze and Guattari 1994) which are experienced as a form of embodiment rather than an intellectualised agreement that such a personification is apposite.

Embodied Cognition and Knowing Through Experience

The rhizome of image-affects that makes this becoming available is contained by the temporary and newly created space of the matrix. It is, as you would expect from a space filled with dreams, a space of the unconscious, with the main difference between this concept of the unconscious and more traditional descriptions being that this is an unconscious that is shared in a matrix rather than belonging to each individual teller of a dream. I have been calling this kind of unconscious space, following

Long and Harney (2013), the 'associative unconscious', which follows more closely both Deleuze's and Latour's conceptualisations of rhizomes or networks. The result of this sharing of associations is what I have called 'associative thinking' (Manley, in press). It is important, as I have already insisted upon, to recall that dream sharing and related associations in the matrix are indeed forms of thinking, and this thinking is only made possible through shared associations which are interconnected rhizomatically. It is through maintaining the rhizome (rather than cutting its infinite thread of interconnectivity through interpretation, rendering the connections potentially lost) that the associative unconscious can be produced. The rhizome, therefore produces the unconscious, as Deleuze and Guattari explicitly state:

> The issue is to *produce the unconscious*, and with it new statements, different desires: the rhizome is precisely this production of the unconscious. (Deleuze and Guattari 1988, p. 18 (authors' italics))

As the rhizome in the matrix is more than the sum of each individual unconscious, because it becomes the associative unconscious, the self as an individual body is temporarily displaced (which resonates with the one of the mantras of social dreaming practitioners, that we are interested in the dream and not the dreamer) and a new 'body' is created, the BwO, which contains the blocs of sensations consisting of groupings of intensities of affect that form the rhizome. The reason that this is described as 'without organs' is to emphasise the fact that it is not the eye as an organ that connects an external object to the body through the retina, but some inner mental image that is created, so to speak, without the organs that together constitute a human being. This is not a scientific explanation, it is a philosophical one that seeks to create a new way of understanding the associative rhizomatic process of social dreaming. Clearly the brain is an organ and the mental images under discussion here are presumably from the brain; however, what is being emphasised here is that the brain is not being used in its Cartesian sense, a definition that emphasises the centrality of the individual self as its most important feature and which actually defines the human being. The brain, in social dreaming, is thinking differently and a sense of self is temporarily placed on a secondary plane in favour of a shared associative unconscious. The ensuing sensations of becoming then, although they are sensations in each individual in the matrix, are sensations that arise as a result of this process. They are experienced as embodied sensations precisely because the brain as an individual organ has been placed in a different position in relation to the BwO of the accumulated image–affects of the rhizome. This enables it to 'see' the rhizome in all its potential interconnectivities and hold back from cutting up, categorising and placing the image-affects into rational sequences of content that erase the interfering affect that is otherwise produced. The affect, when it remains, is understood partly through this process of becoming (rather than through the cognitive process of the Cartesian brain). In the 'becoming seal' of Chap. 9, the participants in the matrix are involved in a process that is more than a comparison between human and animal, it is a sensation of actually becoming that animal, and in doing so becoming the affects associated with the image and the other associated images at the same time. This is what Deleuze and Guattari mean by becoming, which they differentiate from 'conceptual becoming'. In *What is Philosophy?* they make this explicit:

> Sensory becoming is the action by which something or someone is ceaselessly becoming-other (while continuing to be what they are) … Conceptual becoming is heterogeneity grasped in an absolute form; sensory becoming is otherness caught in a matter of expression. (Deleuze and Guattari 1994, p. 177)

This is how it is possible to disembody the individual self in social dreaming, in favour of the BwO and at the same time to experience the sensation of knowledge through affect.

The Limits of Knowledge in the Individual

Although the BwO and the sensations of sensory becoming in the social dreaming matrix are not science, empirical philosophy does offer different perspectives that are interesting in the context of this study. With the onset of virtual technology, questions arise about the Cartesian claim for the individual. It seems that the individual does not necessarily harbour such a separate and autonomous body and mind that can be easily separated from the environment. According to Andy Clark, and as a result of experimentation with virtual limbs and sensations of pain that arise from these, the border between self and context is not as obvious as maybe we would like it to be:

> The image of the physical body with which we so readily align our pains and pleasures is highly negotiable. It is a mental construct, open to continual renewal and reconfiguration. (Clark 2003, p. 61)

Elsewhere, Clark discusses the 'extended' mind as opposed to the 'brain-bound' mind, where the extended mind acknowledges the functions of the body and the external environment in the process of cognition. He also calls this the 'parity principle' where if part of the external world (just as the BwO becomes externalised from the individual in social dreaming) engages in a process with the mind that the mind acknowledges as part of the thinking process, then that part of the world is, at least temporarily, part of the thinking mind (Clark 2011; Clark and Chalmers 1998). Although this theory has its detractors and objections (see Rowlands 2009 for a summary; see also Sutton et al. 2010; Rupert 2004) it is not difficult to associate this idea of extended cognition to the social dreaming process that I have been exploring in this book. Not only does this support an understanding of the individual as not being an isolated island from fellow individuals and the environmental context, (in other words, supporting the idea that knowledge is shared or associative through constant interaction), but it also suggests that the Deleuzian experience of becoming is not so strange or as unusual as some people might initially think. This way of conceiving of cognition also makes more obviously appropriate Long and Harney's (2013) adoption of Charles Peirce's abduction theory to describe the value of the working hypothesis in social dreaming, where hypothesising is constructed through ever expanding additions of possibilities in order to open out a framework for possible meaning. As the rhizome of image-affects is under construction in the process of social dreaming, it also tends to continuous expansion, in theory at least. The sense of knowledge in social dreaming is therefore one of continuous expansion, abductive rather than deductive. This expansion is, therefore, potentially infinite. In social dreaming, Lawrence was given to discussing the unconscious processes in the matrix as being infinite, without being able to truly define what he meant by that. On the one hand he claimed that the infinite in social dreaming was an exploration of the 'social unconscious' which is 'boundless expansion, or progression, of cultural experiences, images, and emotions', but on the other hand he would go on to say that this same 'social unconscious' had a 'finite limit' and that 'the way of accessing the infinite is to pursue the finite in all its dimensions and directions' (Lawrence 2007, p. 15). This logic is in danger of becoming an oxymoron. Lawrence correctly identified the sense of expansion to infinity of the social dreaming experience, but was unable to provide a theoretical basis for this which would also allow for the justification of the social dreaming process (i.e. his argument implies that the infinite is finite within the container of the social dreaming matrix, and therefore this justifies the use of social dreaming to explore the infinite). The idea of the infinite in the philosophy of Deleuze and Guattari, however, needs no finite boundaries. From a Deleuzian perspective, the infinite is related to 'smooth space' and therefore to the way of the nomad, defined as directionless movement that can lead to new, creative thoughts and ideas in constant expansion, which goes against the 'striated' spaces of restricted and preordained thoughts of a state, system or territory. Movement of thoughts and affect in the smooth space leads away from this territory and into a new space of deterritorialization:

> *It* [the movement into the unknown] *is like a passage from the finite to the infinite*, but also from a territory to deterritorialization. It is indeed the moment of the infinite: infinitely varied infinites. (Deleuze and Guattari 1994, pp. 180–181 (authors' italics))

Whereas Lawrence attempts to separate the individual unconscious from the 'social unconscious' (Lawrence, 2007 pp. 14–15) – with the individual unconscious being a regression in a personal historical and biographical past, a series of memories that can be known through psychoanalysis – the

Deleuzian perspective, which is more in tune with the idea of extended cognition, suggests that the infinite unconscious is in the rhizome, which, in social dreaming, is the rhizome of the image-affects of the matrix that has no end.

Thought as Affect

The embodiment of the image-affects of the BwO of the matrix consists of movements between intensities of affect, which can, in its rhizomatic form, constitute knowledge. This is a defining feature of social dreaming. The rhizomatic interconnections of image-affects are the equivalents of a thought process experienced and understood as and through affect. It is vital, however, to reaffirm the status of affect as knowledge, even if it does not emanate from the thinking brain. Fortunately, advances in theories of cognition and in neuroscience now suggest that thought and feelings are inseparable, that is to say they are bound and linked in embodiment (for example, Nuñez and Freeman 1999; Varela et al. 1993; Damasio 2000, 2003, 2006). Damasio is able to talk about the 'feeling brain' in his book *Looking for Spinoza* (2003). The figure of Spinoza in this happy coincidence, brings together neuroscience and Deleuzian thought. Damasio points out how Spinozian ideas of the inseparability of mind and body are mirrored in contemporary neuroscience, in particular, he points to the Spinozian postulate that the mind is the image of the body and that the images in the mind are received internally rather than externally. Damasio quotes the following Propositions from Spinoza's *Ethics*:

> 15: "The human mind is capable of perceiving a great number of things, and is so in proportion as its body is capable of receiving a great number of impressions."
>
> 26: "The human Mind does not perceive any external body as actually existing except through the ideas of the modification (affections) of its own body." (Quoted in Damasio 2003, p. 212)

In Damasio's work on Spinoza and neuroscientific explorations of the role of the emotions in the body, there is a connecting strand leading from Spinoza to Deleuze, through Damasio and, I am suggesting, to social dreaming, where internal images are affects that are equivalent to thinking in a way that recognises the transitions between internal and external worlds and gives sense to the idea that dreams can emerge from a shared internal space to interconnect and create knowledge through shared and embodied affect.

References

Clark, A. (2003). *Natural-Born Cyborgs. Minds, technologies, and the future of human intelligence*. Oxford: OUP.

Clark, A. (2011). *Supersizing the Mind: Embodiment, action and cognitive extension*. Oxford: OUP.

Clark, A. and Chalmers, D.S. (1998). The Extended Mind. *Analysis*, 58(1), pp. 7–19.

Damasio, A. (2000). *The Feeling of What Happens*. London: Vintage.

Damasio, A. (2003). *Looking for Spinoza*. London: William Heinemann.

Damasio, A. (2006). *Descartes' Error*. London: Vintage.

Deleuze, G. and Guattari, F. (1988). *A Thousand Plateaus*. London: Continuum.

Deleuze, G. and Guattari, F. (1994). *What is Philosophy?* London: Verso.

Lawrence, W.G. (Ed.). (2007). *Infinite Possibilities of Social Dreaming*. London: Karnac.

Long, S. and Harney, M. (2013). The associative unconscious. In Long, S. (Ed.), *Socioanalytic Methods*. London: Karnac.

Manley, J. (in press). Associative thinking: A Deleuzian perspective on social dreaming. In Long, S. and Manley, J. (Eds.), *Social Dreaming: Philosophy, research and practice*. London: Routledge.

Nuñez, R. and Freeman, W.J. (1999). *Reclaiming Cognition*. Thorverton: Imprint Academic.

Rowlands, M. (2009). Extended cognition and the mark of the cognitive. *Philosophical Psychology*, 22(1), pp. 1–19.

Rupert, R.D. (2004). Challenges to the Hypothesis of Extended Cognition. *The Journal of Philosophy*, 101(8), (Aug., 2004), pp. 389–428.

Sutton, J., Harris, C.B., Keil, P.G., and Barnier, A.J. (2010). The psychology of memory, extended cognition, and socially distributed remembering. *Phenomenology and the Cognitive Sciences*, 9(4), pp. 521–560.

Varela, F.J., Thompson, E., and Rosch, E. (1993). *The Embodied Mind*. London: The MIT Press.

13

A Note on Post-Lawrence Research on Social Dreaming

During the development years of social dreaming and while Lawrence was alive, most of the thinking around social dreaming was centred on the figure of its 'discoverer'. There are very few, if any, publications on social dreaming that were published while Lawrence was alive without either his direct input or very much framed by Lawrence, both as person and thinker (for a complete bibliography of publications by Gordon Lawrence, see http://www.socialdreaming.com/resources/). The reasons for this are mainly biographical, as noted in the beginning of this book. This created a stasis in quality of intellectual debate during this period, with much of the writing, for example the chapters in the books that Lawrence edited, sounding like reiterations of Lawrencian ideas. It was difficult at that time to write otherwise, such was Lawrence's grip on the process.

J. Manley, *Social Dreaming, Associative Thinking and Intensities of Affect*,
Studies in the Psychosocial, https://doi.org/10.1007/978-3-319-92555-4_13

Post-Lawrence Research Publications

Since 2010, the date of Lawrence's last edited book on social dreaming (Lawrence 2010), and increasingly since then, there has been a growing interest in the potential for social dreaming as an academic research method in different academic disciplines. For example, Ruth Balogh has explored the potential of social dreaming as used in action research (Balogh 2010, 2015, in press). Francesca La Nave and Hayley Berman have separately explored the use of social dreaming in art therapy (Berman and Manley 2018; La Nave 2010, in press); Karolia and Manley have investigated its potential in the psycho-social context of uncovering the hidden affect, fear and anxieties of contemporary British Muslim identity (2018); Manley and Trustram place social dreaming in the context of a psycho-social approach to museum studies (2018). Long and Manley have pursued defining social dreaming in academic and philosophical terms (Long and Harney 2013; Long and Manley in press); Gosling and others have been locating social dreaming within the sphere of Business and Organisational Studies (Gosling and Case 2013; Manley et al. forthcoming); and Agresta uses social dreaming in the context of social anthropology research (in press).

The Emergence of Hybrid Methods

Alongside the publications, there have been a series of attempts to re-invent, use in a mixed methods context or give a different perspective to social dreaming as a method. For example, Page et al. (2014) use social dreaming as part of a mixed arts-based approach to the work space; Sievers (among other publications, see 2008, 2013, 2014) uses photos as the means of encouraging a dream reflection space in the 'social photo-matrix'. Mersky uses 'social dream-drawing' (2013). Along with experiments in social dreaming using art therapy, these different uses of social dreaming-influenced methods all use some form of physical visual aid in support of the method. It may be that this is an interesting area for future research. In the method I myself have experimented with – the 'visual matrix' – the emphasis remains on the mental images of social dreaming (even though I have used participant drawings in one case (Manley and Roy 2017)).

The Development of the Visual Matrix

The visual matrix is a social dreaming matrix without the dreams, often using some form of stimulus to begin the associative process, since without the dreams this may not be automatic. It makes the claim that the data can be more focussed on a research question through this use of stimulus that provides a context and framework for the session (Manley et al. 2015; Froggett et al. 2015; Manley and Roy 2017; Roy and Manley 2017; Manley 2018).

In the course of my early work on social dreaming, I became aware of the preponderance of associations and other images in the matrix, compared to dreams. In some cases, I noted that after an initial burst of dream images from the participants in the matrix, the contributions would settle into providing a stream of associations; in extreme cases, the dreams were consigned to the very beginning of the matrix only. In my (2010) chapter on the use of social dreaming following the visit of a museum exhibition on the subject of the abolition of the slave trade, I began to notice the way the images from the museum exhibits were finding their way into the social dreaming matrices, and how many of the emerging concerns of the participants in the matrix were expressed purely as associations, with no reference to dream material at all. In fact, in quoting from the original transcripts for the purposes of this paper, there were only 10 instances of dreams compared with 32 instances of associations. This was the beginning of my thinking leading to the visual matrix by suggesting the possibility of a visual stimulus or framework, such as the context of an exhibition, to begin the associative process. In the following extract from this research, the contributions are inspired by associations to the images of ships and the sailors who crossed the Atlantic with their holds full of slaves, images that came from the museum exhibits rather than the dreams of the participants. In this extract the 'A' before each contribution indicates an association or similar, but not a dream. It is, to all intents and purposes, a 'mini' visual matrix:

> Another image that emerged in the course of the second matrix was that of the sailor and his songs. In a similar way to the image of the enslaving of innocent children combined with the hope they represented discussed above, the sailor's song was representative of the double possibility of joy and despair, just as the negro spiritual represented both hope and despair and contained hidden messages:
>
> *A That's the funny thing about the human species, minor differences are highlighted. I have this song going around in my head, I don't know if anyone else can hear it. It goes something like 'Sailor … Sailor…' in a voice that isn't mine, like a song from the deep…*
> *A Is it a waltz, a tango or a foxtrot…?*
> *A As if it came from a mermaid, deeply inviting…*
> *A Spirituals were made on hidden songs and hidden codes… (II)*
>
> As the matrix developed, this sailor's song became ever more sinister as a song that could be expressed in childlike innocence and yet embrace the corruption of reality, such as the reality of the sailors' cargo, representative, therefore, of our blind turning away from the truth through a screen of song and drunkenness:
>
> *A I wonder if the sailor's song referred to had something to do with soul music…*
> *A Sailors had a brutal life, the song reminds me of 'What shall we do with the drunken sailor'. I remember singing this at school, how sailors had to cope with such a hard life, maybe by being drunk, and how innocent this was singing the song as a child at school, how the innocent mixes with the harsh realities…*
> *A The song is quite a violent one too, one of the lines being 'shave his balls with a rusty razor'. (II)* (Manley 2010, pp. 76–77)

The easy flow of associations as demonstrated in this extract prompts some difficult questions about the absolute necessity or not of the use of dreams in social dreaming; whether dreams bring anything different or specifically useful that the associations in the visual matrix cannot; and whether the visual matrix method has any advantages over the use of social dreaming in its original form. As usual, Lawrence, in his intuitive way, had already considered the importance of associations compared to the actual dreams, but he did not follow this through:

> While the dreams may be the currency of the matrix, it is the free associations and the thinking that gives them value. (Lawrence 2003, p. 270)

This is an area for further research. My own experiences of the two methods is that they are surprisingly alike, and this must be an indication of the importance of associations in the social dreaming process, which, although acknowledged by Lawrence, was never given as much importance as the dreams themselves. Having emphasised this aspect of social dreaming, my feeling is that the dreams locate social dreaming squarely in the unconscious. Interestingly, Long and Harney (2013) have combined this essential aspect of social dreaming with the idea of the importance of associations in their coining of the term the 'associative unconscious'. On the other hand, it is not clear to what extent the visual matrix consists of unconscious processes; undoubtedly, it does to some degree, but is it less embedded in this sense than social dreaming? Is there more of a Freudian 'preconscious' presence in the visual matrix than in social dreaming? Can the use of stimulus material at the start of a visual matrix be justifiably interpreted as a manipulation on the part of the researcher or host of the process of the matrix? Is the narrowing effect of excluding dreams from the visual matrix justified by a greater focus and clarity on the topic of research? These are matters of interest for future research and reflection. Whatever the direction of research from this moment on, it is clear that a Deleuzian approach, as explained in this book and in other publications on social dreaming and the visual matrix (Manley, 2018, in press) can provide an overall philosophy that embraces social dreaming in its original version and in its later development in the form of the visual matrix.

Social Dreaming and Hyperobjects

As a clue to what might be appropriate as a research topic for social dreaming, it is interesting to note some recent work on climate change, including the case study in this book. Since Lawrence and many authors in his edited series of books on social dreaming are or were mainly practitioners rather than researchers, their concern was with the effect and utility of social dreaming, not the information that was gathered as data for research purposes. In Lawrence's case, he was keen to use social dreaming as a consultancy tool. Furthermore, there is often a feeling, even if this is not the specific aim of social dreaming, of some form of wellbeing resulting from participating in a matrix, even some form of therapeutic outcome.

These concerns are not those of the researcher. However, the areas that social dreaming can be usefully applied to in research are topics that could be too enormous or grand to be easily assimilated by human comprehension, topics which possibly defy all other qualitative and/or psychosocial methods. There are at the time of writing several small research projects using social dreaming in such contexts. An example of one of these projects, which I discuss below, is the use of social dreaming to investigate climate change and, in particular, the relationship of each of us as single human entities with the whole planetary and ecological system that is threatened by the consequences of global warming. It may be that the appropriateness of social dreaming as a method resides in the nature of the topic as a 'hyperobject', with 'hyperobject' referring to entities that are massively complex in space and time, so much so that they defy human situation and comprehension (Morton 2013).[1] In a case such as this, the 'infinite' nature of social dreaming, interpreted as an ever expanding Deleuzian rhizome, may present us with a criterion for choosing social dreaming as a research method. This too – whether the hyperobject be climate change or some other area of massive complexity – may be a reason for future uses of social dreaming in research.

[1] My thanks to Wendy Hollway, (personal communication), who brought my attention to Morton's definition of 'hyperobject' and its potential as a focus for social dreaming.

In the research currently under discussion, social dreaming is being combined with the experience of art as another means of attempting to grasp the meaning of climate change as a hyperobject. There is a sense today that life's problems and challenges are essentially different to our ancestors' concerns; ours are ineluctably global and universal, inextricably intertwined. Morton calls this sensation – that everything touches and connects to everything else – 'viscous'. By viscous, Morton means that a hyperobject touches all aspects of our daily and mundane lives, even if we cannot 'see' the entire object at once:

> A hyperobject is a thing so vast in both temporal and spatial terms that we can only see slices of it at a time; hyperobjects come in and out of phase with human time; they end up 'contaminating' everything, if we find ourselves inside them (I call this phenomenon *viscosity*). (Morton 2018, p. 125, (author's italics))

An example of this would be the way plastic is connected to the hyperobject of climate change, the fact that there is no innocent local use of plastic in our little home and household, that this plastic will go vast distances and find its way to remote islands in the middle of distant oceans affecting marine life and coming back to haunt us in our local spheres of existence. If this is indeed a definition of human and ecological existence today, then social dreaming, perhaps, is an appropriate method to help us make sense of it. The following extract from a presentation I gave at the Slow Violence art exhibition and conference (University of Hertfordshire, 29 November 2017)[2] illustrates how this can work. There is a dream, then an association, followed by a commentary:

> Dream- "I had a dream about stairs last night, I was going up the stairs. I was entrusted with the care of some toddler. I don't know who the toddler was. We're in this house which was square, but it was a tall like a tower,

[2] This presentation included some of the thinking from another (not the case study in this book) social dreaming/art and climate change event I co-hosted with Paul Hoggett in Dorset. It will be the subject of a forthcoming chapter, co-authored with Wendy Hollway, in a book on climate change, edited by Paul Hoggett (forthcoming).

with stairs going up, around the tower, up and up and up, but with no bannister, so as we went up, there is just a drop right down into the centre of the building. The stairs were sort of incomplete, with bits of building material, and there are gaps in the stairs, you have to get ladders to get further up, but despite all the difficulties we seem to be managing and there's quite a feeling of omnipotence."

Association- "The image of the stairs reminds me of the image of the carbon molecule on the barn wall outside, incredibly intricate and beautiful structure, which I found very moving, and then I noticed one of the ladders on the stairs was broken or only half formed in this microcosmic molecule, and I was wondering what kind of stresses that expresses or whether they were never perfectly formed for some reason. But that image of the broken stairs reminded me of the imperfect but perfectly beautiful cellular structure."

Commentary- In our shared dreams we can walk around the atom and feel it and see it. The reality of our climate dilemma is made visible through the dream, we see the unseen of the carbon atom, and we think the unknown. We move through the gaps, the spaces between the lines, the energy between the words. We feel the responsibility for the toddler. The climb is hard but it can be done. The danger is real but can be overcome. The stairs that take us up are flawed, like the step-like patterns on the atom, but they are still beautiful and can be negotiated. Now we can talk. Now I feel a belonging, a being-becoming part of this system. Now I can see it and feel it.

Association- "So for me it's like the greatest safety that we're all able to kind of just talk … about 'it', because 'it' is the most terrifying thing that there is."

Association- We can feel the fear that hides behind the scientific text, the fear of climbing up the steps for nothing… (Manley 2017)

As explained in the extract, in this example – in which reference is made to an art work featuring a hugely magnified coccolithophore, (a microscopic, unicellular organism found in the sea) – the hyperobject of climate change is opened out to the imagination through the art work and then through the dream and the ensuing association so that what is impossible to see (and therefore to comprehend) is given to the viewer and presented both to the perceiving eye and retina and to the 'inner' eye of the dream. The fact that the coccolithophore is misidentified as a 'carbon molecule' is not a problem. In fact, it indicates how its inspiration as part of an art work and its creative transformation or interpretation into a carbon atom is conducive to the understanding of the matrix. Since the story of climate change is centred around carbon emissions (although in fact science tells us that there is more to these emissions than simply carbon), it is important that the dream and the participants in the matrix can imagine it as a carbon molecule, which, *in the context of the matrix*, is actually true.

The social dreaming matrix, then, enables participants to 'see' the hyperobject of climate change in this fashion. The way this works brings to mind Deleuze's discussion of Bergson's work on images and perception (Deleuze 2005a). An image or an image of a thing perceives itself and perceives all other things in proportion to the actions it receives from other images and things and all its consequent reactions. That is to say that the image is not necessarily perceived as the thing in itself but perceived nevertheless through the gaps and intervals between itself and other images. This is why movement is so vital to Bergson and Deleuze, the movement in the intervals between images is part of the image-perceiving process. In social dreaming this movement is the constantly fluctuating and pulsing movement in the intensities of affect between images. This is what is implied in the dream quoted above which refers to gaps in the stairs, and the ensuing association that connects theses gaps with the broken stair formation of the molecule. The images from the dreams and associations are not perceived as things in themselves but through the movements of affect *between* the images that constitute the rhizome. This helps us to understand how, through the image of the 'carbon molecule' and the way it is injected with the affect of the dreams in the example given above (not the image in and of itself), we can perceive the hyperobject. The gap between the dream image and the physical image of the microscopic 'molecule' is connected by an affect identified as 'fear', which is hiding, so to speak, behind the words of rational science. The thinking of the matrix suggests that the facts of science obscure the fear by presenting facts free of emotion and therefore blind us to the hyperobject of climate change which, without the fear associated to it cannot be perceived. In this process, the participants in the matrix are able to 'see' the hyperobject in the smallest example of what cannot normally be seen, the image of the 'carbon molecule', which we know is responsible for climate change. The idea that this tiny 'carbon molecule' can be responsible for vast and catastrophic disaster is only comprehended through this process. It is rather like William Blake's idea of being able to 'see a World in a Grain of Sand' (Blake 1977, p. 506), but through social dreaming, it is an experience to be felt by all in the matrix, and not just by a genius poet.

In something so little, we perceive the vastness of the hyperobject. In the gap between the dream image and the physical microscopic image, the hyperobject is perceived as a 'prehension', something that is perceived but not cognitively apprehended – within the space that connects them as part objects. This is how Deleuze puts it:

> An atom, for example, perceives infinitely more than we do and, at the limit perceives the whole universe – from the point where the actions which are exercised on it begin, to the point where the actions which it emits go. (Deleuze 2005b, p. 66)

The associated affect that includes fear is brought out and made explicit because the matrix provides a safe space for doing so; the implication is that without this safe space, (made safe through the creative and imaginative process of the image-affects of the rhizome), there would be no possibility of sharing the fear, which therefore might be repressed or ignored, and no consequent understanding of the hyperobject which is here given imaginative and affective form.

References

Agresta, D. (in press). Festino di San Silvestro: Rites and social dreaming. In Long, S. and Manley, J. (Eds.), *Social Dreaming: Philosophy research and practice*. London: Routledge.

Balogh, R. (2010). 'In dreams begins responsibility': A self-study about how insights from dreams may be brought into the sphere of action research. *Educational Action Research*, 18(4), pp. 517–529.

Balogh, R. (2015). In the Forests of the Night: An inquiry into the relevance of social dreaming for action research. *Educational Action Research*, 21(3), pp. 312–330.

Balogh, R. (in press). An action research study of dream-sharing as socially constituted practice. In Long, S. and Manley, J. (Eds.), *Social Dreaming: Philosophy research and practice*. London: Routledge.

Berman, H. and Manley, J. (2018). Social Dreaming and creativity in South Africa: Imagi(ni)ng the unthought known. In Adlam, J., Gilligan, J., Kluttig, T., and Lee, B.X. (Eds.), *Creative States: Overcoming Violence*. Vol 1, Part 4, Ch. 2, pp. 221–237. London: Jessica Kingsley.

Blake, W. (1977). *The Complete Poems*. London: Penguin.

Deleuze, G. (2005a). *Bergsonism*. New York: Zone Books.

Deleuze, G. (2005b). *Cinema 1*. London: Continuum.

Froggett, L., Manley, J., and Roy, A. (2015). The Visual Matrix Method: Imagery and Affect in a Group-based Research Setting. *Forum: Qualitative Social Research./ Forum Qualitative Sozialforschung / Forum: Qualitative Social Research*, 16 (3).

Gosling, J. and Case, P. (2013). Social dreaming and ecocentric ethics: Sources of non-rational insight in the face of climate change catastrophe. *Organization*, pp. 1–17.

Hoggett, P. (Ed.). (forthcoming). *Climate Psychology: Psycho-Social Research on Human/Nature Relations in the Age of Climate Change*. Basingstoke: Palgrave Macmillan.

Karolia, I. and Manley, J. (2018). 1 in 5 Brit Muslims' Sympathy for Jihadis': An insight into the Lived Experience of UK Muslims following the Terror Attacks in Paris. In Adlam, J., Gilligan, J., Kluttig, T., and Lee, B.X. (Eds.), *Creative States: Overcoming Violence*, Vol. 1, Part III, pp. 161–177. London: Jessica Kingsley.

La Nave, F. (2010). Image: Reflections on the treatment of images and dreams in art psychotherapy groups. *International Journal of Art Therapy*, 15(1), pp. 13–24.

La Nave, F. (in press). Looking for Treasure in Dream Water. In Long, S. and Manley, J. (Eds.), *Social Dreaming: Philosophy research and practice*. London: Routledge.

Lawrence, W.G. (Ed.). (2003). *Experiences in Social Dreaming*. London: Karnac.

Lawrence, W.G. (Ed.). (2010). *The Creativity of Social Dreaming*. London: Karnac.

Long, S. and Harney, M. (2013). The associative unconscious. In Long, S. (Ed.), *Socioanalytic Methods*. London: Karnac.

Long, S. and Manley, J. (Eds.). (in press). *Social Dreaming: Philosophy, research and practice*. London: Routledge.

Manley, J. (2010). The slavery in the mind: Inhibition and exhibition. Chapter 6 in Lawrence, W. Gordon (Ed.), *The Creativity of Social Dreaming*. London: Karnac, pp. 65–82.

Manley, J. (2017). The Unthought Known of Climate Change, unpublished paper presented at the Slow Violence Conference, University of Hertfordshire.

Manley, J. (2018). 'Every human being is an artist': From social representation to creative experiences of self. In Cummins, A.M. and Williams, N. (Eds.), *Researching Beneath the Surface*, Vol. 2. London: Routledge.

Manley, J. (in press). Associative thinking: A Deleuzian perspective on social dreaming. In Long, S. and Manley, J. (Eds.), *Social dreaming: Philosophy, research and practice*. London: Routledge.

Manley, J., Roy, A., and Froggett, L. (2015). Researching Recovery from Substance Misuse Using Visual Methods. In Hardwick, L., Smith, R., and Worsley, A. (Eds.), *Innovation in Social Work Research*. London: Jessica Kingsley, pp. 191–210.

Manley, J. and Roy, A. (2017). The visual matrix: A psycho-social method for discovering unspoken complexities in social care practice. *Psychoanalysis, Culture and Society*, 22(2), pp. 132–153.

Manley, J. and Trustram, M. (2018). 'Such endings that are not over': The slave trade, social dreaming and affect in a museum. *Psychoanalysis, Culture and Society*, 23(1), pp. 77–96.

Manley, J., Gosling, J., and Patman, D. (submitted for publication) Full of dreams: Social dreaming as liminal psychic space.

Mersky, R. (2013). Social dream-drawing "Drawing brings the inside out". In Long, S. (Ed.), *Socioanalytic Methods*. London: Karnac.

Morton, T. (2013). *Hyperobjects. Philosophy and Ecology after the End of the World*. London: University of Minnesota Press.

Morton, T. (2018). *Being Ecological*. Milton Keyes: Pelican.

Page, M., Grisoni, L., and Turner, A. (2014). Dreaming fairness and re-imagining equality and diversity through participative aesthetic inquiry. *Management Learning*, 45(5), pp. 577–592.

Roy, A. and Manley, J. (2017). Recovery and Movement: Allegory and 'journey' as a means of exploring recovery from substance misuse. *Journal of Social Work Practice*, 31(2), pp. 191–204.

Sievers, B. (2008). 'Perhaps It Is The Role of Pictures To Get In Contact with the Uncanny': The Social Photo Matrix as a Method to Promote the Understanding of the Unconscious in Organizations. *Organisational and Social Dynamics*, Number 2 / 2008, pp. 234–254(21).

Sievers, B. (2013). Thinking organisations through photographs: The social photo-matrix as a method for understanding organisations in depth. In Long, S. (Ed.), *Socioanalytic Methods*. London: Karnac, pp. 129–153.

Sievers, B. (2014). It is difficult to think in the slammer: A social-photo matrix in a penal institution. In *The Psychosocial and Organization Studies*. Basingstoke: Palgrave Macmillan.

14

Using the Virtual for the Real

From Virtual to Real and Back Again

The difficulty of a hyperobject is in its massiveness compared to the actors within it, of whom our beings are tiny parts. However, as indicated above, a process such as social dreaming may facilitate the location of self in relation to the hyper which makes for a form of 'seeing' that would otherwise be impossible to achieve. This kind of 'seeing' is virtual, it is the mind's (and the body's) eye. It is connected to creativity and imagination and yet at the same time it is connected to our bodies and, moving outwards from our bodies, to the external world – let's call this the 'real' – which we are either experiencing or have experienced as a self in the world. There is no barrier or doorway that can be traversed to go from one state to another. The border or boundary is unclear and gradual. I have referred to this space, which is between the virtual of social dreaming and the real of external experience as a liminal space (Manley et al. forthcoming). In her seminal work on virtual technology, *Alone Together* (2011), Sherry Turkle touches upon the same term to describe the virtual world as being connected to the external world in this sense, which is why the virtual is not separate from or an escape from the real but an informing and contributing part of the real in the way it liminally connects virtual and real,

J. Manley, *Social Dreaming, Associative Thinking and Intensities of Affect*,
Studies in the Psychosocial, https://doi.org/10.1007/978-3-319-92555-4_14

occupying a space that is 'literally on the boundary of things' (Turkle 2011, p. 213). To be on or in the boundary is tantamount to saying there is no such boundary, or that a new boundary is created outside the space created within the old boundary, and then this new boundary is liable to be inhabited in its turn, so that the boundaries are forever being newly created, pushed away and then recreated forever, as long as the virtual is in constant play and movement with the real. In the virtual, and so in social dreaming, the psychic boundary is an inchoate space. The importance of this realisation in social dreaming is to grasp the fact that the business of social dreaming is not about providing an escape from the real world, or an alternative world of the imagination and creativity. Whatever space is created in the social dreaming matrix it is never out of touch with the experience of the matrix and the experienced world of the participants that exists with reference both to the liminal space of the matrix as well as the actual reality of the room and situation of the social dreaming event, all combined with the memories of each of the participants, either individually and as part of their internal biographies and narratives, or in the social world that they inevitably share outside the experience of the matrix. This is why it is not infrequent to have participants in social dreaming refer directly to the physical space that they occupy. This actual space can then be expanded to physical spaces that have been experienced but are recent experiences and then further expanded to the social world beyond, with none of this process necessarily following the linear sequence I have just described, but becoming part of a spontaneous and haphazard rhizomatic constellation that gives meaning to and interconnects to all levels of the virtual and the real. For example, in the social dreaming matrices that were run in a museum to celebrate the abolition of the slave trade (Manley 2010; Manley and Trustram 2018), a reference to the wooden panelling of the room, which was the actual physical space of the social dreaming event, was merged into the image-affects of the matrix:

> …the 'past' image of the slaves in the hold of the slave ship became the 'present' image and affect of the participants in the SD 'locked' inside a 'wooden' room: 'I was struck about coming through the door here and the door being locked behind us, a sense of claustrophobia … like in the ships,

> being left here but in this case we're in a gracious Jacobean room' (Social Dreaming Workshop). (Manley and Trustram 2018)

The physical space that was outside this room but still in the museum, i.e. the exhibition space, also became part of the matrix:

> By this time it was clear to the shared thinking in the second Matrix that the exhibition was like a dream space that enabled participants to carry 'the dream of the past' and allowed them to go to a place they had never physically been to but yet, at the same time, had in some sense 'been to'. (Manley 2010, p. 70)

Finally, the memories of the social dreaming experience survive or live on as potential memories or ripples that themselves connect further with the social worlds of the participants – another time, another place – which may also include further images, as in my experience of the same series of social dreaming matrices on slavery:

> The effects of the Matrix on creative thinking can last beyond the Matrix itself. At the moment of writing, for example, my mind sees the painting 'The Last of England' by Ford Maddox Brown – where an emigrating couple cling to their child's little hand as they make their journey to a new land – in a new light. It is as if the couple in the painting represent the inhumanity of being forced away from one's homeland, slaves to circumstance, as if the little child will never experience the freedom of childhood as understood in the Matrix. This thought helps me to understand the plight of the slaves on their transatlantic journey. (Manley 2010, p. 75)

Where Is Your Comfort Zone?

As Turkle says, in her study of the virtual, 'it is not unusual for people to feel more comfortable in an unreal place than a real one because they feel that in simulation they show their better and perhaps truer self' (Turkle 2011, p. 212). She goes on to describe how some of the 'experimentation and self-reflection' that comes about as a result of creating an online identity that is different to your externally experienced self can almost become unwittingly 'therapeutic' (pp. 212–213). This sensation of experimentation and self-reflection and a sense of wellbeing is also true of people's experience of social dreaming; and although participants in social dreaming are not specifically finding another identity, they are in a sense losing their routinely experienced identity for the duration of the matrix in favour of something other than themselves, that I have been calling the BwO. This object that is created by the matrix in a circular and ever moving collaboration with others, consists of the accumulated dreams, images and associations of all the participants, with the added effect of a certain freedom of expression engendered by being able to address thoughts and feelings in the guise of dreams and figurative language in a non-judgemental fashion, as and when each participant desires to do so. In this way, complex thoughts and affects that might not normally surface in standard discourse, replete with anxieties and defences, may be given an expression that may appear to be 'truer to the self' in each participant's contribution. Similarly, this individual 'truth', garnered from the sharing of 'truths', is a sensation that might be assigned to the virtual in the matrix as opposed to the external 'truths' of the world outside this reverie that are not the concern of the shared experience of social dreaming, or at least are placed as secondary, though linked, to the concerns of the matrix. It then turns out, as a result of this, that many people who participate in social dreaming matrices for the first time are at first apprehensive about the idea of sharing dreams with strangers, but by the time they finish, they mostly report having experienced sensations of feeling good, a sense of surprise, of being fired up emotionally, of engagement, bonding and creativity.

From Images to Action

If social dreaming helps in the production of this liminal space of the virtual with a permanent connection to the real, avoiding false barriers and boundaries, auto-creating a space for 'experimentation and self-reflection', it may be legitimate to ask 'what for', or what does it 'do'? Epistemologically speaking, this is not necessarily a question that needs to be asked, since the self-generated support that is implied in creative thinking for the participants in the matrix is its own justification. However, living as we do in a world of measuring targets and outcomes, it is still a question that will be asked. Indeed, in Gordon Lawrence's experiences in trying to introduce social dreaming to the world of organisational consultancy, this may have been one of the problems he faced in attempting to persuade corporate leaders of its utility or to demonstrate a practical outcome beyond that of the managing directors of a company reporting social dreaming as having been 'a liberating experience in terms of thinking' (Lawrence 1998, p. 140).

According to Ellis (2005), 'appropriate imagery helps us to trigger feelings that in turn will trigger appropriate actions' (p. 154). Ellis points to the role of imagery to allow for an exploration of the intentionality of an emotion. By suggesting that the image is more than the reflection or embodiment of emotion, a purpose is given to the image, which can lead to action. In an intriguing way, in his discussion of the role of images in discovering emotional sense, Ellis describes many of the features of social dreaming. For example, without using the term 'affect', he distinguishes between emotions such as 'angry' or 'hurt' and what can be discovered instead through finding 'fresh imagery that is specific to the particular felt sense of the moment' (Ellis 2005, p. 153). He points to the value of 'a conglomerate of intentional felt senses' (p. 153) in a way that resonates with the 'collage' of images of social dreaming. He continues by suggesting two ways that human beings may be able to use images:

> … there is an ability to temper and refine imagery, and to use imagery in the service not only of understanding the intentionality of emotions, but also in the service of meta-emotions that allow us to imagine ways that we would like to feel, but are not yet feeling. (Ellis 2005, p. 154)

Emotions, therefore, when they are contained within an image, become complex and multi-layered evocations of affect. The blankness of a simple emotion on its own (such as 'anger') may not lead to any understanding of its complexity or genuine source or, therefore, to any kind of effective action. However, when held in an image, and, in social dreaming, when this image is given further depth and perspective through accumulation and interconnectivity with other images, the simple emotion is converted into the richness of shared affect that not only rings true but can be presented as open for exploration with others. Someone's anger may be another's pain, but together they are something else that needs to be understood, since the anger will contain pain and the pain anger, even if this conjoining may be too difficult for one person on her own to discover. In my work with Ismail Karolia on British Muslim identity (2018), this became clear in the social dreaming sessions that revealed emotions beyond pain and anger. Traditional discourse might reveal the anger, pain and frustration of British Muslims, but the social dreaming revealed something more, something like the 'state of the impossible' that British Muslims were expressing in the social dreaming sessions, where multiple emotions are inextricably layered over one another in a communication of nuanced and desperate conflicting and unresolvable affect:

> It is as if 'mainstream' discrimination has been replaced with what British Muslims experience as a wholesale attack on all manifestations of Islamic culture and identity; as if this identity were evil and impossible to maintain, requiring a dismantling of inherited identities and roots with nothing to replace them, except cultural rejection and a pragmatic acceptance of a 'better' and 'Christian' British version of identity, euphemistically labelled 'integration'. The impossibility of accepting this as the only solution to solving an identity crisis comes across in the social dreaming in the vacillations between waking realities and dream states, leaving a sense of identity in limbo between an exterior reality that cannot be embraced and an interior dream state that cannot be made real. (Karolia and Manley 2018)

As a complex iteration from Muslims themselves, they, as community, are able to express a complex felt truth that would otherwise have had to be filtered through some observer, analyst or interpreter, possibly watered down or otherwise reduced.

As such, we suggest, this is the kind of knowledge that could be used to inform the controversial Government Prevent programme, where simple truths are taken for granted and are easily interpreted as being racist or close to racist:

> … despite the claim that the Prevent duty is solely about safeguarding, it is not applicable in Northern Ireland, even though the MI5 threat rating for

> Northern Ireland-related terrorism is the same as from international terrorism. A government official is reported to have told Gavin Robinson MP: "Don't push the issue too far. It is really a counter-Islamic strategy"…
>
> Yet in the UK, the idea of referring innocent Muslims is not deemed to be equally counter-productive. (Versi 2017)

Through understanding the almost Catch 22 situation of British Muslims as expressed in these social dreaming sessions, the complexity of wanting to be both British and Muslim at the same time and this being a possible source of suspicion, maybe initiatives such as the Prevent programme could be better managed to become more effective, sustainable and ethical. Social dreaming used in this way can lead towards action through the identification of what Ellis calls the 'intentionality' of the emotion.

Ellis' second suggestion, that imagery can create 'meta-emotions' that can enable people to imagine emotions that they might like to feel, may explain the agency that is sometimes observed in social dreaming for eliciting what Turkle calls our 'better' selves. There may be several levels of psychological blocks and/or defences against accessing this better self, and this may hinder certain forms of progress. If this were the case, social dreaming could positively contribute to progressive debates. An example of this was discussed in the previously cited work on social dreaming and the abolition of the slave trade (Manley and Trustram 2018) where it was noted that a social dreaming group was more likely than a debating group to accept the relevance of a social apology for the slave trade. The shame, anger and humiliation of apology was defended against mainly through the argument that it happened so long ago that people today cannot feel responsible for the actions of their ancestors. In the social dreaming sessions, the use of image-affects contained in the dreams and associations facilitated and enabled an imaginative empathy with the plight of the African slaves that made apology more possible through a greater affective connection with the issues. The desire to apologise was a feeling that could be given space in the matrix, something that was deeply 'known', to return to Bollas' terminology, but had until then been 'unthought'.

'Perception Is Master of Space in the Exact Measure in Which Action Is Master of Time'

Bergson's linking of perception to space, and action to time, quoted above (in Deleuze 2005, p. 67), provides a framework for demonstrating how social dreaming can go from image to action, as discussed above. The social dreaming matrix can thus be conceived as a space of perception of image-affects, which works in a function of timelessness defined as 'reverie', while the ensuing action occurs in a situation of time. In terms of language, which is the main 'translator' of the images of the matrix, it is interesting to note that perception in this sense is compared by Deleuze to a noun, and the action in time to a verb (2005, p. 67). In terms of boundaries between perception and action, space and time, as already suggested above, there are none, or if there are, they are constantly shifting: 'One passes imperceptibly from perception to action' (Deleuze 2005, p. 67). What I have been calling the image-affect of social dreaming is a description of the original image (dream or association) in the matrix and the space of affect between this image and the action, in Deleuzian terms. Deleuze describes this as passing through an interval from 'perception-image' to 'action-image' with 'affection' in the in-between space between these manifestations of image, (remembering at all times that this 'affection' is always the Spinozian affect, as adopted by Bergson and Deleuze). This affect, which is the most important aspect of the images, is indefinable as or by any of the images but is nevertheless inextricably part of those images as it defines it at any moment (moments that come and go) as it travels along the spectrum of the interval between them. This is described by Deleuze as a "quality' as a lived state (adjective)' (2005, p. 67). In a way that exquisitely describes the rhizome of the social dreaming matrix, it is possible to see how Deleuze's description of that which is most important – the affect – being nevertheless not the centre from which other pieces or strands evolve. Instead, since this is a rhizomatic description, affect is situated in the 'centre of indetermination' (Deleuze 2005, p. 67). The nexus between image and action, in this schema, is therefore affect, and by definition, therefore, the quality of the action is dependent on the quality of the affect, while this, in turn, is mutually dependent on the quality of the images of the matrix and the space that is created for that perception to occur. In other words, if this is indeed a valid description of the process of social dreaming, it suggests that the relevance of social dreaming to action, or decision-making leading to action, is that it can provide a more complete, nuanced, rich and enriching quality of affective knowledge to a particular question or issue, without which the action risks being impoverished.

The Objects of Action and Acting on Objects

As already discussed in Chap. 10, intersubjectivity is key to the matrix's rhizomatic structure, and it is clear from the way that the image-affect is connected to the potential for action that this intersubjectivity extends beyond the timeless space of the matrix and into the action movement of time. There is a delicate balance to be had here between this perception of intersubjectivity and the handling of objects, especially if we are to move from perception to action. One way to understand the place of action is to move away from the rhizome, which is always intersubjective by definition, and allow for the creation of an object. Arguably, this happens the minute the fluctuating image-affects of the BwO consisting of the dreams and associations of the rhizome are written down. This changes the process and quality of the thinking in the matrix from rhizome to object, into thinking about thinking, and in doing so makes an object of thinking itself, which Clark suggests is a defining feature of human beings. According to Clark (who of course is not referring to social dreaming):

> … as soon as we formulate a thought in words or on paper, it becomes an object for both ourselves and for others. As an object, it is the kind of thing we can have thoughts about. In creating the object, we need to have no thoughts about thoughts, but once it is there, the opportunity immediately exists to attend to it as an object in its own right.' (Clark 2011, p. 58)

Sometimes, the post-matrix discussion or reflection dialogue consists of an unannotated conversation, but often, and certainly for research purposes, the post-matrix discussion consists of the host noting down the comments and ideas from the participants of the matrix. This then, would be the first instance of writing down. The second instance would be the writing of the transcript. The post-matrix discussion provides a hybrid condition that bridges the matrix space and the 'real world' space. As such, although an object is being created through the notes, some of the experience of reverie and intersubjectivity remains. However, when the transcript is written, there is a definite object to analyse. This has both advantages and disadvantages, and much thought and time has gone into developing a method of data analysis that can retain and recreate the rhizomatic structure of image-affects, with its subjective content, while simultaneously recognising the transcript as an object for analysis. This development of an analytical protocol has mostly been developed as part of the elaboration of the visual matrix, discussed above. The analytical process is very much about the tension between maintaining the original intersubjective rhizomatic communication of the original matrix while moving simultaneously towards some degree of objectivisation:

> The interpretation process is designed to allow the visual thinking of the matrix to 'speak its own language'. That is to say, it respects the emotional and image-based expression of the visual matrix. It does so by allowing the images to retain their multiple meanings and complexity by incorporating further association and returning to the original material as part of the analysis. In this way, the process attempts to avoid foreclosure through premature interpretation. (Manley et al. 2015, p. 196)

Eventually, after a series of research panels and the writing up of results, the data is made into an object where interpretation has closed off the possibility of further intersubjective associations. This is a process that inevitably loses the richness of the multi-layered rhizome in the name of clarity. It may be that there are other ways of approaching the data by somehow retaining the rhizomatic structure of the original experience, and this would be an interesting pursuit for further research. I believe that it was a similar concern (although not related to social dreaming) that may have guided Deleuze and Guattari to use creative and often poetic-sounding language in the pursuit of philosophy, which may also account for what some people regard as a frustrating opacity and long-windedness in some of their work. This is especially true of the book they wrote as a rhizome, *A Thousand Plateaus*, which they call an 'image-book', written in 'plateaus' rather than in conventional and logical sequences (Deleuze and Guattari 1988, p. 22). Maybe there is something that can be learnt from their original experiment for future analysis of social dreaming data.

References

Clark, A. (2011). *Supersizing the Mind: Embodiment, action and cognitive extension*. Oxford: OUP.

Deleuze, G. (2005). *Cinema 1*. London: Continuum.

Deleuze, G. and Guattari, F. (1988). *A Thousand Plateaus*. London: Continuum.

Ellis, R.D. (2005). The roles of imagery and meta-emotion in deliberate choice and moral psychology. *Journal of Consciousness Studies*, 12(8–10), pp. 140–157.

Karolia, I. and Manley, J. (2018). 1 in 5 Brit Muslims' Sympathy for Jihadis': An insight into the Lived Experience of UK Muslims following the Terror Attacks in Paris. In Adlam, J., Gilligan, J., Kluttig, T., and Lee, B.X. (Eds.), *Creative States: Overcoming Violence*, Vol. 1, Part III, pp. 161–177. London: Jessica Kingsley.

Lawrence, W.G. (Ed.). (1998). *Social Dreaming @ Work*. London: Karnac.

Manley, J. (2010). The slavery in the mind: Inhibition and exhibition. Chapter 6 in Lawrence, W. Gordon (Ed.), *The Creativity of Social Dreaming*. London: Karnac, pp. 65–82.

Manley, J., Roy, A., and Froggett, L. (2015). Researching Recovery from Substance Misuse Using Visual Methods. In Hardwick, L., Smith, R., and Worsley, A. (Eds.), *Innovation in Social Work Research*. London: Jessica Kingsley.

Manley, J. and Trustram, M. (2018). 'Such endings that are not over': The slave trade, social dreaming and affect in a museum. *Psychoanalysis, Culture and Society*, 23(1), pp. 77–96.

Manley, J., Gosling, J. and Patman, D. (submitted for publication). *Full of dreams: Social dreaming as liminal psychic space*.

Turkle, S. (2011). *Alone Together*. NY: Basic Books.

Versi, M. (2017). 'The latest Prevent figures show why the strategy needs an independent review'. In *The Guardian*. (www.theguardian.com/commentisfree/2017/nov/10/prevent-strategy-statistics-independent-review-home-office-muslims) Accessed 14.02.18.

15

The Final Plateau

Deleuze and Guattari's final plateau will never arrive, although even they twisted their image-book into a circle so as to prevent its rhizome from ever expanding:

> It is composed of plateaus. We have given it a circular form, but only for laughs. (Deleuze and Guattari 1988, p. 22)

This speaks to the difficulty and the creative wonder of social dreaming, discussed in the section above on analysis and interpretation. The difficulty is knowing when to stop the accumulation of image-affects and associations. There is no answer to this, except through the cut-off point of the hosting of the matrix and some form of control of the interpretation process. But these are both artificial stops designed so that we can grasp something of the meaning of the image-affects in continuous expansion. This need to grasp is that of the cognitive mind, since there appears to be no end of the ability of the human experience of knowing that constitutes the social dreaming process, a knowing that is beyond the merely cognitive. Thankfully, this book has not been written as a rhizome, so it is now drawing to a close.

J. Manley, *Social Dreaming, Associative Thinking and Intensities of Affect*,
Studies in the Psychosocial, https://doi.org/10.1007/978-3-319-92555-4_15

In this chapter, I want to summarise the principle features of social dreaming as they have been discussed above.

Visual Thinking

Above all, the social dreaming matrix is about thinking visually. Unlike many other visual methods (for example Photovoice, the social photo-matrix, dream drawing-matrix, which include physical images and/or objects), the visual aspect is almost always internal and mental. There are exceptions to this, especially with those social dreaming practitioners who use social dreaming in the context of art therapy, including mark making and artefacts, but in the vast majority of cases, social dreaming is about internal mental images.

Visualisations of Affect: The Image-Affect

The images in social dreaming, whether they emanate from dreams or associations, are always harbouring affect. They are a means of transmitting affect that would otherwise not be expressed due to the inherent complexity of affect (not to be confused with emotion) or for other reasons, for example the presence of taboo subjects or hyperobjects that are difficult to explain or explore in standard discourse. This combination of image and affect has been referred to in this book as the image-affect.

Social Dreaming Creates a Rhizome

Although the delivery of the dreams and associations is necessarily sequential, due to the passing of time, the creation of the matrix as a container encourages a sense of reverie and a certain feeling of timelessness within this temporary space. These are the conditions for the creation of the matrix of images and associations of the social dreaming process. The way the images and affects begin to interconnect during the course of the matrix is rhizomatic rather than sequential. An image from the beginning of the matrix may resonate more strongly and create a connection with another image much later on in the matrix, and there may be other, less relevant images in between. The rhizome is multi-layered, like the Deleuzian plateaus, and the images are interconnected like a collage that is in constant movement according to the varying intensities of affect of the interconnecting image-affects that are forever changing according to participant perception and as long as further and continuing images and associations are added to the rhizome.

More Than One Meaning

As a result of this rhizomatic structure, the matrix may offer more than one meaning emerging from the images and affects at any given time, with none of these different meanings being any more correct or incorrect than another.

States of Becoming

The way that affect can be converted into knowledge is through the Deleuzian idea of becoming. Since affect is more than simply stated emotions (rage, sadness, hate… and so on), the complexity of the multifarious cluster of emotions in the form of a 'bloc of sensations' is best experienced through a feeling of being drawn into the image-affect in such a way as to become immersed in the sensation of becoming-affect. Since this is normally an affect contained within an image, the sensation of becoming-affect is equivalent to becoming-[the image]. In the case study in Chap. 9, an example of this was becoming-seal.

The Unthought Known

This term, which was originally coined by Christopher Bollas, refers to the idea that the process of social dreaming enables the creation of a space called the matrix where aspects of the participants' social experience which are subliminally known to them are given an opportunity to emerge into consciousness through the recounting of dream images, and in this way they become thoughts. What was known but hidden acquires a space for being thought about, and therefore to be considered, as part of the shared thinking of the matrix.

The Social Dreaming Process Is Intersubjective

One of the features of the rhizomatic matrix is that all the relationships, whether these are between participants or the combinations of image-affects of the rhizome, are intersubjective. There is no dominant item and neither is there a dyadic relationship based on a form of power that would produce a doer and done to dynamic. It is only at a later stage of analysis and interpretation that this intersubjectivity is disturbed and gives way to the creation of an object in the form of a transcript prepared for analysis, in the case of research.

The Body Without Organs

The oft mentioned idea of social dreaming that the participants are interested in the dream, not the dreamer is one of the most persistent and important aspects of social dreaming, particularly so because dreams in psychoanalysis are traditionally expected to be a private communication between analyst and analysand, with no social content worth sharing. The opposite is true of social dreaming, where the dreamer in part loses possession of the dream as it is offered to the participants in the matrix. Once in the social dreaming matrix, the individuals are no longer directly connected to the dream and the dream is not linked to the dreamer by others. In other words, no interpretation is made about the possible meaning of the dream content in relation to any one person. From a Deleuzian perspective, this is the same as saying that the individual 'bodies *with* organs' (the participants) recede from any personalised connection with the process of the shared dreams and associations; instead, these image-affects create a new 'body', a 'body without organs', consisting of a living entity which is not viewed from inside a body outwards, but rather exists as an entity in itself.

Creativity and Social Dreaming

Social dreaming is most often reported as being an enjoyable experience for participants. This may be due, in part, to the inherent creativity of the process, where people are being invited to 'play' (in a Winnicottian sense of the word) with the image-affects of the dreams and associations in order to imagine different configurations and possible meanings in the shared, safe space of the matrix. The resonance with the creative imagination of art and culture seems to have made the connections between social dreaming and exhibitions and art therapy especially fruitful.

Timelessness and Reverie

The imagination at work in the matrix is facilitated by a sense of reverie and an uncanny sensation of timelessness, which encourages calm and reflexivity. This sensation of the matrix is contrasted with the time bound action that might take place outside the matrix, which might provide an internal/external combination as a result of the social dreaming process. This 'timeless space' is an experience that the social dreaming matrix can offer to participants and provides an experiential experience of Foucauldian and Bergsonian time. Maybe social dreaming can use this knowledge of time as experienced in the matrix to enable or encourage an all-encompassing view of history that makes the past relevant to present-future time, duration in a Bergsonian sense.

Transforming Thinking

Lawrence claimed that social dreaming transformed thinking. This book has tried to show how this might be so using largely a Deleuzian lens. Social dreaming, by bringing into consideration the sharing of dreams and associations in the social space of the matrix transforms thinking by providing a forum for this kind of thinking to emerge and be considered as interesting and valuable in its own right. This kind of thinking is closely linked to knowing through affect, rather than intellectual cognition on its own. The eventual transformation will reside in the way such thinking can be used beyond the space of the matrix, in the 'real' world. This is an area for further research. The use of dreams in this way is far removed from a Freudian approach that understands dreams to be only the result of repression, which need to be removed from the unconscious in order to better manage a healthy mind. In social dreaming, the positive aspects of dreams, and by implication the unconscious, become part of a way of thinking that recognises the validity of thought in its multi-layered possibilities that include dreams and the importance of the associative unconscious.

The Working Hypothesis

The thinking described in the previous section requires a willingness to think with uncertainty, a kind of negative capability that allows for the thinking to occur without a need to immediately seek out an answer or some concrete direction. Instead of creating a hypothesis to be proved or defined (which may leave out other possible meanings, ideas and affects), the way of working with thinking in social dreaming encourages the development of working hypotheses. That is to say, an indication or idea of what might be happening as the image-affects are being produced and presented to the space, without a need to reach definitive conclusions. A working hypothesis is suggestive and not requiring of proof.

Difficulties, Conflicts and Hyperobjects

It might be that social dreaming has a particular use in the context of attempting to visualise and transform into knowledge situations that are in some sense hyperobjects. The example I have used in this book is that of climate change, however, something can be 'hyper' when it is too difficult for the cognitive mind to grasp in other ways too. For example, social dreaming can be used to bring to knowledge the unfathomable in situations that include trauma or apparently irreconcilable disparities, such as the question of British-Muslim identity, which I also mention above.

Social Dreaming and Ecology

The rhizomatic patterns that emerge in social dreaming mirror in some ways the patterns of nature. It may be that to participate in social dreaming therefore creates a patterning of thought that more closely resembles the systems and structures of ecology. The sharing of images, dreams and associations in the social dreaming matrix is autopoietic, self-generating and autonomous, and creates, in this fashion, the BwO. It can be usefully compared to a 'dissipative structure' and in a sense can be seen as imitating the process of living systems.

Reference

Deleuze, G. and Guattari, F. (1988). *A Thousand Plateaus*. London: Continuum.

16

Concluding

Applicability and Relevance

There is something ineludibly esoteric about social dreaming. A quick glance at popular publications on dreams and associated topics that seem to be linked to dreams and dream work would be sufficient to make this unfortunate connection. There are many who, before experiencing the process, are sceptical about its value beyond some form of marginalised activity for dreamers and communities, groups and thinkers, more concerned with the so-called mind-body problem and closely associated with various spiritual approaches to life, rather than concerned with research. My personal experience of the process is that all such thoughts are dissipated when someone actually experiences a matrix. This book has, therefore, attempted to place social dreaming in a psychosocial and philosophical context, which, while not mainstream, is not aligned to the spiritual and/or mystical. There is nothing strange about dreaming: we spend half our lives thinking in this way.

The relevance of thinking within the social dreaming process can be understood in two ways: firstly, the intrinsic value of this way of thinking; and secondly the practical applications the method might have in different scenarios.

J. Manley, *Social Dreaming, Associative Thinking and Intensities of Affect*,
Studies in the Psychosocial, https://doi.org/10.1007/978-3-319-92555-4_16

Intrinsic Relevance

In terms of the intrinsic value of the thinking process, it seems to me that the opportunity of participating in the creative process of social dreaming has a value all of its own. Winnicott has a beautiful paragraph in *Playing and Reality* (1991) that discusses the essential nature of creativity. It seems to me that this description of creativity and how it can take a person beyond the 'compliant' thinking of everyday life can be directly applied to social dreaming:

> It is creative apperception more than anything else that makes the individual feel that life is worth living. Contrasted with this is a relationship to external reality which is one of compliance, the world and its details being recognized but only as something to be fitted in with or demanding adaptation. Compliance carries with it a sense of futility for the individual and is associated with the idea that nothing matters and that life is not worth living. (Winnicott 1991, p. 65)

By 'creativity', then, Winnicott means a use of the mind that ignites a sense of play. In considering the nature of the thought activity of the matrix, it seems to me that the source of the creativity of social dreaming can be traced to childhood experiences and as such we may be prone to relegating this quality to the realm of childhood. An adult in this scenario thinks more closely along the lines of what might be considered the 'rational' mind, a linear, cause-and-effect way of thinking that I have been arguing as a one-sided 'Cartesian' way of approaching the world. This is why Winnicott discusses the particular value of child play in relation to perceived 'reality' and emphasises how this play can become part of adult life through participation in culture. Social dreaming is, I would argue, a direct experience in culture. It is a happy coincidence, therefore, that Winnicott also compares the creativity of the child as expressed in play to the dream:

> Into this play area the child gathers objects or phenomena from external reality and uses these in the service of some sample derived from inner or personal reality. Without hallucinating the child puts out a sample of dream potential and lives with this sample in a chosen setting of fragments from external reality. (Winnicott 1991, p. 51)

As adults, I believe we can access this 'dream potential' through the 'play' and creativity of social dreaming. Social dreaming can provide adults with an access to this part of ourselves that we might have left behind in childhood. It allows 'personal reality' to be shared intersubjectively with others and to become better balanced with our adult tendency for 'objectivity'.

The second relevant feature of the matrix that immediately follows on from this discussion is the place of affect among the participants. The images that arise in the social dreaming matrix are directly associated to shared affect. They are visual affects in a collage that this book identifies as a rhizome. Like Winnicott, but taking a neuroscientific line, Susan Greenfield suggests that the subjective emotional states of the brain are key to our understanding of how the brain functions and that as adults we can only access this process through cultural experience:

> The nearest we may come to sharing someone else's consciousness is via poetry, paintings, and music. (Greenfield 2002, 180)

Away from poetry, painting and music, the social dreaming matrix can provide a safe space for the containment of shared affect (what Greenfield calls 'emotions'). The social dreaming matrix, therefore, provides a space for the expression of personal emotional truths that become social in the sharing process of social dreaming, and these truths are often hidden or hiding behind contrary rational truths. In a world of ever-increasing difficulties, doubts and conflicts, where the rational may sometimes appear to flounder in the face of complexity, the thinking-in-affect process of social dreaming may be a significant way of transforming thought.

Practical Applicability

It is worth considering how difficult it is to be specific about clearly stating the benefits of social dreaming. As we have seen, the intrinsic value of social dreaming is in the opportunity it affords for participating in creative processes that are imbued in complexities and intensities of affect; this can also lead to a feeling of empathic 'bonding' between participants.

There are elements of the very nature of the process, with its free flowing mass of images that emerge from the associative unconscious, rather than ideas that have been well thought out, discussed as a result of Cartesian or linear thinking, that militate against any need or desire for sharply delineated results and conclusions. It may be that the social dreaming experience feels to be a space for thinking that is more revealing and more deeply relevant than other, more familiar spaces, and yet the experience may remain unclearly defined in terms of concrete or specific conclusions. The thinking presented in this book suggests that incorporating social dreaming into decision making, especially where decisions are to be taken by and/or affecting people, and especially if the area of debate is emotionally difficult or complex, would lead to a more complete picture of the issues around such a situation or problem and, therefore, theoretically at least, lead to better decision-making. An example of this, which has been suggested in this book, would be deciding whether or not a local government authority should apologise for its part in the slave trade.

As an academic research method, either in its original form or in one of its other guises, social dreaming is being used more and more as a means of gathering affective data in a shared or social context. It is a method that can be especially effective where knowledge of affect is needed or where the subject matter is so difficult that other data collection methods, such as focus groups for example, would be ineffective in gathering the data. Examples of this, referred to in this book include gathering data about people's attitudes to climate change and understanding the nuances of British-Muslim identity.

A Deleuzian *and* Psychosocial Method

As I have pointed out elsewhere (Manley 2018, in press), Deleuzian thinking is sometimes applied to provide perspectives on research methods, to contribute to discussion of results and analysis, but in the case of social dreaming as a research method, I have been arguing here that social dreaming can be construed as a Deleuzian research method in all its aspects, its theory, process and application. It conforms to Deleuze and Guattari's descriptions of schizoanalysis. Schizoanalysis celebrates the continuous expansion of affect in a rhizomatic fashion, challenges the border between phantasy and reality, encourages the creation of new concepts and therefore the creativity that can lead to such concepts; it rejects a narrow Freudian view of the unconscious as a site of repression, and replaces this with self-expression and vitality of desire, and the 'production of desire' as a quality of vibrancy, not a problem; it associates this process with liberation from the 'striated' channels of state power and domination that would seek to stifle the 'smooth' spaces of free, 'nomadic' activity of exploration and discovery. Schizoanalysis is itself an assemblage that includes expression and content in spaces of the real and the 'possible'. Compared to social dreaming, the schizoanalysis process corresponds most closely to a content of 'incorporeal complexity', that is to say Deleuze and Guattari's BwO, the 'body' of the rhizome in the matrix. What Guattari has to say of schizoanalysis is equally true of social dreaming:

> Schizoanalysis, rather than moving in the direction of reductionist modelisations which simplify the complex, will work towards its complexification, its processual enrichment, towards the consistency of its virtual lines of bifurcation and differentiation, in short towards its ontological heterogeneity. (Guattari 1995, p. 61)

Deleuze and Guattari have often been labelled as the enemies of psychoanalysis, especially that of Freud and Lacan, but we may be seeing a reconsideration of that radical and somewhat narrowly focussed point of view, and this book certainly attempts to contribute to that debate. Indeed, it is crucial to a Deleuzian and psychosocial interpretation of social dreaming that we do so.

The Unconscious in Schizoanalysis

Between Deleuze/Guattari, it was the latter who was psychoanalytically trained and a practising psychotherapist, (albeit a radical one), so it is normal to turn to Guattari to try to understand how their work can sit more comfortably with the psychosocial. The first thing to note is that

Guattari himself explicitly denies that his work with Deleuze is anti-psychoanalysis. He claims for schizoanalysis a different rather than opposing view of the role of the psyche in human existence. According to Guattari, schizoanalysis and traditional psychoanalysis share and accept the existence of the unconscious:

> This model of the unconscious is not opposed point-by-point to the old psychoanalytic model. It takes up some of its elements… (Guattari 2009, p. 198)

He goes on to accept the basic tenets of psychoanalysis, but suggests that they are occasionally outdated and easily superseded by schizoanalysis:

> Actually, an unconscious pattern really does exist within an intrapsychic "familialized" space where certain mental materials elaborated during early stages of psychic life are tied together. No one can deny that such a place where hidden and forbidden desires, a sort of secret kingdom, a state within the state exists, which seeks to impose its law over the whole psychism and its behaviors. But this formula, a private individualized and Oedipal unconscious, assumes premier importance in developed societies where most of their power depends upon systems of guilt and internalizations of norms. (Guattari 2009, p. 198)

In terms of the psychosocial, Guattari's emphasis on the social – which he strongly claims is an essential part of understanding the way the unconscious needs to be analysed, not just from the intrapsychic and dyadic perspective of the analyst and analysand duality – seems to locate schizoanalysis in an epistemological paradigm that could make it very relevant to psychosocial approaches. Since this point is so crucial to the thesis that this book claims for social dreaming, and the concerns that researchers in the psychosocial sometimes display about adopting a Deleuzian perspective, I will quote extensively from Guattari below. According to Guattari, the unconscious – to which he attaches the adjective 'machinic', meaning that it has rhizomatic qualities – that is the subject matter of schizoanalysis has the following characteristics:

1. It is *not* the exclusive seat of representative contents (representations of things or representations of words, etc.). Rather it is the site of *interaction between semiotic components and extreme diverse systems of intensity*, like linguistic semiotics, "iconic" semiotics, ethological semiotics, economic semiotics, etc. As a consequence, it no longer answers to the famous axiom formulated by Lacan, of being "structured like a language."
2. Its different components *do not depend upon a universal syntax*. The configuration of its contents and its systems of intensity (as these may be manifested in dreams, fantasies, and symptoms) depend upon *processes of singularization* which necessarily resist reductive analytic descriptions, like castration or Oedipus complexes (or intrafamilial systematizations). Collective arrangements that relate to specific cultural or social contexts account for such machinic instances.
3. *Unconscious interindividual relationships do not depend on universal structures* (like those that the disciples of Lacan try to base on a sort of "game theory" of intersubjectivity). Both imaginary and symbolic interpersonal relations obviously occupy a nodal point at the heart of unconscious arrangements, but they don't account for them all. Other, no less essential dispositions, come from systems of abstract entities and concrete machines that operate outside human identifications. The machinic unconscious is like a department store—you can find whatever you want there. This explains both its subservience to consumer society, its rich creativity and openness to innovation.
4. The unconscious can fall back on a nostalgic imaginary, *open up to the here and now*, or take chances on the future. Archaic fixations on narcissism, the death instinct, and the fear of castration can be avoided. They are not, as Freud assumed, the rock bottom of the whole edifice.
5. The machinic unconscious is not the same all over the world: *it evolves with history*. Obviously, the economy of desire of Malinowsky's Trobrianders is different from the inhabitants of Brooklyn, and the fantasies of Precolumbian Teotihuacans have little to do with those of contemporary Mexicans.
6. The structures of unconscious analytic enunciations do not necessarily require the services of the corporation of analysts. *Analysis can be pur-*

> *sued individually or collectively*. The notions of transference, interpretation and neutrality, based on a "typical cure," should also be revised. They are only admissible in very particular cases, within a very limited range of circumstances. (Guattari 2009, pp. 199–200)

Clearly, then, whether one agrees or not with Guattari's specific definition of the unconscious, the way this connects the intrapsychic with an extra-subjective psyche, and the way this is indissolubly related to the socio-historical realities of human ecologies, is not unrelated to some psychosocial approaches. Indeed, Joseph Dodds goes as far as to say that psychoanalysts should embrace the challenge:

> Their [Deleuze and Guattari] writings on psychoanalysis do not constitute a cheap dismissal, which could be achieved in a few throwaway paragraphs, but instead emphasize schizoanalysis which involves an extended and detailed critical engagement with psychoanalytical thought which is at times subtle and nuanced even if at other times it can be rather overblown. In this sense, it is not something to be disparaged by psychoanalysts, but rather, however cautiously, to be welcomed.' (Dodds 2011, p. 113)

Guattari, Bateson and Deleuze

Walkerdine has pointed to the need for psychosocial studies to better understand Guattari's work, but this could and should be extended to his joint work with Deleuze, and the latter's far more substantial work as a sole author. Guattari's reference to Bateson, cited by Walkerdine as being where we should 'begin to think about Guattari and the psychosocial' (Walkerdine 2014, p. 147) is a much later reference than the original reference to Bateson in *Anti-Oedipus* (1972 in French), where Deleuze and Guattari also credit Bateson with discussing schizophrenia 'from which he extracts an interesting psychoanalytic theory' (Deleuze and Guattari 2004, p. 257), and in *A Thousand Plateaus* (1980 in French), where Deleuze and Guattari unusually credit Bateson with the idea that gives itself to the title of their book, the 'plateau' (Deleuze and Guattari 1988, pp. 21–22).

In a detailed and helpful account of the influence of Bateson on Deleuze and Guattari, Shaw (2015) lists some of the concepts in Deleuze and Guattari's work that resonate or seem to have their sources in Bateson's work. These are: 'plateaus', the 'rhizome', the 'double-bind', 'ecosophy', and 'schizoanalysis' (Shaw 2015, p. 152). One of the key links between Bateson's thought and Deleuze and Guattari's is the way they all are intent on thinking across disciplines by weaving in and out (in a rhizomatic fashion) the various creative possibilities that might arise if one were to break down barriers and boundaries, and this to a certain extent is what the psychosocial is about: moving from the inner world to the external, from the conscious through various stages of the unconscious, and admitting the influence of culture and politics on the way individuals, groups, and society behave, think and react. This way of proceeding is also the way that schizoanalysis and the philosophical work of Deleuze perceives creative thought, a thinking that unexpectedly can bring together opposites or strange bedfellows and thus create new ideas, a smooth space of new ideas created spontaneously in the right conditions. Shaw draws our attention to such a Bateson-influenced heterogeneous splash of thought in the following extract:

> Bateson's work can thus be characterized as seeking connections between behavioral sciences, anthropology, psychiatry, cybernetics and biology, in order to explore the relationship between selves and the world. His influential conclusion is that, as Guattari paraphrases, 'nature cannot be separated from culture; in order to comprehend the interactions between ecosystems, the mechanosphere and the social and individual Universes of reference, we must learn to think "transversally"' (Guattari 2000: 29). (Shaw 2015, p. 155)

In social dreaming, all possibilities are opened out in this fashion. Through the holding back from interpretation, the tentative suggestions of working hypotheses, the efforts of the hosts to allow for the free flowing associations to emerge without hindrance within the container of the matrix, and the validity given to the dreams and therefore the unconscious in the shared space, and finally via the relative de-subjectivisation of the participants in favour of a mutually created and rhizomatic BwO, thinking becomes 'transversal' and is transformed into new thinking. This is true of both Deleuze and Guattari.

Some have suggested that Guattari developed a branch of thinking that is arguably more his own and can be found in his sole authored work (1995, 2000, 2009) and in his work with Deleuze *What is Philosophy?* which brings together some of Guattari's interest in ecology and chaos theory, influenced by thinkers such as Prigogine and Stengers (1984). In particular, Guattari's bringing together of ecology and schizoanalysis under the label of 'ecosophy' has been pointed out as a development distinct from Deleuze. This strikes me as doubtful, however, in part because it is interesting to note (as Shaw does, but without further comment, (see note p. 168)) that Arne Naess, the Norwegian philosopher, coined this idea at the same time or even before Guattari. It seems highly improbable that Guattari and Deleuze did not know this, especially when you consider that Naess' ideas emanated not from any general philosophy, but that of Spinoza, which puts his thinking in direct contact with that of Deleuze. Naess specifically connects his ecosophy with Spinoza's *Natura*, (Naess 1990, p. 39) which Deleuze pointed out was a conceptualisation that drew out the subjectivity of the human being to make her at one with a meta-subjectivity of deeper nature (Deleuze 1988, pp. 92–94).

How Does It Feel?

When the host at the beginning of a social dreaming matrix asks 'what is the first dream?', she is subliminally simultaneously asking 'what is the feeling?' It is the same question, image and affect, the image-affect. In this way, the image and its affect (or vice versa) is being solicited from its existence which is located outside of the subject(s), in a way that corresponds to Spinoza's concept of knowledge, as summarised by Deleuze:

> Knowledge is not the operation of a subject but the affirmation of the idea in the mind: "It is never we who affirm or deny something of a thing; it is the thing itself that affirms or denies something of itself in us"' (Spinoza, quoted in Deleuze 1988, p. 81)

This is the beginning of the BwO – or the dreams in search of a dreamer, Lawrence would have said – that can include everything in potential (not only things in an individual), literally anything, what Deleuze and Guattari called 'an inorganic life of things' (1994, p. 213). It is hardly an epistemology as it exists in itself. It can hardly be proved, either rationally or empirically. But it is closer to an ontology, a way of being and through that a certain kind of knowing. Dreams present a knowledge of affect. Words can be assigned to dream images, but they do not have to mean what they say. They are no longer the recipients of knowledge. Foucault makes this point in his discussion of Magritte's famous painting 'Ceci n'est pas une pipe' (this is not a pipe), where the image of a pipe is denied by the word. Where is the knowledge here? As Foucault implies it may reside in the French exclamation 'Nom d'une pipe!' ('for goodness' sake!') rather than in the words that seem to contradict the image. The knowledge is that of the dream, says Foucault:

> … it is in dream that men, at last reduced to silence, commune with the signification of things and allow themselves to be touched by enigmatic, insistent words that come from elsewhere. *Ceci n'est pas une pipe* exemplifies the penetration of discourse into the form of things… (Foucault 2000, p. 197)

This well describes the sensation of participating and grasping meaning from a social dreaming matrix, where the words of discourse clash and tussle with the images of dreams and associations, all in the shadow of affect.

> It is here that concepts, sensations, and functions become undecidable, at the same time as philosophy, art, and science become indiscernible, as if they shared the same shadow that extends itself across their different nature and constantly accompanies them. (Deleuze and Guattari 1994, p. 218)

It is tempting to ignore the implication of the affect contained in the dream, then gather the dreams and images of the matrix as if they were representations and/or symbols of something, and then to decode or translate these in data analysis in order to reach for something that looks like empirical results: to reduce the condensation of dreams to meaning, to *say something*. But saying the unsayable is more than difficult, if words are not enough. Maturana and Varela talk of consciousness of mind and self as 'languaging', emphasising that even language has to be a continuous, lived experience rather than a system of representation:

> Language was never invented by anyone only to take in an outside world. Therefore, it cannot be used as a tool to reveal that world. Rather it is by languaging that the act of knowing, in the behavioural coordination which is language, brings forth a world. (Maturana and Varela 1998, p. 234)

The act of knowing in social dreaming is that process of placing dreams, dream images, associations and affect in the forefront of our experience. It is a different kind of knowledge; it is not like Maturana and Varela's *Tree of Knowledge* (1998), although it is, like languaging, experienced knowledge, or knowledge through experience. The knowledge system that has served us so well since Descartes is not primarily available to us in social dreaming. The knowledge of words, representations and symbols, the worlds of words and facts has become amorphous but not less powerful in our shared world of dreams. The world and words of conscious knowledge making is still the offer of a certain apple from a certain tree that we might sometimes want to refuse, as angels before the fall.

References

Deleuze, G. (1988). *Spinoza: Practical Philosophy* (Hurley, R. Trans.). San Francisco: City Light Books.

Deleuze, G. (2004). *Difference and Repetition*. London: Continuum.

Deleuze, G. and Guattari, F. (1988). *A Thousand Plateaus*. London: Continuum.

Deleuze, G. and Guattari, F. (1994). *What is Philosophy?* London: Verso.

Deleuze, G. and Guattari, F. (2004). *Anti-Oedipus. Capitalism and Schizophrenia*. London: Continuum.

Dodds, J. (2011). *Psychoanalysis and ecology at the edge of chaos: Complexity Theory, Deleuze/Guattari and Psychoanalysis from a Climate in Crisis*. New York: Routledge.

Foucault, M. (2000). This is not a pipe. In Faubion, J.D. (Ed.), *Essential Works of Foucault 1954–1984, Volume* 2. London: Penguin.
Greenfield, S. (2002). *The Private Life of the Brain*. London: Penguin.
Guattari, F. (2000). *The Three Ecologies*. London: Athlone Press.
Guattari, F. (1995). *Chaosmosis*. Sydney: Power Publications.
Guattari, F. (2009). *Chaosophy. Texts and interviews 1972–1977*. South Pasadena, CA: Semiotext(e).
Manley, J. (2018). 'Every human being is an artist': From social representation to creative experiences of self. In Cummins, A.M. and Williams, N. (Eds.), *Researching Beneath the Surface*, Vol. 2. London: Routledge.
Manley, J. (in press). Associative thinking: A Deleuzian perspective on social dreaming. In Long, S. and Manley, J. (Eds.), *Social dreaming: Philosophy, research and practice*. London: Routledge.
Maturana, H.R. and Varela, F.J. (1998). *The Tree of Knowledge: The Biological Roots of Human Understanding*. Boston: Shambhala.
Naess, A. (1990). *Ecology, Community and Lifestyle*. Cambridge: CUP.
Prigogine, I. and Stengers, I. (1984). *Order out of Chaos*. London: Fontana.
Shaw, R. (2015). Bringing Deleuze and Guattari down to Earth through Gregory Bateson: Plateaus, Rhizomes and Ecosophical Subjectivity. *Theory, Culture & Society*, 32(7–8), pp. 151–171.
Walkerdine, V. (2014) Felix Guattari and the psychosocial imagination. *Journal of Psycho-Social Studies*, 8, pp. 146–158.
Winnicott, D.W. (1991). *Playing and Reality*. London: Routledge.

References

Abram, D. (1996). *The Spell of the Sensuous*. New York: Vintage Books.

Agresta, D. (in press). Festino di San Silvestro: Rites and social dreaming. In Long, S. and Manley, J. (Eds.), *Social Dreaming: Philosophy research and practice*. London: Routledge.

Armstrong, D. (2004). Emotions in organizations: Disturbance or intelligence? In Huffington, Clare, et al., (Eds.), *Working Below the Surface. The Emotional Life of Contemporary Organizations*. London: Karnac.

Armstrong, D. (2005). *Organization in the Mind*. London: Karnac.

Bain, A. (2007). The organization as a container for dreams. In Lawrence, W. Gordon (Ed.), *Infinite Possibilities of Social Dreaming*. London: Karnac.

Balogh, R. (2010). 'In dreams begins responsibility': A self-study about how insights from dreams may be brought into the sphere of action research. *Educational Action Research*, 18(4), pp. 517–529.

Balogh, R. (2015). In the Forests of the Night: An inquiry into the relevance of social dreaming for action research. *Educational Action Research*, 21(3), pp. 312–330.

Balogh, R. (in press). An action research study of dream-sharing as socially constituted practice. In Long, S. and Manley, J. (Eds.), *Social Dreaming: Philosophy research and practice*. London: Routledge.

Bateson, G. (2000). *Steps to an Ecology of Mind*. Chicago: University Press of Chicago.

J. Manley, *Social Dreaming, Associative Thinking and Intensities of Affect*,
Studies in the Psychosocial, https://doi.org/10.1007/978-3-319-92555-4

Bateson, G. (2002). *Mind and Nature*. New Jersey: Hampton Press.

Benjamin, J. (1988). *The Bonds of Love*. New York: Pantheon.

Benjamin, J. (1995). *Like Subjects, Love Objects*. New Haven and London: Yale University Press.

Benjamin, J. (1998). *The Shadow of the Other*. London and NY: Routledge.

Benjamin, J. (2018). *Beyond Doer and Done to*. London and NY: Routledge.

Benvenuto, B. (1994). *Concerning the Rites of Psychoanalysis*. Cambridge: Polity Press.

Beradt, C. (1968). *The Third Reich of Dreams. The Nightmares of a Nation 1933–1939*. Chicago, IL: Quadrangle B.

Bergson, H. (2005). *Matter and Memory* in *Key Writings*. London: Continuum.

Berman, H. and Manley, J. (2018). Social Dreaming and creativity in South Africa: Imagi(ni)ng the unthought known. In Adlam, J., Gilligan, J., Kluttig, T., and Lee, B.X. (Eds.), *Creative States: Overcoming Violence*. Vol 1, Part 4, Ch. 2, pp. 221–237. London: Jessica Kingsley.

Bermudez, G. and Silverstein, M. (2013). Social Dreaming Applications in Academic and Community Settings. *Other/wise*, 1(Spring), pp. 33–54. (https://ifpe.wordpress.com/2013-issues/volume-1-spring-2013/) Accessed 07.05.18.

Bion, W.R. (1961). *Experiences in Groups and Other Papers*. London: Routledge.

Bion, W.R. (1967). *Second thoughts*. London: Maresfield.

Bion, W.R. (1970). *Attention and interpretation*. London: Karnac.

Bion, W.R. (2000). *Experiences in Groups and other papers*. London: Routledge

Bion Talamo, P., Borgogno, F., and Merciai, S.A. (Eds.). (1998). *Bion's Legacy to Groups*. London: Karnac.

Blake, W. (1977). *The Complete Poems*. London: Penguin.

Bohm, D. (1980). *Wholeness and the Implicate Order*. London: Routledge.

Bohm, D. (1996). *On Dialogue*. London: Routledge.

Bollas, C. (1987). *The Shadow of the Object*. London: Free Association.

Bourassa, A. (2002). Literature, language and the non-human. In Massumi, B. (Ed.), *A Shock to Thought*, pp. 60–77. London: Routledge.

Breton, A. (1992). First manifesto of surrealism 1924. In Harrison, C. and Wood, P. (Eds.), *Art in Theory 1900–2000*. Padstow: Blackwell.

Breton, A., Eluard, P., and Soupault, P. (1997). *The Automatic Message*. London: BCM Atlas Press.

Capra, F. (1989). *Uncommon Wisdom. Conversations With Remarkable People*. London: Flamingo.

Capra, F. (1997). *The Web of Life. A New Synthesis of Mind and Matter*. London: Flamingo.

Capra, F. (2003). *The Hidden Connections*. London: Flamingo.

Capra, F. and Luigi Luisi, P. (2014). *The Systems View of Life*. Cambridge: CUP.

Chancer, L. and Andrews, J. (Eds.). (2014). *The Unhappy Divorce of Sociology and Psychoanalysis*. Basingstoke: Palgrave Macmillan.

Clare, J. and Zarbafi, A. (2009). *Social Dreaming in the 21st Century*. London: Karnac.

Clark, A. (2003). *Natural-Born Cyborgs. Minds, technologies, and the future of human intelligence*. Oxford: OUP.

Clark, A. (2011). *Supersizing the Mind: Embodiment, action and cognitive extension*. Oxford: OUP.

Clark, A. and Chalmers, D.S. (1998). The Extended Mind. *Analysis*, 58(1), pp. 7–19.

Coleman, R. and Ringrose, J. (2013). *Deleuze and Research Methodologies*. Edinburgh: Edinburgh University Press.

Crociani-Windland, L. (2009). How to live and learn: Learning, duration, and the virtual. In Clarke, S. and Hoggett, P. (Eds.), *Researching Beneath the Surface*, pp. 51–79. London: Karnac.

Cummins, A.M. and Williams, N. (Eds). (2018). Further *Researching Beneath the Surface*. London: Routledge.

Damasio, A. (2000). *The Feeling of What Happens*. London: Vintage.

Damasio, A. (2003). *Looking for Spinoza*. London: William Heinemann.

Damasio, A. (2006). *Descartes' Error*. London: Vintage.

de Quincey, C. (2005). *Radical Knowing*. Vermont: Park Street Press.

Deleuze, G. (1978). Lecture transcripts on Spinoza's concept of *Affect*. (https://www.gold.ac.uk/media/images-by-section/departments/research-centres-and-units/research-centres/centre-for-invention-and-social-process/deleuze_spinoza_affect.pdf) Accessed 05.03.18.

Deleuze, G. (1988a). *Bergsonism*. New York: Zone Books.

Deleuze, G. (1988b). *Spinoza: Practical Philosophy* (Hurley, R. Trans.). San Francisco: City Light Books.

Deleuze, G. (2004). *Difference and Repetition*. London: Continuum.

Deleuze, G. (2005a). *Bergsonism*. New York: Zone Books.

Deleuze, G. (2005b). *Cinema 1*. London: Continuum.

Deleuze, G. and Guattari, F. (1988). *A Thousand Plateaus*. London: Continuum.

Deleuze, G. and Guattari, F. (1994). *What is Philosophy?* London: Verso.

Deleuze, G. and Guattari, F. (2004). *Anti-Oedipus. Capitalism and Schizophrenia.* London: Continuum.

Dodds, J. (2011). *Psychoanalysis and ecology at the edge of chaos: Complexity Theory, Deleuze/Guattari and Psychoanalysis from a Climate in Crisis.* New York: Routledge.

Driver, S. (2005). Intersubjective openings: Rethinking feminist psychoanalytics of desire beyond heteronormative ambivalence. *Feminist Theory* 6 (1): 5–24.

Ellis, R.D. (2005). The roles of imagery and meta-emotion in deliberate choice and moral psychology. *Journal of Consciousness Studies*, 12(8–10), pp. 140–157.

Ettinger, B.L. (2002). Trans-subjective transferential borderspace. In Massumi, B. (Ed.), *A Shock to Thought*, pp. 215–240. London: Routledge.

Ferrero, A. (2002). Some implications of Bion's thought. The waking dream and narrative derivatives. *The International Journal of Psychoanalysis*, 83(3), pp. 597–607.

Foucault, M. (1991). *Discipline and Punish.* London: Penguin.

Foucault, M. (2000a). This is not a pipe. In Faubion, J.D. (Ed.), *Essential Works of Foucault 1954–1984, Volume* 2. London: Penguin.

Foucault, M. (2000b). On the Archaeology of the sciences: Response to the epistemology circle. In Faubion, J.D. (Ed.), *Essential Works of Foucault 1954–1984, Volume* 2. London: Penguin.

Foucault, M. (2000c). Philosophy and psychology. In Faubion, J.D. (Ed.), *Essential Works of Foucault 1954–1984, Volume* 2. London: Penguin.

Foucault, M. (2001). *Madness and Civilization.* Abingdon: Routledge.

Foulkes, S.H. (1964). *Therapeutic Group Analysis.* London: George Allen & Unwin.

Freeman, W. (1999). *How Brains Make up their Minds.* London: Phoenix.

French, R. and Vince, R. (Eds.). (2002). *Group Relations, Management, and Organization.* Oxford: Oxford University Press.

Freud, S. (Strachey, J. (Trans.). (1991a [1900]). *The Interpretation of Dreams.* London: Penguin.

Freud, S. (Strachey, J. (Trans.). (1991b). Civilization and its Discontents. In *Civilization, Society and Religion, Vol.* 12. London: Penguin.

Froggett, L., Manley, J., and Roy, A. (2015). The Visual Matrix Method: Imagery and Affect in a Group-based Research Setting. *Forum: Qualitative Social Research./ Forum Qualitative Sozialforschung / Forum: Qualitative Social Research*, 16 (3).

Fromm, E. (1962). *Beyond the Chains of Illusion: My encounter with Marx and Freud.* NY: Simon & Schuster.

Frosh, S. (2008). On negative critique: A reply. *Psychoanalysis, Culture & Society,* 13, pp. 416–422.

Goleman, D. (1999). *Working With Emotional Intelligence.* New York: Bantam.

Gosling, J. and Case, P. (2013). Social dreaming and ecocentric ethics: Sources of non-rational insight in the face of climate change catastrophe. *Organization,* pp. 1–17.

Greenfield, S. (2002). *The Private Life of the Brain.* London: Penguin.

Guattari, F. (2000). *The Three Ecologies.* London: Athlone Press.

Guattari, F. (1995). *Chaosmosis.* Sydney: Power Publications.

Guattari, F. (2009). *Chaosophy. Texts and interviews 1972–1977.* South Pasadena, CA: Semiotext(e).

Henderson, J.L. (1988). The cultural unconscious. *Quadrant: Journal of the C. G. Jung Foundation for Analytical Psychology,* 21(2), pp. 7–16.

Hoggett, P. (Ed.). (forthcoming). *Climate Psychology: Psycho-Social Research on Human/Nature Relations in the Age of Climate Change.* Basingstoke: Palgrave Macmillan.

Holland, E.W. (1999). *Deleuze and Guattari's Anti-Oedipus: Introduction to Schizoanalysis.* London: Routledge.

Hollway, W. and Jefferson, T. (2013). *Doing Qualitiative Research Differently: A Psychosocial Approach.* New Delhi: Sage.

Hollway, W. (2015). *Knowing Mothers.* Basingstoke: Palgrave Macmillan.

Hollway, W. and Manley, J. (2018 forthcoming). *The Unthought Known of Climate Change: How Social Dreaming and Art can be used to think the unthinkable.*

Hopper, E. (2003). *The Social Unconscious.* International Library of Group Analysis 22. London: Jessica Kingsley Publishers.

Ingold, T. (2007). *Lines: A brief History.* Abingdon: Routledge.

Ingold, T. (2008). When ANT meets SPIDER: Social theory for arthropods. In Knappett, C. and Malafouris, L. (Eds.), *Material Agency: Towards a Non-Anthropocentric Approach.*

Johnson, S. (1755). Dictionary. (https://johnsonsdictionaryonline.com/search-johnsons-dictionary/?SearchValue=cat)

Jung, C.G.(1972). *Man and his Symbols.* London: Aldus.

Jung, C.G. (1978). *Man and his Symbols.* London: Picador.

Jung, C.G. (1991). *The Archetypes and the Collective Unconscious (Collected Works of C. G. Jung).* London: Routledge.

Jung, C.G. (2002 [1931]). The practical use of dream-analysis. In *Dreams*, pp. 85–109. London: Routledge.

Jung, C.G. (2004). *Dreams*. London and New York: Routledge.

Karolia, I. and Manley, J. (2018). 1 in 5 Brit Muslims' Sympathy for Jihadis': An insight into the Lived Experience of UK Muslims following the Terror Attacks in Paris. In Adlam, J., Gilligan, J., Kluttig, T., and Lee, B.X. (Eds.), *Creative States: Overcoming Violence*, Vol. 1, Part III, pp. 161–177. London: Jessica Kingsley.

Keats, J. (Gittings, G. Ed.). (1970). *Letters of John Keats*. Oxford: OUP.

Kimble Wrye, H. (1999). The Shadow of the Other: Intersubjectivity and Gender in Psychoanalysis. By Jessica Benjamin. *Journal of the American Psychoanalytic Association*, 47, pp. 1455–1461.

Kuhn, T.S. (1996). *The Structure of Scientific Revolutions*. Chicago: Chicago University Press.

La Nave, F. (2010). Image: Reflections on the treatment of images and dreams in art psychotherapy groups. *International Journal of Art Therapy*, 15(1), pp. 13–24.

La Nave, F. (in press). Looking for Treasure in Dream Water. In Long, S. and Manley, J. (Eds.), *Social Dreaming: Philosophy research and practice*. London: Karnac.

Lacan, J. (1981). *The Language of the Self*. London: John Hopkins.

Lacan, J. (2001). *Écrits: A Selection*. London and New York: Routledge.

Lacan, J. (2008). *My Teaching*. London: Verso.

Langer, S. (1948). *A Philosophy in a New Key*. NY: Mentor New American Library.

Latour, B. (2005). *Reassembling the Social*. Oxford: OUP.

Latour, B. and Hermant, E. (1998). *Paris ville invisible*. (http://www.bruno-latour.fr/virtual/EN/index.html) Accessed 05.03.18.

Lawrence, W.G. (Ed.). (1998). *Social Dreaming @ Work*. London: Karnac.

Lawrence, W.G. (2000). *Tongued with Fire: Groups in experience*. London: Karnac.

Lawrence, W.G. (2002). The complementarity of social dreaming and therapeutic dreaming. In Neri, C., Pines, M., and Friedman, R. (Eds.), *Dreams in Group Psychotherapy*, pp. 220–233. London: JKP.

Lawrence, W.G. (Ed.). (2003a). *Experiences in Social Dreaming*. London: Karnac.

Lawrence, W.G. (2003b). Social dreaming as sustained thinking. *Human Relations*, 56(5), pp. 609–624.

Lawrence, W. G. (2005). *Introduction to Social Dreaming. Transforming Thinking*. London: Karnac.

Lawrence, W.G. (2006). Organizational analysis: The birth and growth of ideas. In Newton, J., Long, S., and Sievers, B. (Eds.), *Coaching in Depth: The Organizational Role Analysis Approach*. London: Karnac.

Lawrence, W.G. (Ed.). (2007a). *Infinite Possibilities of Social Dreaming*. London: Karnac.

Lawrence, W.G. (2007b). Dream Reflection Group. In Lawrence, W.G. (Ed.), (2007). *Infinite Possibilities of Social Dreaming*. London: Karnac.

Lawrence, W.G. (2007c). Creative Role Synthesis. In Lawrence, W.G. (Ed.), (2007). *Infinite Possibilities of Social Dreaming*. London: Karnac.

Lawrence, W.G. (Ed.). (2010). *The Creativity of Social Dreaming*. London: Karnac.

Lawrence, W.G. and Long, S. (2010). The creative frame of mind. In Lawrence, W.G. (Ed.), *The Creativity of Social Dreaming*. London: Karnac.

Lawrence, W.G. and Armstrong, D. (1998). Destructiveness and creativity in organizational life: Experiencing the psychotic edge. In Bion Talamo, Parthenope, et al. (Eds.), *Bion's Legacy to Groups*. London: Karnac.

LeDoux, J. (1999). *The Emotional Brain*. London: Phoenix.

Leigh-Ross, S. (2003). The science, spirit, chaos, and order of social dreaming. In Lawrence, W.G. (Ed.), *Experiences in Social Dreaming*, pp. 72–90. London: Karnac.

Long, S. (2013). *Socioanalytic Methods*. London: Karnac.

Long, S. (in press). Dreams and Dreaming: A Socioanalytic and Semiotic Perspective. In Long, S. and Manley, J. (Eds.), *Social Dreaming: Philosophy research and practice*. London: Routledge.

Long, S. and Harney, M. (2013). The associative unconscious. In Long, S. (Ed.), *Socioanalytic Methods*. London: Karnac.

Long, S. and Manley, J. (Eds.). (in press). *Social Dreaming: Philosophy, research and practice*. London: Routledge.

Lovelock, J.E. (2000). *Gaia, a new look at life on Earth*. Oxford: OUP.

Manley, J. (2009). When words are not enough. In Clarke, S. and Hoggett, P. (Eds.), *Researching Beneath the Surface*, pp. 79–99. London: Karnac.

Manley, J. (2010). The slavery in the mind: Inhibition and exhibition. Chapter 6 in Lawrence, W. Gordon (Ed.), *The Creativity of Social Dreaming*. London: Karnac, pp. 65–82.

Manley, J. (2014). Gordon Lawrence's Social Dreaming Matrix: Background, origins, history and developments. *Organisational and Social Dynamics*, 14(2), pp. 322–342.

Manley, J. (2017). The Unthought Known of Climate Change, unpublished paper presented at the Slow Violence Conference, University of Hertfordshire.

Manley, J. (2018). 'Every human being is an artist': From social representation to creative experiences of self. In Cummins, A.M. and Williams, N. (Eds.), *Researching Beneath the Surface*, Vol. 2. London: Routledge.

Manley, J. (in press). Associative thinking: A Deleuzian perspective on social dreaming. In Long, S. and Manley, J. (Eds.), *Social dreaming: Philosophy, research and practice*. London: Routledge.

Manley, J. and Roy, A. (2017). The visual matrix: A psycho-social method for discovering unspoken complexities in social care practice. *Psychoanalysis, Culture and Society*, 22(2), pp. 132–153.

Manley, J., Roy, A., and Froggett, L. (2015). Researching Recovery from Substance Misuse Using Visual Methods. In Hardwick, L., Smith, R., and Worsley, A. (Eds.), *Innovation in Social Work Research*. London: Jessica Kingsley, pp. 191–210.

Manley, J. and Trustram, M. (2018). 'Such endings that are not over': The slave trade, social dreaming and affect in a museum. *Psychoanalysis, Culture and Society*, 23(1), pp. 77–96.

Manley, J. and Hollway, W. (2018 forthcoming). The Unthought Known of Climate Change: How Social Dreaming and Art can be used to think the unthinkable. In Hoggett, P. (Ed.), *Climate Psychology: Psycho-Social Research on Human/Nature Relations in the Age of Climate Change*. Basingstoke: Palgrave Macmillan.

Manley, J., Gosling, J. and Patman, D. (submitted for publication). *Full of dreams: Social dreaming as liminal psychic space*.

Margulis, L. (2001). *The Symbiotic Planet*. London: Phoenix.

Masny, D. and Waterhouse, M. (2011). Mapping Territories and Creating Nomadic Pathways with Multiple Literacies Theory. *Journal of Curriculum Theorizing*, 27(3), pp. 287–307. Retrieved from http://journal.jctonline.org/index.php/jct/article/viewFile/155/21MasnyWaterhouse.pdf.

Masny, D. (2013). Rhizoanalytic Pathways in Qualitative Research. *Qualitative Inquiry*, 19(5), pp. 339–348. https://doi.org/10.1177/1077800413479559.

Masssumi, B. (Ed.). (2002). *A Shock to Thought*. London: Routledge.

Matte-Blanco, I. (1975). *The Unconscious as Infinite Sets*. London: Duckworth.

Matte-Blanco, I. (1988). *Thinking, Feeling, and Being*. London: Routledge.

Morgan, H. (2007a). Shedding light on organizational shadows. In Lawrence, W.G. (Ed.), *Infinite Possibilities of Social Dreaming*, pp. 106–113. London: Karnac.

Maturana, H.R. and Varela, F.J. (1998). *The Tree of Knowledge: The Biological Roots of Human Understanding*. Boston: Shambhala.

Maturana, H.R. and Poerksen, B. (2004). *From being to Doing*. Heidelberg: Carl-Auer.

Mersky, R. (2013). Social dream-drawing "Drawing brings the inside out". In Long, S. (Ed.), *Socioanalytic Methods*. London: Karnac.

Morgan, G. (2006). *Images of Organization*. Thousand Oaks, CA: Sage.

Morgan, G. (2016). Commentary: Beyond Morgan's eight metaphors. *Human Relations*, 69(4), pp. 1029–1042.

Morgan, H. (2007b). Shedding light on organizational shadows. In Lawrence, W.G. (Ed.), *Infinite Possibilities of Social Dreaming*, pp. 106–112. London: Karnac.

Morton, T. (2013). *Hyperobjects. Philosophy and Ecology after the End of the World*. London: University of Minnesota Press.

Morton, T. (2018). *Being Ecological*. Milton Keyes: Pelican.

Müller, M. and Schurr, C. (2016). Assemblage thinking and actor-network theory: Conjunctions, disjunctions, cross-fertilisations. *Transactions of the Institute of British Geographers*, 41(3), pp. 217–229.

Naess, A. (1990). *Ecology, Community and Lifestyle*. Cambridge: CUP.

Neri, C. (2003). Social dreaming: Report on the workshops held in Mauiburg, Raissa, and Clarice Town. In Lawrence, W.G. (Ed.), *Experiences in Social Dreaming*, pp 15–36. London: Karnac.

Nixon, R. (2011). *Slow Violence and the Environmentalism of the Poor*. Harvard: Harvard University Press.

Noack, A. (2010). Social dreaming: Competition or complementation to individual dreaming? *The Journal of Analytical Psychology*, 55(5), pp. 672–690.

Nuñez, R. (1999). Could the Future Taste Purple? Reclaiming Mind, Body and Cognition. In Nuñez, R., and Freeman, W.J. (Eds.), *Reclaiming Cognition. The Primacy of Action, Intention and Emotion*, pp. 41–61. Thorverton: Imprint Academic.

Nuñez, R. and Freeman, W.J. (1999). *Reclaiming Cognition*. Thorverton: Imprint Academic.

Page, M., Grisoni, L., and Turner, A. (2014). Dreaming fairness and re-imagining equality and diversity through participative aesthetic inquiry. *Management Learning*, 45(5), pp. 577–592.

Pinker, S. (1999). *How the Mind Works*. London: Penguin.

Pistiner de Cortinas, L. (2009). *The aesthetic dimension of the mind*. London: Karnac.

Prigogine, I. (2003). *Is Future Given?* New Jersey: World Scientific.

Prigogine, I. and Stengers, I. (1984). *Order out of Chaos*. London: Fontana.

Psychoanalysis, Culture and Society, Volume 13, Issue 4, December 2008 Special Issue: British Psycho(-) Social Studies.

Rowlands, M. (2009). Extended cognition and the mark of the cognitive. *Philosophical Psychology*, 22(1), pp. 1–19.

Roy, A. and Manley, J. (2017). Recovery and Movement: Allegory and 'journey' as a means of exploring recovery from substance misuse. *Journal of Social Work Practice*, 31(2), pp. 191–204.

Rupert, R.D. (2004). Challenges to the Hypothesis of Extended Cognition. *The Journal of Philosophy*, 101(8), (Aug., 2004), pp. 389–428.

Ryan, R.E. (2002). *Shamanism and The Psychology of C.G.Jung*. London: Vega.

Sievers, B. (2008). 'Perhaps It Is The Role of Pictures To Get In Contact with the Uncanny': The Social Photo Matrix as a Method to Promote the Understanding of the Unconscious in Organizations. *Organisational and Social Dynamics*, Number 2 / 2008, pp. 234–254(21).

Sievers, B. (2013). Thinking organisations through photographs: The social photo-matrix as a method for understanding organisations in depth. In Long, S. (Ed.), *Socioanalytic Methods*, pp. 129–153. London: Karnac.

Sievers, B. (2014). It is difficult to think in the slammer: A social-photo matrix in a penal institution. In *The Psychosocial and Organization Studies*. Basingstoke: Palgrave Macmillan.

Silverstein, M. (2013). Dreaming personality theory forward: Creating pedagogical change from the ground up. *Otherwise*, 1(Spring 2013), pp. 3–33. (https://ifpe.wordpress.com/2013-issues/volume-1-spring-2013/) Accessed 07.05.18.

Simpson, P. and French, R. (2006). Negative Capability and the Capacity to Think in the Present Moment. *Leadership*, 2(2), pp. 245–255.

Shaw, R. (2015). Bringing Deleuze and Guattari down to Earth through Gregory Bateson: Plateaus, Rhizomes and Ecosophical Subjectivity. *Theory, Culture & Society*, 32(7–8), pp. 151–171.

Spinoza, B. (1992). *Ethics. Treatise on the Emendation of the Intellect and Selected Letters* (Shirley, S, Ed). Indianapolis: Hackett.

Sutton, J., Harris, C.B., Keil, P.G., and Barnier, A.J. (2010). The psychology of memory, extended cognition, and socially distributed remembering. *Phenomenology and the Cognitive Sciences*, 9(4), pp. 521–560.

Tatham, P. (2003). Social dreaming and the senior managers' programme. In Lawrence, W.G. (Ed.), *Experiences in Social Dreaming*, pp. 179–189. London: Karnac.

Tatham, P. (2007). Social Dreaming at the Jung Congress. In Lawrence, W.G. (Ed.), *Infinite Possibilities of Social Dreaming*, pp. 113–120. London: Karnac.

Tatham, P. and Morgan, H. (1998). The social dreaming matrix. In Lawrence, W.G. (Ed.), *Social Dreaming @ Work*. London: Karnac.

Taylor, F.W. (1911). Shop Management, The Principles of Scientific Management. Harper & Row (consulted in. www.marxists.org/reference/subject/economics/taylor/principles/index.htm).

Thomas, J. (2018). "As easy as to know...": On the tensions between psychoanalysis and psychosocial research. In Cummins, A.M. and Williams, N., *Further Researching Beneath the Surface*. London: Routledge, pp. 3–26.

Thrift, N. (2008). *Non-Representational Theory*. London: Routledge.

Turkle, S. (2011). *Alone Together*. NY: Basic Books.

Ullman, M. (1975). The transformation process in dreams. *American Academy of Psychoanalysis*, 19(2), pp. 8–10.

Ullman, M. (2006). *Appreciating Dreams, a Group Approach*. New York: Cosimo.

Varela, F.J., Thompson, E., and Rosch, E. (1993). *The Embodied Mind*. London: The MIT Press.

Versi, M. (2017). 'The latest Prevent figures show why the strategy needs an independent review'. In *The Guardian*. (www.theguardian.com/commentisfree/2017/nov/10/prevent-strategy-statistics-independent-review-home-office-muslims) Accessed 14.02.18.

Walkerdine, V. (2014) Felix Guattari and the psychosocial imagination. *Journal of Psycho-Social Studies*, 8, pp. 146–158.

Weizenbaum, J. (1993). *Computer Power and Human Reason*. London: Penguin.

Wheatley, M.J. (2006). *Leadership and the New Science*. San Francisco: Berret-Koehler.

Winnicott, D.W. (1991). *Playing and Reality*. London: Routledge.

Zwicky, J. (2002). Dream logic and the politics of interpretation. In Lilburn, Tim (Ed.), *Thinking and Singing, Poetry and the Practice of Philosophy*. Cormorant Books.

Index[1]

[1] Note: Page numbers followed by 'n' refer to notes.

J. Manley, *Social Dreaming, Associative Thinking and Intensities of Affect*, Studies in the Psychosocial, https://doi.org/10.1007/978-3-319-92555-4

Printed by Books on Demand, Germany